Rhapsody in
Schmaltz

Michael Wex

Rhapsody in Schmaltz

Yiddish Food and Why We Can't Stop Eating It

St. Martin's Press
New York

641.5676
Wex

www.stmartins.com

The Library of Congress Cataloging-in-Publication Data is available upon request.

ISBN 978-1-250-07151-4 (hardcover)
ISBN 978-1-4668-8265-2 (e-book)

Our books may be purchased in bulk for promotional, educational, or business use. Please contact your local bookseller or the Macmillan Corporate and Premium Sales Department at 1-800-221-7945, extension 5442, or by e-mail at Macmillan SpecialMarkets@macmillan.com.

First Edition: April 2016

10 9 8 7 6 5 4 3 2 1

In Memory of

Theo Bikel
Tamara Brooks
Adrienne Cooper
Sybil Goldstein
Albert Winn
Chana Yachness

Sit eis terra levis

Table of Contents

Introduction
An Oral Fixation

I

Researching and writing this book has been one of the most unpleasant experiences of my life.

"You're writing a book on Jewish food?"

"Yiddish food."

"Yiddish, Jewish, same thing. You're going to talk about bagels, I guess." I nod. "You live in Toronto, right?" I nod again, my interlocutor snorts. "Then how the hell can you write about bagels? There isn't a decent bagel in the whole bloody city. Toronto bagels are dough pucks with a hole in the middle. You want a real bagel, go to Montreal— and there's only one place there that still knows what they're doing. You never even lived in Montreal, you're gonna write about bagels; you're gonna write about my ass. And don't get me started on those horse turds they've got in New York."

It isn't only bagels. Dishes come and dishes go—it's the law of the kitchen. Chala and kugel, bagels and lox, gefilte fish, brisket, latkes, and schmaltz; the mighty *cholent* itself could go the way of *pashtet*, the now-forgotten medieval meat pie for which our ancestors drooled on Sabbaths and holidays—it wouldn't make any difference. The Yiddish-speaking kitchen's principle product isn't chewable and cannot be swallowed. It isn't boiled, broiled, baked, or fried; it's far from kosher and can't be legally killed. It is, of course, the nudnik, from the Yiddish "to bore, to feel nauseous"—a flesh-coated windbag stuffed tightly with opinions that tend to repeat.

And repeat they did. I developed a fear of dinner parties and social events. If I didn't lie about what I was writing, I had to have the same conversation six, eight, ten times a night. The dish might change, but the theme was constant, invariable. The nudnik's favorite dish was the essence of Jewish food and there was only one way to make it; anyone who did it differently was a fool and a fraud who needed to be exposed for the sake of authentically ethnic nutrition and the speaker's peace of mind. And if that meant trying to record their screeds into my cell phone, just to make sure that I got everything right . . . it wasn't their fault that I said no.

It had been decades since some of these people had eaten the dishes that they were so worked up about and few had ever cooked the things—that's what mothers were for—but none of that mattered: The tradition of talking—and pontificating and complaining— about Jewish food goes all the way back to the Bible. Jewish cuisine, especially its Yiddish branch, is as focused on fight as on flavor. Centuries of rigorous schooling in dietary laws have helped to insure that statutory principles and the arguments they provoke will almost always take precedence over matters of taste. "How do you cook swordfish?" isn't really a Jewish question. "If the swordfish loses its scales as part of its maturation process, am I still allowed to eat it?"—*that's* the kind of home ec that we were put on earth to practice.

The answer, of course, depends on who you ask. Orthodox rabbis say no, Conservative and Reform say yes. And since we're dealing with Jewish law and tradition, there are a few Orthodox dissenters who agree with the Conservatives in principle, but not on the plate: Sure as they are that swordfish is kosher, they're still not about to eat it.

When what's forbidden for Abraham is permitted for Isaac, when Jacob agrees with Isaac but behaves like Abe, recipes are the last thing anyone needs. When you're dealing with a cuisine whose signature dish has no fixed ingredients and is based entirely on the idea of eating a hot meal on a day when cooking is forbidden (see Chapter Five), the main course can all too often turn into an abstraction.

This tendency to think in categories instead of ingredients produces a way of looking at food that doesn't depend on the presence of food, a definite advantage once want began to pervade the lives of most East European Yiddish speakers. They were a nation of food critics without enough to eat and their tastes—such as they were—were more often a matter of theory than of practice: They were as happy to eat anything kosher as they were to argue about it. The Yiddish folk song "Bulbes," in which no one ever eats anything but the potatoes named in the title, was sung by people who were happy to be able to complain; too many potatoes meant that they were still eating *something*, that whatever problems they might have, at least they weren't in Ireland.

Hungry as the Jews might have been, though, there was still plenty that they wouldn't normally eat. Lifelong engagement with the dietary laws, the endless watch for forbidden ingredients or illicit combinations, gives rise to a way of thinking in which looking at food becomes looking for trouble. Attitudes developed to help safeguard the will of God have persisted as a kind of cultural reflex among less traditionally oriented Jews. Narrowly religious queries—Is turkey permitted? What about gelatin? Can permitted food A be eaten with permitted food B without incurring a metaphysical penalty?—are easily secularized into equally hairsplitting concerns with a food's origins, calorie content, or methods of production. Looking for faults in the food—even when it's free—might be the one traditional activity at which contemporary, non-kosher-keeping Jews are more adept than their forebears. They have expanded their range of distaste, allowed their dissatisfaction to embrace foods that God told them not to eat in the first place. Standards of judgment might have changed, but the traditional Talmudically based approach to eating has only, if unconsciously, been refined.

II

Most of what we know about Central and East European Jewish eating before the mid-nineteenth century comes from rabbinic writing about the dietary laws rather than cookbooks or guides to home economy. Until the first Yiddish cookbook was published in 1896, vernacular food writing was a matter of handbooks explaining which of the half dozen preingestion blessings were to be recited over foods that readers were supposed to know how to make. *Halachically*—according to Jewish law—the finished product was all that mattered. So, for example, cheese takes one blessing, blintzes and cheesecake another, a cheese sandwich takes a third and also requires ritual hand washing. The preliminary blessings determine which of the three closing benedictions has to be recited once you finish eating. Traditional Jewish eating is so complicated that rabbis used to spend much of their time answering basic questions about the dietary laws: "I spilled a tablespoon of milk into a pot of chicken soup. What do I do, and can I still eat the soup?" The pot is affected, the soup is affected, the spoon is affected if it touched the soup. Relative amounts of milk and chicken soup can play a part in the decision. There's also a human element: if the rabbi forbids the soup, will the questioner and her family be forced to go hungry? If so, maybe, just maybe, he can find some little-known ruling that will permit him to allow it without angering the Lord or upsetting the neighbors.

There is no respite. As long as you can even think about eating, this is how you're going to do so. It's an obsession that has nothing to do with aesthetics. Every mouthful of every meal is packed with moral and ritual drama, and the show goes on long after the script has been changed:

> "Glass of milk with your ham hock, Mr. Schwartz?"
> "Milk? With ham? Feh!"

Difficult as keeping the dietary laws can be, trying to silence their echoes once you stop observing them isn't always any easier. As the Hebrew has it, *im poga noga:* touch, and it touches back. The alacrity with which Chinese food was embraced by the first generation of East European immigrants to stop observing the dietary laws en masse—at least when out of the house—rests to some degree on the fact that Chinese food lay well beyond the pale of culinary respectability, so suspect with regard to hygiene and ingredients, so outré in cooking technique, that most people didn't *want* to know what was in it and couldn't always recognize it when they did. It was the "somewheres east of Suez" of the restaurant world, "where there aren't no Ten Commandments" and ideas of Jewish and Christian were completely irrelevant. The common "white" concerns with Chinese restaurant hygiene were meaningless to people accustomed to being called dirty Jews. Indeed, Chinese food gave the Jewish consumer an unprecedented chance to pass for white. More than just a cheap and tasty break from kosher food (if that's all you wanted, you could have eaten almost anything), Chinese food was a rare chance to take a vacation from kosher thinking.

Although the dietary laws no longer play a central role in the day-to-day lives of most American Jews, many of them continue to associate various "Jewish" times of year with "Jewish" food, generally in large amounts. For most American Jews, the age-old schedule of holidays—beginning with the weekly Sabbath—has been whittled down to occasional family dinners featuring dishes that the family considers traditional. Along with funerals and circumcisions, such dinners are often as close as these families get to traditional Jewish activities, and the food served at them comes to represent the entire aggregate of social and religious factors that make Jews so distinct. It's the other side of their great-grandparents' Chinese-food coin, a vacation from the unhyphenated homogeneity of American culture.

In a society that claims not to discriminate on grounds of faith, even more than in one that does, food becomes the all-purpose, immediately comprehensible expression of Jewish identity. Invoking Jewish dishes or dietary laws is a way of marking oneself—sometimes as different, sometimes as one of us. In more incongruous contexts, mentioning Jewish food becomes a way of taunting the dominant culture or trying to mask a certain self-consciousness about one's own difference. Such references are always gratuitous, but never accidental. As with other Yiddish words and phrases that are as out of place in regular English as matzoh balls in eggnog, the names of Jewish foods are a way of telling anyone in on the joke that there's more to the speaker (or writer or performer) than he or she usually displays in public. My attitude to *The Simpsons'* Mr. Burns changed forever when he turned up for dinner at the Simpson house and announced, "Look, I've brought noodle kugel." The very next week I asked for gefilte fish in Delmonico's.

III

All observant Jews follow the same basic set of rules and observe the same holidays, but there are plenty of regional variations. The Jewish food that we'll be talking about is the food of Ashkenazi Jews. Ashkenaz is an old Hebrew term for Germany, and Jews of Central and East European descent—roughly 80 percent of the Jewish population—are known as Ashkenazim. Their forebears are thought to have settled along the Rhine, then migrated east to such places as the Czech Republic, Slovakia, Hungary, Romania, Poland, Ukraine, Russia, Belarus, and the Baltic states. Despite the considerable territory involved, Ashkenazi culture changed little from country to country; minor variants in dress and religious customs were no more decisive than minor variants in the Yiddish once spoken in all these communities.

Unlike their Sephardic coreligionists whose ancestors were expelled from Spain and Portugal in the fifteenth century, Ashkenazim made a point of resisting acculturation. While Sephardim were (and are) no less religious than Ashkenazim, they were much more comfortable with the outward trappings of the societies in which they lived, and were quick to take on many of the manners and habits of their non-Jewish neighbors in places as diverse as Holland and Thessaloniki, Serbia, and Egypt. Although Ashkenazim were hardly immune to outside influence, Frankfurt is more like Kiev than Amsterdam is like Rabat. Where Sephardic cookery thus varies considerably from country to country, Ashkenazi cuisine is primarily a matter of slight regional variations on a relatively small number of themes.

Heavy, unsubtle and, once it emerged from Eastern Europe, redolent of an elsewhere that nobody missed, the food of Yiddish speakers and their descendants is a cuisine that none dares call haute, the gastronomic complement to the language in which so many generations grumbled about it and its effects. This vernacular food continues to turn up in vernacular form in the mouths of people who have never eaten it, or who don't always realize the Jewish origin of the strawberry swirl bagel onto which they're spreading their Marmite. We'll be looking at the aftertaste of Ashkenazi food as much as at the cuisine itself. But before we can do so, we have to go back to the Bible to see why Jewish food exists and what it really is.

A NOTE ON TERMINOLOGY, TRANSLITERATION, AND TRANSLATION

Aside from the idea of kosher, which is explained in the text, the terms that come up most often are:

Treyf—the opposite of kosher, both literally and metaphorically.

Milkhik—dairy. The noun is **milkhiks.**

Fleyshik—meat. The noun is **fleyshiks**

Parve—neutral, neither dairy nor meat. All vegetables are parve. The final *e* is pronounced.

Kashrus—kosherness.

Mishna—the first part of the Talmud, finished around 200 CE. Basically an attempt to work out rules of day-to-day life and behavior on the basis of the commandments in the Bible.

Gemore–the later part of the Talmud, compiled around 500 CE. An attempt to do for the Mishna what the Mishna attempted to do for the Bible. The final *e* is pronounced.

Halacha is Jewish law. People who act according to its dictates are said to behave **halachically.**

The Yiddish that appears in this book is transliterated according to the system of YIVO, the *Yidisher Visnshaftlikher Institut* (Institute for Jewish Research). The main points to note are:

1. Final *e* is not silent. So, for example, the Yiddish version of kasha would be *kashe.*
2. The hard "h" sound, as at the beginning of Chanukah, is rendered with *kh.* The Yiddish version of Chanukah would be *khanike.*
3. *Ey* is pronounced as in the English "hey." A bagel in Yiddish is a *beygl.*
4. *Ay* is like the English long *y* in "my."

Hebrew and Yiddish words that have come into English, including the names of many of the dishes discussed, are given in their common English versions. So, kreplach, Rosh Hashana, bar mitzvah all look like this. If used in Yiddish, they follow the rules above: *kreplekh, rosheshone, bar mitsve.*

Biblical quotations follow either the Jewish Publication Society or the Revised Standard versions, often with my own emendations. All other translations not credited in the endnotes are my own.

Rhapsody in
Schmaltz

ONE

Who Says It's Supposed to Taste Good?
The Prehistory of Yiddish Food

For that night I will go through the land of Egypt and strike down every first-born in the land of Egypt, both man and beast; and I will mete out punishments to all the gods of Egypt. (Ex 12:12)

Most national cuisines owe their character to flora and fauna, crops and quarry, domesticated animals and international trade. Jewish food starts off with a plague.

As God goes through Egypt, killing the firstborn males, He takes care to pass over the houses of the Israelite slaves, who are eating a hearty, if not wholly voluntary, dinner. Each household has been ordered to slaughter a lamb or kid on the fourteenth night of the month of Nisan—a month revealed to the Israelites only two weeks earlier and which no Egyptian has heard of—smear its blood on their doorposts and lintels, and eat the rest.

They shall eat the flesh that same night; they shall eat it roasted over the fire, with unleavened bread and with bitter herbs. Do not eat any of it raw, or cooked in any way with water, but roasted—head, legs, and entrails—over the fire. You shall not leave any of it over until morning; if any of it is left until morning, you shall burn it. This is how you shall eat it: your loins girded, your sandals on your feet, and your staff in your

1

hand; and you shall eat it hurriedly; it is a passover offering to the Lord. (Ex 12:8–11)

Although God has been speaking to the Israelites through Moses for the last few chapters, this passage marks the first time that He has given them something to do—two things, in fact. The first is mental; they have to change their notion of time. "This is the beginning of your months, the first of the months of the year for you." (Ex 12:2) God is telling the Israelites to put the Egyptian calendar aside. Egyptian time is slave time, but the Children of Israel are on God's time now. The sun, the moon, the earth haven't changed at all, but the cosmos to which they belong has just become a whole different place.

Changing your calendar means reconfiguring your view of the world. In abandoning the Egyptian calendar, the Israelites are starting to shrug off their slavery, together with the attitudes and beliefs of the people who enslaved them: There is no place for the ten-day Egyptian week in a system that is about to make every seventh day a major religious festival. Other peoples and their customs will now enter the Israelite world only on terms that the Israelites and their Lord have established and defined. Will they know it's Christmas? Sure. As the Yiddish writer B. Tsivyen once observed, it'll be what someone else celebrates during our month of Kislev.

"Eat the flesh"—the physical part of the Israelites' assignment—is a public display of the same repudiation of everything Egyptian. Killing a lamb or kid, celebrating its death by smearing its blood on your doorposts and eating its flesh for supper is more than a sign of obedience to God's will or a sort of metaphysical barrier tape to protect your own firstborn; it's a giant fuck you to the whole pantheon of Egyptian deities. Rashi, the popular acronym for Rabbi Solomon ben Isaac, whose eleventh-century commentaries on the Bible and Talmud have been taught together with the texts for the past thousand years, remarks that "sheep are Egyptian deities"

(Gen 46:34) and explains that when Moses tells Pharaoh that the Israelites have to offer their sacrifices in the desert because the Egyptians will stone them if they see what's being offered (see Ex 8:22), what he's really saying is, "We're going to be killing your god."

Not entirely accurate, perhaps, but still a fair reflection of the traditional Jewish understanding of Egyptian religion. Khnum, one of the oldest Egyptian deities, and Amun, one of the best known, are both identified with the ram, especially as a symbol of fertility, and there is a wealth of ancient tradition—rumor, to be sure, but sanctified by time—concerning Egyptians and their ovine stock. Herodotus, the fifth century BCE historian who has been called both "the father of history" and "the father of lies"—regrettably not by the same person—asserts that some Egyptians loved their goats even better than they loved their kids:

> *Certain Egyptians (the Mendesians) will not sacrifice goats, either male or female . . . The Mendesians hold all goats in veneration, especially male ones . . . One of them is held in particular reverence, and when he dies the whole province goes into mourning . . . In this province not long ago a goat [sh]tupped a woman, in full view of everybody—a most surprising incident.*

It's hard to tell whether Herodotus is more surprised by the tupping or the viewing, but he was hardly the only one to notice. Classical Greek writers from Pindar to Plutarch make the same connection between Mendesian women and goats.

It doesn't matter if any of these rumors is true. Plenty of modern scholars deny the historicity of the Exodus and claim that the Israelites never went down to Egypt at all, but that doesn't make ham kosher or "Go Down, Moses" a hymn to the glories of slavery. Traditional Jewish culture behaves as if everything described in the Bible really happened and uses these events as the foundation for a system of belief that cannot be fully understood unless you suspend your disbelief and accept them at face value. Whether the Israelites ever set foot in Egypt or not, the blood on their narrative doorposts turns the meaning of the Egyptian ram inside out: It and its aco-lytes die, while its killers walk away into freedom. This is what the Lord means when He promises to "mete out punishments to all the gods of Egypt." He's going to have the Israelites eat them for supper.

As long as the Israelites do as he tells them, that is. The first task imposed upon the Israelites, the first action they are ordered to per-form, is to make dinner. God gives them an annotated menu, speci-fying ingredients, side dishes, methods of cooking, treatment of leftovers, dining time, and dress code—no sandals, no stick, no di-vine service—and tells them to get cracking and do it. The first national Jewish activity is also the first recognizably Jewish meal: Identifiable Jewish behavior begins with a meal designed to sicken anyone not commanded to eat it. It is an act of symbolic deicide that takes place just before the Lord, the one and only Deity-with-a-capital-D, wipes out the Egyptian firstborn, the first fruits of these tutelary spirits of fertility. The roast lamb that would have struck the Egyptians as blasphemous becomes a mocking reminder of their gods' incapacity.

THE PRIMAL JEWISH FOOD

Until that first seder, the Israelites ate only what their masters gave them. Although they later claim to have lived on cucumbers, melons, onions, garlic, and leeks, as well as fish that they got for free (Nm 11:5), neither God nor Moses takes them very seriously. As the Midrash rather pointedly asks, "If the Egyptians wouldn't give them straw [to make bricks, see Ex 5:7], would they have given them fish for free?" The other foods that the Israelites miss so much in the des-ert are recognizable variants of the forced laborers' diet described by Herodotus, who mentions an inscription on the pyramid of

Cheops "recording the amount spent on radishes, onions, and leeks for the labourers." If the Israelites' list is any indication, they didn't even get the radishes that the ethnic Egyptians received. Until that first Passover, the Israelites ate only what was tossed to them.

The change of diet turned them into Jews. Killing lambs or kids and eating them with matzoh and bitter herbs instead of waiting for a ration of onions and leeks is a declaration of the end of dependence. Ignoring the foods that they later long for in the desert— the only other food they would ever have eaten, if we follow the Bible's logic—is the first step to getting out of Egypt and into that desert.

The Bible also tells us that they didn't prepare any food for the trip (Ex 12:39); they were being pursued by hordes of Egyptians, God wouldn't let them eat the leftover lamb, and the food prohibitions associated with Passover had already come into effect:

> *No leaven shall be found in your dwellings for seven days, for the soul of anyone who eats anything leavened will be cut off from the community of Israel . . . in all of your settlements you shall eat matzoh. (Ex 12:19–20)*

Far from taking whatever they were given, the Israelites are commanded to reject what they had on hand and to leave with nothing but leftover matzoh, kneading bowls, and the dough that they had already prepared. Since bitter herbs are really just a side dish that anyone can pull out of the ground, and no one has seen a Passover sacrifice for two thousand years, matzoh—for which the Bible provides an antirecipe—became the basis for Jewish thinking about food. Making and eating it is the first organized activity that the Israelites undertake without Egyptian permission; they eat it for their own benefit, not the Egyptians', and on their own time, not that of their former masters. Once the Israelites abandon the Egyptian calendar and stop thinking like second-class versions of their oppressors, they become free to act in ways that have nothing to do with Egypt.

The matzoh that they baked probably didn't bear much resemblance to the brittle, crackerlike substance that Ashkenazim have been eating for the last few centuries, but flour and water are flour and water, and once we make allowances for the difference between baking on a griddle or pan and doing so in an oven, the basic process cannot have been much different. The first batch, the first few centuries of batches, were probably a lot more relaxed about the ancillary regulations that began to proliferate in the Talmudic era, but the baking itself and the near-obsessive worry about leavening cannot have changed too much. While most of the matzoh produced today is made by machines that hack out thousands of pounds an hour, bakeries in which everything is done by hand have never gone away and, thanks to a growing ultra-Orthodox population, have been undergoing something of a resurgence.

Aside from such modern touches as thermostats and electricity, today's hand-matzoh bakeries aren't much different from those that sprang up in the eighteenth century to spare householders the trouble of making their own. If anything, the modern bakeries are probably more stringent with respect to the law and more specialized in division of labor. A measurer who has been sequestered with the flour pours about 2.7 pounds (the volume, our sages tell us, of 43.2 eggs) into clean, dry, metal bowls. A water bearer then emerges from the water room—a further precaution to keep flour from meeting water before the time is right—and moistens the flour with spring or well water that has been left to stand overnight. The mixture is kneaded into a long strip of dough, which is then cut into smaller strips that are rolled into thin discs. These are perforated with a toothed wheel called a *reydl* to keep the dough from bubbling when it's baked—a bubble bigger than a hazelnut disqualifies the matzoh for Passover use. The discs are given a quick once-over and then slid into the oven for twenty to thirty seconds.

It's all done with breathless haste. The dough has to get from bowl to cooling rack in no more than eighteen minutes, after which any unbaked dough becomes *chometz*—leaven—and has to be discarded. The flour used in this example is enough for about half a dozen bowls of dough, all of which would be kneaded and baked in a single eighteen-minute shift. At the end of every batch, the facility, the equipment, and the workers are cleaned off and the process of making the simplest, least complicated of all baked goods begins anew.

IT ISN'T THE BREAD, IT'S THE AFFLICTION

There are those who say that God gave us cardboard so that we could describe the taste of matzoh, but taste is what matzoh is not about. Since the penalty for eating leaven on Passover is the death-in-life of excision from the Jewish people, matzoh doesn't need to be good, it only needs to be there—inside of eighteen minutes. Or twenty-two, according to some authorities; however long it took to walk to Tiberias from Migdal Nunia, the probable home of Mary Magdalene—a single Roman mile. (*Pesokhim* 46a)

Although all Jewish communities follow the same general rules for baking matzoh, indifference to taste is a direct outgrowth of the obsessive, heart-wrenching concern for halachic niceties that characterizes Ashkenazi civilization and has had a profound influence on Yiddish-speaking attitudes to food. The Talmud (*Pesokhim* 37a) says that matzoh must be baked until a piece can be broken off cleanly, without any dangling threads of dough, and Ashkenazi matzoh started out like all other matzoh, a flatbread or pita made without starter, salt, or yeast.

Soft matzoh of this type seems to have been universal for a couple of millennia and is still eaten by plenty of non-Ashkenazim. Regardless of what it tastes like, though, it grows stale after a day or two, and Ashkenazim, whose approach to Jewish law resembles that of a cartoon Jewish mother to the health of her only child, began to worry about the dangers of baking fresh batches over the holiday: "What if something goes wrong, if there's God forbid an accident and the dough begins to rise? Forget that you wouldn't even think about eating it, just *having* it means that you've transgressed the commandment about having leaven in your dwelling." This was a risk that no one was willing to take, so the community as a whole came up with a solution: Cut the amount of water to the barest minimum and make a dough with the consistency of Portland cement. Such dough—the kneading of which became a seasonal form of Jewish resistance training—is less prone to rise on its own and, once it's been beaten into submission, comes out of the oven not much wider than a hair. The *Shulkhan Arukh*, the Sephardi legal code at the base of all contemporary Jewish practice, says that matzoh must be less than a handbreadth (i.e., four fingers) thick, but Moses Isserles, the sixteenth-century Polish rabbi who adapted the *Shulkhan Arukh* for Ashkenazi use, says, "Matzohs are to be made as wafers, not thick like other breads, because wafers are slower to ferment." In practice, soft matzoh reached a maximum thickness of about an inch, the height of four or five sheets of the hard stuff.

The proof of the pudding might be in the eating, but the measure of the matzoh is in the making: Technique is more important than taste, results take a backseat to theory. Matzoh is the bread of affliction (Dt 16:3), not the artisanal cracker of unleavened heritage grain and pure spring water. It's the food of real slaves on the run, not wage slaves in repose, and what is important about it is what it is not. Matzoh has a duty, if not quite to taste bad, then to not taste like much, "For you left the land of Egypt in a hurry" (Dt 16:3), with nothing but the ancient Near Eastern equivalent of roadside fast food to sustain you, food of dire necessity that you'd avoid if you could. While it's difficult to argue over questions of taste, the fact that a small number of Jews who also observe Passover claim to *like* the taste of matzoh could be seen as a kind of culinary Stockholm syndrome. As a Yiddish proverb has it, "A worm in horseradish thinks that there's nothing so sweet." Matzoh doesn't *need* to stoop to taste, it knows that it has you hostage.

For most observant Jews, matzoh anytime but Passover is usually the bread of last resort, a Torah-true hardtack suitable for shlepping into areas where acceptable bread is hard to come by. It tends to be considered a delicacy primarily by non-Jews and Jews whose ties to the ritual and ceremonial aspects of Judaism are not particularly powerful—there are plenty of "Jewish" or kosher-style restaurants that serve their usual nonkosher fare on Passover, but with a box of matzoh on every table.

People schooled in Jewish law and tradition appreciate matzoh for what it is, an aftertaste of oppression at a feast of deliverance, a reminder of how big a favor the Lord has done us. Whether toasted to perfection or blackened like a kosher campfire marshmallow, matzoh is the original win-win product: If it tastes good, it tastes good; if it doesn't, then it's all the more authentic. It's food for the brain, not the belly, as any Passover seder makes clear.

FEEDING YOUR HEAD

While few contemporary seders are as momentous as the first, those that follow the traditional ritual are largely devoted to reinforcing the attitudes and beliefs that that seder was there to encourage. A sacrifice designed to distinguish Israelites from Egyptians has developed into an annual all-you-can-eat, semiopen bar symposium on the Exodus and its meaning. Like any proper symposium—the word means "drinking together" in Greek—it starts off with a glass of wine, after which the chief symposiast, generally known as Dad or *Zeyde*—Yiddish for grandpa—points to the three matzohs stacked before him and declares, in an Aramaic that he might not understand, "This is the bread of affliction that our ancestors ate in the land of Egypt." For the next few hours, you're his.

The length of the seder depends on the leader's frame of mind, the size of the group, and the number of time-outs needed to threaten or cajole increasingly restive children, whose levels of boredom-stoked hunger rise in proportion to the adults' interest in reciting and discussing the text of the Hagaddah, the ritual GPS—"Raise glass here"; "Dip finger in wineglass now"—that is part program, part menu, part interpretive overview of the Exodus. Hagaddah means narrative, and the ritual that it both embodies and describes is devoted to explaining *why* you're going to eat that matzoh, even as you start to despair of *when*. You look at it, you hold it up, you point to it and discuss its history—but it's a long time before you get to eat it. And even then, you don't just cram it into your mouth; if you don't follow the proper procedure—an olive's worth from each of the top two matzohs in the stack, eaten as you lean to your left after Dad has made the blessing—you might as well watch the hockey game. The matzoh is the climax; the endless waiting and arguing and rehearsal of minority opinions the casuistic *Kama Sutra* that gets you there.

The matzoh is followed by an equally obligatory appetizer of bitter herbs, anything from Romaine lettuce or arugula to the traditional, if halachically suspect, horseradish, strong enough to call forth tears, but not so potent as to raise any gorges. The chosen herb is dipped into *charoses*, a paste of walnuts, apples, cinnamon, and wine meant to remind us of the bricks and mortar with which the Egyptians embittered our ancestors' lives. One final appetizer follows, a party sandwich that fulfills the commandment in Exodus 12:8 about eating matzoh and bitter herbs together. Finally—at ten, ten-thirty or even later—the menu blossoms into a lavish, less over-determined supper that my family always started with hard-boiled eggs in salt water—a little treat for the kids—after which the *second* half of the Hagaddah is recited.

This primal Jewish meal has more to do with discussion than digestion; you're meant to feed your head, not stuff your face. The real treat isn't dinner, which is only standing in for the Paschal sacrifice that can't be offered before the Messiah arrives; the gustatory high point is the matzoh. Tension is supposed to build, the participants are supposed to get more and more anxious, more and more involved in the story, attaining release only when the leader distributes the matzoh, recites the usual blessing over bread, and follows it up with a special, seder-only benediction, "On the eating of matzoh." Then, and only then, does mouth meet matzoh, and longing—fulfillment.

It doesn't matter what it tastes like, we've been jonesing for it, especially since matzoh is otherwise banned on the day of the seder, and bread—if you can find any—has been off-limits since midmorning. It isn't really nourishment that we crave—we invented Yom Kippur, we know from not eating—but a Jew loves matzoh like it was sweet jelly roll:

> *Matzoh is forbidden all day on the eve of Passover, as our sages have told us: "He who eats matzoh on Passover eve is like a man who has sex with his fiancée in her father's house"* [Yerushalmi Pesokhim, 10:1]. *Our sages have decreed that anyone who has sex with his fiancée while she is still a ward of her father is to be flogged for his willful disregard of proper standards of behavior: in displaying his lust, he shows himself lecherous and lewd, unable to restrain himself long enough to hear the Seven Blessings with her beneath the wedding canopy. So does he who eats matzoh on Passover eve display his lust and his gluttony, his inability to restrain himself and wait until nighttime and the seven blessings that must be pronounced before eating matzoh . . . and he is likewise to be flogged for his willfulness.*

It is hard to imagine how something so lacking in the usual attributes of good eating—things like taste, texture, and aroma—could arouse such passion, but matzoh is more than mere food; it's the essence of Judaism—what Yiddish calls *dos pintele yid*, the irreducible nub of Jewishness—wrapped up in a biscuit. Mordechai

Yoffe, the late sixteenth/early seventeenth-century author of the passage just quoted, is expressing the standard idea that even the coarsest, most uncouth Jew can see through the fripperies of moistness and flavor to the real essence of this Diana Prince of the bake pan. Lust he might, but for the freedom of *yidishkayt*, of Jewishness, in all its crunchy, nutlike splendor. The matzoh-hound looks past the matzoh's workaday exterior to the divine spark that makes it what it is; instead of the crudest imaginable cracker, he sees an edible image of his soul, a crispy, immediately tangible version of his spiritual genome, and nothing's going to keep him from it. Without matzoh there would be no Jews, the Torah would have stayed in heaven, and no one would ever have heard of kosher.

WHATTHEHELL FROM HEAVEN

Such dough as the Israelites managed to bring with them from Egypt ran out on the fifteenth day of the month of Iyar, exactly a month after the Exodus, and they wasted no time telling Moses and Aaron: "Would that we had died at the hand of the Lord in the land of Egypt, while we sat by a pot of meat and ate bread until we were full; for you have taken us into this wilderness to starve the whole community to death." (Ex 16:3) Given what eight days of matzoh can still do to Jewish innards, we can only imagine how the Israelites must have been feeling after a solid month of the stuff—sixty-one separate meals, the rabbis tell us—but there's still such a thing as good manners. As Rashi points out, it was fine for them to ask for bread, without which they would have died, but to demand meat, which is hardly necessary for survival, especially when they had plenty of flocks and herds at their disposal . . . Rashi doesn't say that they're still thinking like slaves, and dishonest ones at that, but he leaves us no doubt as to their rudeness.

This isn't the Children of Israel's first complaint. In the preceding chapter they find the water undrinkable; in the chapter before that they accuse Moses—not for the last time—of taking them into the desert to die: "There weren't enough graves in Egypt?" (Ex 14:11). Now they don't even ask to be buried; they want to die with their mouths open, chins on their chests in a food coma they'd prefer not to come out of.

God shrugs his metaphorical shoulders and tells Moses, "Behold, I will rain down bread for you from heaven, and the people will go out every day and collect that day's ration." (Ex 16:4) Since the manna will fall only in the daytime, when the Children of Israel can see it, God sends quail that night, the last real food the Israelites are going to see for a while, and the manna appears the next morning. Each person gets an omer a day, the same 2.7 pounds or so used in the matzoh described above.

The Israelites never give the manna a real name. They just look at each other and ask, *"Man hu?"*—Bible-speak for "What the hell is this?" Since Torah scrolls have no punctuation, though, their question can also be read as a declarative statement, "It's *man*," i.e., manna, even though *man* had never been used as a noun before. Had they been speaking English, countless generations would have been calling any sudden windfall "whatthehell from heaven" without giving the name a second thought. The Book of Exodus describes the manna as white and says that it tasted like wafers in honey; the Book of Numbers—where the Children of Israel let Moses know how much they don't like it—says that the Israelites cooked it and baked it and that it tasted, as generations of Yiddish-speaking schoolboys used to render the verse, *vi di fetkayt fun shmalts*, "like the fatness of schmalts" (Nm 11:8), the very essence of the essence of goodness.

But to the Jews in the desert, it tasted like crap, a fact that puzzles a number of midrashic commentators, according to whom the manna not only tasted *good*, it tasted like whatever you liked best or happened to be craving. One influential source says that the biblical talk of milling and grinding and cooking the manna was strictly metaphorical. The manna "was never milled at all, but [the verb *milled*] teaches us that it was transformed into anything ground between millstones," that is, it took on the taste of whatever flour-based dish a person felt like eating. The same point is then made about foods ground with a mortar, baked in an oven, or cooked in a pot. In other words, as every Jew with a grade-school education once knew, the manna could taste like whatever you wanted it to taste like—as long as you were Jewish: "The nations of the world were not able to savor it, for it was like bitter tendons in their mouths," and the Israelites—who never complain unless they have a chance to speak—must have been aping the mixed multitude of gentile fellow travelers who tagged along with them on the Exodus (see Ex 12:38).

The Bible also tells us that the Children of Israel ate manna for forty years—forty years less one month, if you sit down and count it—from thirty days after they left Egypt to the death of Moses on the seventh of the month of Adar forty years later. No explanation is ever offered as to why they didn't avail themselves of the flocks and herds that they had with them, and there isn't much point in speculating. Except for the quails mentioned above and those that God sends to teach them a lesson after their complaints about the manna in Numbers 11, the Israelites ate nothing else for the whole of their stay in the desert.

GENERATIONS OF NO-GO

Forty years of manna from heaven means that the people who received the dietary laws at Mount Sinai had no real chance to obey them. Since no regular food is consumed in the desert, almost no one who actually gets into Canaan has ever eaten any of the creatures, permitted or not, that figure in these laws. When Moses tells the Jews that man does not live by bread alone (Dt 8:3), he's preaching to people who have never lived by bread at all, most of whom have never so much as seen it. Try to avoid pork when you're not sure what a pig's supposed to look like; go worry about seething a kid in its mother's milk when you're trying to figure out how to get the milk out of the mother. The uncertainty that must have attached to the earliest efforts to put the dietary laws into practice finds an echo in the almost compulsive attention that Jews have been paying to virtually every aspect of food preparation and consumption ever since. But the manna had a more immediate, more visceral effect on the Children of Israel, giving rise to a tradition that has survived its initial cause by thousands of years.

Rabbinic tradition holds that the manna was absorbed directly into the Israelites' bodies rather than processed by their digestive systems, and that "none of them had any need to evacuate." A midrash fills in the details:

> They said, "The manna is going to swell inside our bellies and kill us. Is there any one born of woman who does not eliminate what he has eaten?" Rabbi Shimon was asked his interpretation of the verse, "With your gear you shall have a spike, and when you have squatted you shall dig a hole with it and cover up your excrement" [Dt 23:14]. He said, "That which you buy from merchants who belong to the nations of the world comes out of you, but the manna will never come out of you."

The first sentence of this midrash is the earliest recorded instance of the anxiety about bowel movements that has come to play so large a part in Ashkenazi culture. Israelites by the thousands must have been telling Moses exactly how long it had been since they last squatted and used a spike.

If nothing else, this bit of early rabbinic lore (which is expanded even further in the Talmud, in tractate *Yoma* 75b) might help to refute one of the main arguments against the historicity of the Exodus: the lack of coprolites, the fossilized feces that you'd expect to find after a couple of million people spend forty years relieving themselves in close and conveniently arid quarters. Given the scarcity of leaves in the desert, it is probably just as well that any Israelite BMs were likely to have been bar mitzvahs.

THAT OLD TIME DIGESTION

The Bible is silent about the consequences of four decades of intestinal stasis; Jewish life and history are not. Although the Bible mentions hemorrhoids in passing (Dt 28:27, 1 Sam., chapters 5 and 6), it took Western civilization to transform them into the Jewish affliction par excellence. Painful and bloody, chronic but not fatal, associated with sedentary occupations and confined to an indelicate, otherwise humorous, part of the body, hemorrhoids were so common as to have been taken for granted among Yiddish-speaking Jews. Medieval Christian medical texts characterize hemorrhoids as a congenital Jewish affliction, a form of divine punishment—as if being Jewish wasn't already enough. It was also suggested—less often, but often enough—that Jews considered Christian blood the only effective remedy.

The *Jewish Encyclopedia* of 1906 describes hemorrhoids as "more common to Jews than to any other people," and goes on to say that "among the Hasidim in Galicia and Poland a Jew without hemorrhoids is considered a curiosity." The blame is assigned, as usual, to long hours of sitting in study and prayer (not to mention tailoring and shoemaking), and the constipation that today's insurance companies would probably try to write off as a pre-existing condition: East European Jewish culture *assumes* the presence of hemorrhoids. *A yid mit meridin*, a Jew with hemorrhoids, was once a jocular way of describing a garden variety, everyday sort of person, a Jewish John Q. Public; Joe the Plumber, but with different pipes.

Of course, a diet almost completely lacking in fresh fruit and raw vegetables might have had something to do with it. A Yiddish cookbook published in New York in 1914 states explicitly that "human beings cannot eat raw vegetables and one must know how to cook them," then goes on to tell readers just how to do so. Ears of corn are to be boiled for thirty minutes, carrots for forty, red cabbage for two-and-a-half hours. The only roughage these people absorbed came from treatment at the hands of others. *Bubbies*, those Yiddish-American grandmothers who used to urge their grandchildren—or anyone else who happened by—to "take a piece fruit" were consciously striving to create a new breed of hemorrhoid-free, nonghetto Jew. That fruit might have been food for the body, but it was intended as medicine for the soul. It meant that here in America the grandchildren would be Jews who needn't groan to sit up straight, Jews who walk proudly with their hands at their sides, clear-eyed and smiling as they stride to the nearest washroom, unencumbered by Europe and its venous baggage.

A BEEF IN THE BAKERY

The circle won't be broken. My generation's *bubbies* are gone now, but the prophylactic "piece fruit" lives on in the form of the compote that traditionally closes the seder meal in a last-ditch attempt to counter the binding effects of the matzoh. Participants skip it at their peril. For eight days every year (seven in the land of Israel), we remember our ancestors' liberation and share the pain that they feared the manna would bring them. Observant Jews live in terror of Passover constipation, and the shelves of dried fruit in the Passover section of any supermarket are there to try to lighten their burden.

Things needn't be this way, of course. The fear that gave birth to the Ashkenazi matzoh with which most of us are familiar is only one product of a way of thinking that has shaped the larger Ashkenazi attitude to food. Before looking at what this mode of thought has made of the dietary laws contained in the Bible, it might be best to see what else it has done to a food so basic that it could be made in strictly kosher fashion—kosher enough for God, at any rate—before anyone knew what kosher was supposed to mean. The shape of a Jew's matzoh is a reliable guide to that Jew's approach to religion.

As mentioned above, matzoh has been baked by hand for as long as matzoh has been baked, and until early in the modern era it was baked more often than not by the family that was going to eat it. The baking itself, which usually took place in public at large community ovens, often took on a festive social quality, like something between a quilting bee and a bar mitzvah. As Yitskhok Lipiec describes it in his *Seyfer Matamim*, a late-nineteenth-century encyclopedia of Jewish folk customs (the title means *Book of Tasty Treats*, though very little of it has anything to do with food):

> *It is a custom in Israel that while one is baking matzohs, his near neighbors bless him and say, "May you bake matzohs in kosherness again next year," and it says in Midrash Tanchuma that when they brought first fruits [to the Temple], a heavenly voice would cry out and say, "May you merit to do this next year."*

The matzoh-making machine, invented in 1838 by the otherwise rather obscure Isaac Singer (not to be confused with the sewing machine magnate, who was not Jewish), eventually changed the shape of matzoh as we know it. It had been round from time immemorial. The Hebrew word for "cake"(*ugà*) resembles both the adjective for "round" and the verb meaning "to make a circle," so the matzohs mentioned in Exodus 12:39 ("unleavened cakes") were assumed to look like unrisen pitas; although the *Shulkhan Arukh* forbids making patterns or depicting birds or animals on the matzoh, the author neither prescribes nor forbids any specific shape—it probably never occurred to him that matzohs would be anything but round.

Machine-made matzohs started out round, but cutting the dough into circles raised a possible halachic problem. The edges that were cut away to round off the matzohs were put back into the machine to avoid waste, a process that could compromise the eighteen-minute time limit. "Since," as Hebrew writer J. D. Eisenstein says, "they were afraid lest too much time elapse before [this] dough was baked, they

[also] invented a machine to cut the matzoh [dough] into squares" before it was baked. And the modern matzoh, which also turned out to be much easier to package, was born.

It would be a mistake, however, to look at the difference between the two types of matzoh or a preference for one over the other as having anything to do with taste, aesthetics, or a predilection for either the handmade or the mass-produced. There's no nutritional difference between the two; there's no sweet, sour, or salty; no guarantee that one type will be any more appetizing than the other. The difference lies outside the box, in the informed consumer's attitude toward God and Jewish tradition, and the vehemence with which he chooses to defend this attitude from the ceaseless depredations of that ineducable mass of Jews-Who-Don't-Agree-With-Him-About-Everything.

Almost every Jew who attends a synagogue, however sporadically, also has at least one synagogue into which he or she rather loudly refuses to set foot. Anyone unaware of this fact, anyone who might not know that we are looking at the primal food of the people who pioneered this notion of negative ownership, can be excused for expecting machine matzoh to have been received as enthusiastically as the sliced bread that it preceded by nearly a century. Indeed, matzoh machines spread quickly and without apparent controversy for twenty years, until a rabbi named Solomon Kluger, who had already led an impassioned struggle against horse-drawn hearses, published an attack on them in 1859. Kluger was learned, influential, and extremely conservative; aside from the edge-trimmings mentioned above, his halachic objections to machine-made matzoh concerned bits of dough that could cling to small or hard-to-reach parts of the machine, where they might then begin to leaven.

To complicate matters further, Jewish law demands that matzoh eaten at the seder, the only matzoh to which a Jew is never allowed to say no, be made with the specific intention of fulfilling the commandment to eat matzoh at the seder; even today, workers in hand-matzoh bakeries repeat the Hebrew phrase *le-sheym matses mitsve*—for the sake of matzoh to fulfill the commandment—over and over again while they work. Until such time as Skynet goes active, though, machines cannot be said to behave with intent, and Kluger, the John Connor of halachic argumentation, was also concerned lest they deprive matzoh workers of their income.

This latter worry was not entirely unfounded, as matzoh baking was the kosher original of Christmas work in the post office, a temporary stopgap for people who were otherwise unemployed. As the Yiddish saying has it, *er zitst vi a matse-beker*, he sits around like a matzoh-baker, idle for most of the year. A man with no visible means of support was often called a *matse-reydler*, a guy who makes holes in matzohs.

The leading Hasidic *rebbes* all backed Kluger, who also marshaled some very influential non-Hasidic support, as did his chief opponent, Joseph Saul Nathansohn, one of the preeminent halachic authorities of the time. Kluger's Luddite pamphlet was called *Declaration to the House of Israel*; Nathansohn's response, *Declaration Cancelled*, was a systematic refutation of Kluger's arguments. He admitted the potential problem with round matzohs, thus initiating the shape-shift to which we are now inured, but argued that machines could be cleaned more easily and efficiently than the rolling pins, bowls, workers, and other equipment in traditional bakeries. The question of intention was taken care of by invoking an argument that today's NRA would unquestionably approve: Machines don't make matzoh, Jews do. And as long as the Jew who turns the machine on does so with the explicit intention of baking matzoh for the seder—and why else would he be in the matzoh business?—there is no problem. As for the social aspects of Kluger's critique, Nathansohn compared matzoh workers with scribes rendered redundant by the printing press and argued that the superior kashrus of machine-made matzoh was as good for the souls of the poor as the lower price was for their wallets.

Anyone who's ever heard the name Manischewitz knows who finally won, but we're dealing with a culture in which a controversy that has a chance to ossify almost never dissolves. While contemporary opponents of machine-made matzoh are a minority within the overall Jewish community, they tend to be noisier about proclaiming their unwavering fidelity to ancient ways, no matter how recently uncovered, than those Jews—Orthodox, Conservative, or Reform—who are satisfied with the supermarket matzoh that is being dismissed as worse than donuts. Yet—and in these matters there's always a yet—many Jews who eat regular machine-made matzoh for the rest of the holiday use a different, "kosherer" kind, or else go for the hand-baked, on seder nights. Why take chances, especially when we know that all those arguments about time limits and valid intentions mean that not every piece of unleavened bread counts as matzoh in the Passover sense of the word?

The Bible commands us to "keep close watch on the matzohs" (Ex 12:17), an injunction traditionally understood to mean that since matzoh eaten on Passover has to be made specially for the holiday, it must be made with flour that has been guarded against contact with water or other leavening agents. Raba, a major Talmudic figure, goes a step further, though, and says that the wheat must be guarded from the time of harvest (*Pesokhim* 40a), a difference of opinion that has persisted into the present. According to the *Arbo'oh ha-Turim*, the thirteenth-century legal code on which the *Shulkhan Arukh* is modeled:

> Rabbi Alfasi [1013–1103] wrote that wheat for Passover matzoh must be guarded from the time of its harvesting, lest it come into contact with water, but my father, Rabbi Asher [ca.1250–1327], wrote that it is not necessary to guard the wheat until it has been ground. "In France and Germany," he says, "they are accustomed to guard [the wheat] from the time of milling, when it comes into proximity with water in water-powered mills."

Roughly 150 years later, the same point was made by the tremendously influential Jacob Moelin, better known as Maharil (c. 1365–1427), whose works are an important source of information about the life and customs of the German Jews of his time. "The Passover matzohs of our pious forebears," he writes, "were supervised from the time of harvesting. We are not so punctilious, though, and are accustomed to guard [the wheat for] our Passover matzohs from the time when it is milled."

Such unabashed laxness would get Rabbi Moelin censured in any contemporary yeshiva and very likely cashiered from most. For centuries, *shmura* matzoh—matzoh that's been guarded from the time of harvest, the kosher counterpart of bottled in bond—was the exclusive prerogative of a tiny number of elite scholars and mystics. Ezekiel Landau, a native of Poland who became chief rabbi of Prague, wrote in 1778, "No one but the most punctilious of the punctilious is accustomed to give any thought to *shmura* matzoh in any of the Polish territories." Although the Gaon of Vilna, arguably the most important scholar and certainly the most proficient kabbalist of the past few hundred years, ate only *shmura* matzoh for the duration of the festival, none of his students—an elite and highly prestigious group—followed his example.

Shmura matzoh owes its popularity in the West almost entirely to the Hasidic movement, a particular bête noire of the Gaon, who excommunicated its adherents on more than one occasion. *Shmura* was one of many stringencies assumed by early Hasidic leaders, and anyone who's ever been within kvetching distance of Yiddish folk culture already knows that whatever the *rebbe* does now, his followers will do five minutes from now, though probably not as well. A practice originally adopted for mystical reasons was turned into one more thing that you didn't really think about until *shmura* was unavailable. By the second or third decade of the eighteenth century, when Hasidism had become the dominant trend in most of Jewish Eastern Europe, it was rarely unavailable.

If nothing else, *shmura* matzoh lives up to its name; it's the Greta Garbo of Jewish food, pining for a solitude that it never quite gets. As Gil Marks describes it in his *Encyclopedia of Jewish Food*, "The wheat for matzah is harvested in the early afternoon of a sunny day, after the moisture level in the kernels has decreased to less than 13 percent. After threshing, the kernels are stored in bins and watched over until ready for grinding into flour."

And harvest day better come in a dry spell, a point made by Baila Grunwald, proprietor of the Montreal Matzah Bakery: "Usually we must travel [to the wheat field] a number of times until the wheat is of the right moisture. This year [2009], although we made the trip seven times, due to an excess of rainfall, the wheat wasn't usable, halachically, for shmurah matzah. So for the first time in sixteen years we couldn't harvest wheat for shmurah matzah."

It would be wrong to say that this extra attention makes *shmura* matzoh more kosher for Passover than regular; if it really were, there would be no regular matzoh on Passover—no one who observes the holiday would be willing to risk eating leaven, and even fewer rabbis would be willing to certify such a product as Passover-safe. The furthest any reputable authority will go is to say that *shmura* is preferable or even necessary for a seder, which is often—though not always—a coded way of saying that they don't consider machine-made matzoh real matzoh. It isn't so much that the wheat for *shmura* has been guarded longer, it's that *shmura* is usually made by hand by someone who is making it explicitly for the sake of the seder. While machine-made *shmura* matzoh does exist, it seems to do so only to provide those committed to both *shmura* and machine-made matzoh—people who like to antagonize everyone—with a relatively low-cost way of demonstrating their indifference to the handmade lobby. Not all *shmura* matzoh is handmade, but all handmade matzoh is *shmura*; I'm not aware of any commercially available non-*shmura* handmade matzoh.

It is slightly misleading to describe machine-made *shmura*

matzoh as a low-cost alternative to handmade. A quick check at matzahonline.com reveals an average price of $22.00 a pound (six to eight matzohs) for handmade *shmura* matzohs that have not been certified or endorsed by a prominent Hasidic *rebbe* or other religious celebrity; half-a-dozen organic spelt matzohs cost $29.50 and three gluten-free *shmura* oat matzohs come to $28.00, despite the fact that many authorities do not allow matzoh made of oats to be eaten at a seder. A seven-ounce box of Streit's machine-made *shmura* was going for $9.09 on the Streit's Web site, a net saving of $1.20 per closely watched pound, which suggests either expensive machinery or low-paid workers. That's a lot of lettuce for ersatz bread, especially when five pounds of Osem brand machine-made, non-*shmura* matzoh from Israel, certified by the Orthodox Union, was going for $29.98 on Amazon.com. At $6.00 a pound, roughly double the price of a loaf of fancy bread, it's what my father used to call a *yidishe* bargain.

HEADLONG INTO THE PAST

Among competent rabbis and decently educated laypeople, the question of *shmura* is just one of hundreds, if not thousands, of legal points over which authorities have been wrangling for millennia. The real problem with respect to matzoh is based on a principle expressed in the Yiddish phrase, *oylem goylem*, best translated as, "There's a lot of idiots out there." Popular opinion—which seems to have taken root in plenty of heads that are supposed to know better—has conflated baking technology with the material baked and come up with a syllogistic fallacy:

1. Hand-baked matzoh is the only matzoh that can be used on Passover.
2. All hand-baked matzoh is *shmura*.
3. Only *shmura* matzoh can be eaten on Passover.

Goodbye, Ezekiel Landau, and later for the Maharil and Rabbi Asher's son, Jacob. Two thousand years of Talmudic study and this is the best we can do? Yes, some halachic authorities claim that all machine-made matzoh is *chometz*—*because it's been made by a machine.* The flour that goes into the machine is like Mae West's goodness—it has nothing to do with it. The corollary to the faux syllogism above is that there's no such thing as machine-made *shmura* matzoh, and those boxes in the kosher department that say *shmura* are no more really *there* than the Santas in the toy department.

More thoughtful opponents of machine-made matzoh tend to focus on the question of intent. Among the less sophisticated, the "gimme that old-time unleavened" argument tends to be trotted out more and more frequently: Hand-baked matzoh was all anybody ate for thirty-five hundred years, and if it was good enough for the Hebrew children, it's good enough for me. This principle, known in Hebrew as *minhag avoseynu be-yadeynu*—we do what our fore-bears did—is based on an expression that occurs in the Babylonian Talmud, always in the third person and always in connection with people who insist on doing things the way they've always been done: wrong and by rote. It's a convenient way of dismissing minor varia-tions in Jewish practice: "People there don't do this or that quite the way they're supposed to, but they're following an established custom and are not going to change. Just don't go acting that way yourself."

The continuing use of horseradish for bitter herbs provides a con-temporary illustration of the phenomenon. Horseradish is neither bitter nor a herb. The Talmud lists five vegetables that can be used for *morer*, as the bitter herbs are called; permission to use horseradish when the recommended herbs were unavailable was granted in the fourteenth century and the conditional nature of the permission was soon forgotten. The top recommendation for bitter herbs is lettuce, which was not at all a "Jewish" vegetable. Now, however, when let-tuce and endive and the other plants listed are easily available to anyone within reach of a supermarket, there is no legal justification for continuing to use horseradish as *morer*. After all these centuries, though, it just wouldn't be Pesach without it. Who cares what some rabbi says, *minhag avoseynu be-yadeynu*; that's the way it's always been done and that's how we'll go on doing it.

When people use this phrase about themselves, they're usually rejecting some innovation or reform to which they can't find any valid grounds to object. What they usually mean is, "Yes, you're right, there is good reason to adopt this change, but we aren't going to do it. Our pappies didn't do it, neither did our pappies' pappies or their pappies' pappies, and we're not going to do it, either." It's the vulgar version of the standard Jewish notion that each generation since Moses is slightly weaker than the one before. "Our ancestors were so much greater than we are, so much closer to the revelation at Sinai, that their customs (or at least those for which neither God nor any of His prophets condemned them) must be worthy of emulation. Any failure to grasp their reasoning, any thought that we might understand something that these giants did not, is only further proof of how far we have fallen."

It's a good argument, in the sense that those who invoke it cannot help but get their way: "Evidence, shmevidence we're going to keep on doing things the way we do them now." And, while it is occasionally used to justify the reintroduction of long-abandoned progressive practices ("Look at Abraham, look at Moses, look at Maimonides and the Hasidic movement"), "the custom of our ancestors" is more often a sign of an extreme and rather emotional resistance to change or innovation ("Look at Abraham, look at Moses, look at Maimonides and the Hasidic movement").

This militant conservatism found a motto in the work of Moses Sofer (1762–1839), an educator and halachic authority who was among the more influential figures in nineteenth-century Jewish life. In his negative response to a question about moving the reading desk in a synagogue from the center of the sanctuary to the front,

Sofer turned a Mishnaic remark about grain planted during or after Passover into a mantra for believers in radical belatedness. Such grain, known as *chodosh*, cannot be used before the second day of the following Passover. In explaining that this rule is also in force outside of the land of Israel, the Mishna (*Orla* 3:9) says: "The Torah forbids *chodosh* everywhere." Though used here as a technical term, *chodosh* is an adjective that means "new"; when Sofer quotes this Mishna in support of his decision—and he does so on a number of other occasions, too—what he's actually saying is, "Innovation is forbidden by the Torah."

But only God really knows what's new. Rabbi Sofer's son and successor, who is universally acknowledged to have followed faithfully in his father's footsteps, was an active proponent of machine-made matzoh and contributed a statement of support to Rabbi Nathansohn's automation-friendly pamphlet. Ideas of Jewish authenticity can be just as unpredictable as the gastrointestinal effects of a seder.

TWO

Getting to No
Beginnings of the Dietary Laws

More than mere sources of nutrition, the matzoh and the manna also come with rules that help prep the Israelites for the dietary laws that they don't know they're about to receive. Though often characterized as nothing more than a series of prohibitions, these laws are only incidentally about abstention and have nothing to do with doing without. They rest upon an assumption of freedom and were intended, at least at the outset, as expressions of liberality, in the original sense of liberal as "unsuited to the servile, fit for nonslaves." They are about eating in a way that befits the Israelites' new status as God's "treasured possession" (Ex 19:5), and the Israelites aren't supposed to feel any more deprived of the right to eat certain creatures than most of us usually do of the right to get high on crystal meth or pee in the street. Just as the Lord announces the Israelite calendar with the words, "The first of the months of the year *for you*," so the prohibited species are described as abominable or unclean "for you." There might be nothing wrong with them per se, and if the nation down the street wants to eat them—*bon appetit*. They're just not good enough for the Lord's firstborn. (Ex 4:22) Think of them as rejected rather than forbidden, not so much a "you can't have it" as a "you don't want it"—but for people who have never done anything but follow orders and are still thinking like slaves who dream of having it all.

Slavery is based on denial; rejection is a prerogative of freedom.

The Israelites' Egyptian diet of fruit, vegetables, and imaginary fish satisfies all the demands of the laws in Leviticus or Deuteronomy, but no one thinks of it as kosher. As long as you're forced to make do with what others hand you, abiding by such laws is strictly a matter of chance—ask any Jew who's ever served in a non-Israeli army. Kosher food is the food of people who can insist upon their choices and control their own supply. Kosher means fit or proper, and kosher food, the healthy choice in a junk-food world, is food that is fit for a Jew to eat. It is also the food of people who can feel guilty or belligerent or proudly indifferent when they fail to make that healthy choice.

It is hardly surprising, then, that adherence to such rules should become a conspicuous pillar of identity, an unambiguous public affirmation of Judaism. It had certainly done so by the second century BCE, when the Maccabees rebelled against a government that sought to force-feed Judea with *treyf*, and it has endured into our own era in a plethora of kosher-certification agencies, as well as less formal and even deliberately provocative public statements:

> *Ikey, Mikey, Jake, and Sam,*
> *We're the boys who eat no ham,*
> *We keep matzohs in our locker,*
> *Aye, aye, aye, Weequahic High.*

For centuries, a Jew was assumed to be someone who would never work on Saturday or think of eating pork; only in modern times have significant numbers of Jews found a way to relax or even jettison such observances while retaining their Jewish identity and sense of membership in the Jewish community. It's one of the perks of an anti-Semitism based on racial origin instead of religious affiliation. Were it not for Wagner, we might never have met General Tso.

Although the decrees enacted in Leviticus and Deuteronomy are incumbent only upon Jews, the Bible doesn't hesitate to impose a couple of food rules on humanity at large. The first "thou shalt not" of all is a straightforward prohibition that applies to everyone on earth. "Do not eat from the tree of knowledge of good and evil, for on the day that you do so, you will most emphatically die." (Gen 2:17) Where Christians see Original Sin, Jews behold The Primal Cookie Jar: If life as we know it sucks, it's because we broke the Dietary Law, and we should try not to do so again.

The second food rule is likewise considered binding on all mankind—once they've consulted the Talmud to find out what it means: "You shall not eat flesh with the life—that is, the blood—still in it." (Gen 9:4) Since the blood of dead animals is explicitly forbidden in Leviticus, Jewish tradition takes this verse to refer to living beings: You can't cut the wings off a live chicken and eat them, let alone take a bite from a chicken that is still breathing. Aside from making it impossible for any Jew to pursue a career as a carnival geek—this commandment should, after all, make such geekery unthinkable for Christians as well—it certainly deprives us of any chance at gefilte ikizukuri. Fresh oysters and drunken shrimp, neither of which is kosher even when dead, are the only forms of live food easily available to most Jews in the West, a fact that allows the enterprising sinner to violate two major food ordinances with one little bite.

The first solely Jewish food prohibition is found in the thirty-second chapter of Genesis and is presented as commentary on a wrestling match. The angel who has been bested by Jacob in hand-to-hand combat "touches" the patriarch in the hollow of his thigh, wrenching it from the socket where it meets the hip and leaving Jacob with a permanent limp. "Therefore," the Bible tells us, "the children of Israel do not eat the *gid ha-noshe*, which is in the hollow of the thigh, unto this day; because he touched the hollow of Jacob's thigh, the *gid ha-noshe*," the sciatic nerve. (Gen 32:32–33) Even though the story is found in Genesis, the Mishna (*Khulin* 7:6) explains that the prohibition itself was enacted only at Mount Sinai and that it is mentioned earlier in the biblical narrative only to make the reasoning behind it explicit.

The sciatic nerve covers a fair bit of territory and is often bound up, in the kosher butcher business at least, with yet another taboo part of the animal. In the third chapter of Leviticus, we are told that "all fat is the Lord's," an idea that is elaborated slightly in chapter seven: "You shall eat no fat of ox or sheep or goat. Fat from animals that died or were torn by beasts may be put to any use, but you must not eat it." (Lev 7:23–24) The fat referred to is called *kheylev* in Hebrew and corresponds roughly to what we call suet, the fat around the kidneys, loins, and abdominal cavity, as distinct from the fat mixed in with the flesh. It was sacrificed to the Lord and it belongs to Him still. While the prohibition of the sciatic nerve applies to all kosher animals, that of *kheylev* concerns only those animals authorized for sacrifice: sheep, goats, and oxen. Deer and moose were never offered and their *kheylev*, like that of the buffalo and giraffe, is completely kosher, as is that of such birds as the chicken, without whose schmaltz we wouldn't be here today.

Banning the sciatic nerve explains a good deal about the rather narrow range of cuts available in most kosher meat departments; *kheylev* takes care of the rest. Because fat and sciatic nerves are the sorts of things that animals who have them can't live without, their presence in a slaughtered animal doesn't render the animal *treyf*. They have only to be removed for the surrounding meat—filet mignon, T-bone, sirloin, porterhouse, rump, leg of lamb—to be perfectly acceptable. But the removal presents problems of its own.

Although Jews have been removing the veins and forbidden fat for thousands of years and continue to do so in Israel and some diaspora Sephardi communities, it is generally considered too difficult and time-consuming to be cost-effective in the relatively limited market for kosher meat. Removal is generally the province of specialists who have to be paid; it is picky and precise even by the standards that apply to kosher meat, and many rabbinic authorities insist that all such work be double-checked to make sure that none of the forbidden matter has been overlooked. It's been done sporadically in many Ashkenazi communities but has not been universal—if it ever was—for centuries. Stories used to circulate about Rabbi Moshe Feinstein, the leading halachic authority of the second half of the twentieth century, pining wistfully for the T-bones and sirloins of his Belarussian youth; until the recent opening of a few high-end kosher restaurants and charcuteries, most American-born Jews who had eaten kosher hind cuts had done so in Israel.

Removing the *kheylev* and sciatic nerve is called *nikkur* (literally, gouging) in Hebrew, *traybern* in Yiddish. The English term, "porging," from the verb "to porge," is one of those handy translations that tends to have no meaning for anyone not already familiar with the original: "The rabbi removed his phylacteries, porged an ox, and headed off to the ritualarium" is English in only the most technical sense.

Though not kosher, unporged or improperly porged meat is perfectly edible and is usually sold to non-Jewish butchers, generally at a higher rate of profit than could be realized from kosherly porged hind cuts. Many Ashkenazi communities thus long ago decided to deal only with the front end of the cow, which requires minimal porging, and sell the hind parts to non-Jews or non-Jewish butchers as a matter of course. Kosher meat in most of the Ashkenazi world thus became synonymous with the five tougher front cuts: rib, chuck, brisket, flank, and shank. The brisket that Howard Wolowitz's mother is always yelling about on *The Big Bang Theory* can trace its lineage back to Jacob's fight with the angel.

Much of the nonkosher beef available in supermarkets and butcher shops consists of the hind parts of animals that have been slaughtered according to Jewish law, a fact that seems to exercise religious bigots and European animal rights advocates, who disapprove of both halal slaughter and kosher *shekhita*, neither of which allows an animal to be stunned before it is killed. Recent attempts in the EU to label such meat as "derived from animals that have not been stunned prior to slaughter"—in the interests, of course, of full disclosure—have managed to bring Jews and Muslims together on the same side of at least one issue.

MEAT, DAIRY, AND DISHES

Even before the biblical Israelites find out what animals they will be allowed to eat once they get out of the desert and stop subsisting on manna, the Lord explains how the permitted species are not to be eaten—and explains it again and again. Three times He commands them not to cook a kid in its mother's milk, twice before the forbidden species are named in Leviticus and once again after they are repeated in Deuteronomy (see Ex 23:19, 34:26; Dt 14:21). According to tradition, the repetition is an allusion to the threefold nature of the prohibition: Don't cook a kid in its mother's milk; don't *eat* a kid that someone else has cooked in its mother's milk; and don't derive any benefit from a kid that has been cooked in its mother's milk (i.e., don't take the kid offered you by the person in the second prohibition and sell it to a non-Jew). Tradition also has it that the kid mentioned in the Bible is merely emblematic, that God really means meat from any land animal, as Rashi explains:

> *Calves and lambs are also subsumed under "kid," which is merely a locution for recently born offspring, as we see in several places in the Torah . . . Whenever the text uses kid on its own, we are meant to understand calf and lamb as well. (Ex 23:19)*

While no one seems to have had any serious quarrel with this interpretation of kid, which was at least a thousand years old when Rashi's students transcribed it, the Talmud contains some rather heated discussion of just what constitutes meat, whether or not the category embraces locusts, fish, and birds, and whether the sages of the Talmud would ever be in a position to invent Chicken à la King. Fish and locusts, some of which are kosher, are easily explained away as parve, no more dairy or meat than fruits and vegetables. Birds are a little more troublesome. Rabbi Yossi of Galilee, one of the major Mishnaic sages, says that since birds do not lactate, there is no reason not to cook them in milk. Rabbi Akiva, *the* major Mishnaic sage, claims that eating fowl and milk together has been forbidden by rabbinic enactment, and he will not be swayed by the fact that cooking birds in milk was customary in Rabbi Yossi's hometown (*Khulin* 116a)—a perfect example of mainstream attitudes to the *minhag avoseynu* principle mentioned a few pages ago. Birds are thus classified as meat; as a precaution, according to Maimonides, lest eating their flesh with milk should lead people to think that they can eat the flesh of sheep and cattle with milk, too.

Akiva's stringency was in keeping with the spirit of his second-century times. *Targum Onkelos*, the slightly earlier Aramaic version of the Bible, which the Talmud instructs us to read every week, goes beyond mother and kid to render all three of the verses in which they are mentioned with "Do not eat meat in milk," while the Mishna prohibits putting cheese and meat (including fowl) onto the same dining table.

The strict separation of meat and dairy products is one of the earliest safeguards—fences, the Talmud calls them—against their ever being likely to be eaten together. Such fences have had a profound effect on traditional Jewish life, behavior, and domestic furnishings. Indeed, the possibility of mixing meat and dairy provoked such anxiety that steps were taken to keep them from mingling in the mouth, even if they hadn't been eaten together. The issue, symptomatic in itself of the kind of *folie du doute* responsible for so many familiar Jewish customs, goes back to a couple of passages in tractate *Khulin*:

1) Rov Khisdo says: If someone has just eaten meat, he is forbidden from eating cheese. If he's eaten cheese, though, he can eat meat, but he should wait a little between the cheese and the meat.

2) Mar Ukvo says: With respect to this [waiting], I am as vinegar in comparison with my father, who was like wine. For if my father were to eat meat now, he would not eat cheese for a full twenty-four hours. Whereas if I were to have meat in this meal, I wouldn't eat cheese; but I would at the next meal. (*Khulin* 105a)

For centuries, no one seems to have been troubled by this. Rov Khisdo establishes the principle of a waiting period between meat and cheese, and Mar Ukvo's remarks are used to fix the length of that period—the time between one meal and the next, however long or short that might be. The now-standard six-hour wait between meat and dairy became official, so to speak, in the sixteenth century, when Moses Isserles gave it his seal of approval. Where the *Shulkhan Arukh* itself presents Sephardi practice as if there were no other— "Whoever eats the meat of birds or animals is to wait six hours before eating cheese"—Isserles admits that not everyone was as enthusiastic about so great a gap between dinner and dessert:

> *There are those who say that there is no need to wait six hours, but that cheese can be eaten immediately afterwards. If one clears the table and says the Grace after Meals, he need only cleanse his mouth and rinse it. The widespread custom in our lands is to wait one hour after eating meat before eating cheese, with the proviso that one say Grace after the meat.*

While some people were happy to go straight from meat to dairy, as long as they were not eaten at the same time, most would wait an hour. Yet there is also evidence of whole communities, not just isolated pious individuals, for whom a six-hour wait after meat was already a norm that let those who embraced it feel a certain kinship with such prominent intellectuals as Isserles or Joseph Karo, the author of the *Shulkhan Arukh*.

Although even so influential and generally stringent an authority as Rashi's grandson Rabeynu Tam says that Rov Khisdo merely prohibits eating cheese after meat without cleaning the mouth and hands, and that Mar Ukvo is referring only to cases where he hadn't rinsed his mouth, his opinion was unable to withstand the *Shulkhan Arukh* and the force of social pressure. As David C. Kraemer points out in *Jewish Eating and Identity Through the Ages*, Isserles was living in Cracow at a time when Polish Jews were enjoying a degree of tolerance and prosperity so unusual as to lead to occasional eating and drinking with non-Jews. While such behavior might have involved no actual violation of Jewish law, it has always been frowned upon by most rabbis and plenty of laypeople; imagine the reaction of even an unobservant contemporary Jew to the sight of a Hasid sitting in McDonald's behind a bunch of empty Big Mac boxes left by someone else.

Similar problems arose in sixteenth century Warsaw and Cracow. Adopting the six-hour waiting period let other observant Jews know that you, Mr. or Mrs. Six-Hours-To-Snack-Time, were a true son or daughter of your people, faithful to its traditions and happy to assume the most stringent obligations rather than coast along with the minimum acceptable effort; no one would ever see *you* in a Renaissance-era McDonald's. This was one of the early stirrings of a powerful impulse in modern Jewish social life: conspicuous kashrus, the practice of going beyond the requirements of a law that you might not understand in the certainty that being more kosher than halacha demands will win you the approval of God and man alike. The whole idea can be summed up in three words: Passover dairy apartment.

Although Isserles's recommended practice quickly became standard in Eastern Europe, Dutch Jews continued to follow Rabeynu Tam—say grace, wait an hour, then rinse their mouths—while the tradition in Germany was to wait three hours, the time from one meal to the next, based on the idea that lunch and supper are closer together in winter and that Jewish law is supposed to follow the least onerous path permitted.

The waiting period after eating dairy is completely different. With the exception of certain hard cheeses, which require the same waiting period as meat, dairy foods are not thought to leave any residue behind; you need only rinse your mouth and wash your hands. The Talmud actually says that there is no waiting period at all (*Khulin* 105a), but no real Jew likes to rely on anything that makes life easy: if you don't want to wait at all, you're supposed to eat some solid parve food between cheese and meat, a rule that most people now apply to any dairy food.

Virtually all observant Jews wait at least half an hour between dairy and meat—and more usually an hour—in accordance with the opinion of the *Zohar*, the central Jewish mystical text, that milk and meat should not be eaten in the same hour. The image of a whole roasted kid is said to appear on the skin of anyone who does so, and to stay there for forty days as a sort of welcome mat for demons on the hunt for transgressors, a mystical idea that helps explain the appeal of kabbalah for so many of today's young Jewish hipsters. The punishment for not waiting long enough between dairy and meat gets the guilty party around another more socially disruptive prohibition; you can't get into trouble for having a tattoo when your body art is a heaven-sent reminder of the importance of keeping kosher.

The need to separate milk from meat has also had far-reaching material effects and is responsible for the kosher kitchen's distinctive abundance. The kitchen-supply trade dreams of an all-kosher America with the slightly moist avidity of a twelve-year-old girl contemplating Ringo Starr in 1964. Consider the needs of a contemporary observant household: two sets of dishes and cutlery, dairy and meat, for weekdays; two nicer sets for Saturdays and holidays; two sets for Passover. Six sets of dishes in all, with yet one more among semiobservant people who appreciate tradition but don't want to feel too guilty for ordering Chinese food or pepperoni pizza. Add two sets of pots and pans; two more sets of pots and pans for Passover; that's four. Separate sink-lining tubs for meat and dairy, for those who can't afford the luxury of designated sinks. Separate cupboards for the separated dishes and cookware, separate drawers for the separate sets of cutlery. Separate dishcloths, scrubbers, and towels; dedicated soap dishes for those too hidebound to use liquid dish detergent, with separate cakes of dish soap—a red dot in the middle of one, a blue dot on the other—to distinguish dairy soap from meat. Separate dishwashers if at all possible. More prosperous people will have a fancy kitchen with an island in the middle, with one side of the room—oven, range, fridge, sink, counters, cupboards, and everything else—dedicated to meat, the other to dairy.

Like so many other customs now taken as sine qua nons of proper Jewish conduct, the idea of keeping separate sets of dishes is relatively modern. Until the seventeenth century, when wooden trenchers, similar to the plates used in steakhouses with corkboard walls and red-velvet trim, became the norm, individual dining plates in Europe were made of bread, which might be fresh if you were rich or lucky. Bowls for holding food, pots for cooking it, and spoons for getting it from one to the other and into your mouth comprised most of the armamentarium for a very long time. So the Tosefta, which was compiled during the Mishnaic era, declares unambiguously that milk cannot be boiled in a pot in which meat has been cooked and vice versa; whatever was cooked first might impart its taste to the other, leading to a violation of the biblical injunction against kids in mothers' milk. This rule is repeated in two separate tractates of the Talmud. Whether it led to different pots being set aside for meat and dairy use we don't know; after twenty-four hours of idleness, a pot was thought to revert to a state of neutrality and many medieval authorities, Ashkenazi and Sephardi alike, permitted a pot in which meat had been cooked to be used for cheese as long as something parve had been cooked in it between times.

Roughly half a millennium has passed since an observant Jew would eat in the home of anyone who would do such a thing. Habits of mind conditioned by the unwavering effort of trying not to violate a single one of the 365 prohibitions recorded in the Torah seem to have encouraged Jews to adopt stringencies that God never asked for, generally out of fear of making a mistake. A single fence might not be enough to keep you off the grass; ten fences with no space between them, pointed on top and strung with barbed wire, make it impossible to get to the grass, which means that there is no chance of its ever being trod on. It might not be visible, either, but there is no law that says that it has to be looked at.

MORE CATHOLIC THAN THE POPE

The urge to assign all utensils and ancillary paraphernalia to one category or the other and then segregate the categories; the impulse to go beyond the strict demands of the law to create new, more rigorous norms of observance seems to go hand-in-hand with the increase in waiting time between meat and dairy and, if anything, to have spread more quickly and been adopted far more widely. We have no evidence for the comprehensive separation of all dishes and utensils until the sixteenth century, when a German apostate named Antonius Margaritha wrote that "the Jews use two kinds of vessels, one for meat and the other for milk. Therefore, they have two kinds of pots, bowls, spoons, platters, and knives."

Margaritha's book, an important source for Martin Luther's *On the Jews and Their Lies*, came out in 1530; the *Shulkhan Arukh*, published thirty-five years later, never really broaches the matter of separate dishes except to tell us not to slice cheese with a knife usually used for meat or put it onto a cloth from which meat has been eaten. Isserles comments that "All Israel are already in the habit of having two knives and of marking one of them so that they can be told apart. They are in the habit of marking the dairy one, and universal Jewish customs are not to be changed." Bits of meat or fat or grease are as likely to stick to a knife as bits of cheese, and no one wanted to end up with a mouthful of forbidden mixture. The same basic logic led to a relatively early doubling up on salt. Since food was dipped in salt rather than sprinkled with it, bits of meat or cheese could be expected to lurk in a salt dish.

The halachic self-medication practiced by the Jewish masses far outstripped anything prescribed by Karo, Isserles, or their immediate successors. Everybody knows the problem: Meat and dairy foods cannot come together in any circumstance, but the rules that determine the meaning of "together" and "circumstance" are so detailed and confusing that even experts disagree as to how and when to enforce them. "No problem," says the still, small voice of the people; separate pots don't make sense without separate everything else to go with them. We've already got separate knives and saltshakers, don't we? If you've got to boil a spoon that you used for cheese if it touches a piece of hot meat, why not have two spoons and save yourself the trouble of shlepping water and wood and laying a fire and everything else? Stuff from the meat pot needs to go into a meat bowl or onto a meat tray or plate; it needs to be eaten with a meat knife and a meat spoon and wiped from your mouth and hands with a cloth devoted to meat wipe.

And the same goes for dairy.

If the plain people of Israel cannot match their leaders in learning, they can more than hold their own when it comes to saying no; if lack of understanding should lead them to forbid the permitted, doing so for safety's sake makes them part of an ancient and venerable tradition. It is no surprise that laypeople living in a society that idealizes rabbis and scholars will try to act "rabbinically" in order to feel good about themselves and gain the respect of others. Should their zeal push them to expand the field of what isn't allowed, at least they'll be farther away from any chance of transgression. Just think of the Hebrew National slogan: they answer to a higher authority and can satisfy their vanity and their deity in one fell swoop.

The Jewish folk-mind may sometimes have been subtler, but it has never been more effective. Double sets of dishes were taken for granted in virtually all European Jewish kitchens by the earlier part of the eighteenth century and have remained so ever since. No contemporary Jew, kosher-keeping or not, can even conceive of a kosher home in which all dishes and utensils are not designated as either dairy or meat. The voice of the people, in this instance at least, really has become the voice of God.

The same might be said of the displacement of regular kosher meat in favor of meat called *glatt*. *Glatt* means smooth and refers here to the lungs of a meat-bearing mammal. In broad outline, if the lungs are smooth and free of adhesions, the animal is *glatt* kosher, "smoothly acceptable." If they are covered in adhesions, the animal is *treyf*; if there are adhesions but the lung has not been punctured, the animal is kosher but not *glatt*. Joseph Karo's opinion on the status of an animal with *any* pulmonary adhesions long ago made *glatt* the only kosher for Sephardim; widespread observance of *glatt* in the Ashkenazi world was a Hasidic custom not widely imitated in other communities, and *glatt* kosher meat was not readily available in the United States until well after World War II.

Today, it is almost impossible to find kosher meat that is not *glatt*. The Orthodox Union will not certify anything else as kosher, and such regular kosher meat as is generally available tends to be treated like *treyf* by people who consider themselves religious. In another generation or so, once the last observant Jews with any personal experience of non-*glatt* meat have gone to the great dairy restaurant in the sky, the idea that a piece of meat could be kosher without being *glatt* will sound as outlandish as the idea of a kosher kitchen that has not been divided into two. The fact that kosher isn't kosher enough, that mortals are rejecting what the Lord has permitted, is of little concern when intramural social boundaries come to be drawn. Traditional Judaism tends to respond to both prosperity and adversity by increasing observance. Anything else could lead to mixed dining.

IN, OUT, AND IN BETWEEN

As categories that virtually every Jew over the age of three was forced to think about nearly every day, *milkhiks* and *fleyshiks*, dairy and meat, occupy a not-insignificant place in Yiddish language and folklore.

Important as *milkhiks* was to the East European Jewish diet, it didn't get much respect. It was generally available—much more so than meat, at any rate—and, since it demands only a minimal waiting period, tended to be equated with things without much staying power or lasting effect. Marshall Brickman, coauthor of *Sleeper*, *Annie Hall*, *Manhattan*, and *Jersey Boys*, writes about a conversation he had with S.J. Perelman, the Horowitz of the well-placed Yiddishism. Speaking of a writer whose work they both disliked, Brickman writes, "I was searching for the precise phrase to characterize what I felt was the pallid quality of the lady's prose when Perelman leaned over and whispered, '*milchedig*' [i.e., *milkhik*];" "light," as Brickman goes on to explain, "bland," making no real impression one way or the other. Parve, but with pretensions. When the world regains its pristine balance and restaurant reviews begin to appear in Yiddish, bitchy critics will be answering the question, "How's the deli?" with the most withering of possible put-downs, "*Milkhik*, strictly dairy." A Yiddish-speaking Wisconsin would never dare replace "America's Dairyland" with *Amerikes milkhiker shtat*; it's like saying, "Land of the Bland."

Hence the *milkhiker khesed*, the meatless good turn, the pointless minor favor that someone does you instead of the favor you really need; and the *milkhiker nes*, the not-so-miraculous miracle that happens all the time. "A Republican who dislikes Obama? *A milkhiker nes*, who woulda thunk it?" As the Talmud says, "There is no celebration without meat" (*Pesokhim* 109a), no reason to get excited about something that has no substance. There is also the once widespread "to hear someone *vi dem milkhikn klingl*, like the *milkhik* blade" which means to pay no attention to them at all. Imagine the sound of a cheese cutter or a knife moving through butter or cottage cheese, then compare it with the noise of the *hakmeser*, or meat cleaver, and you'll have the general idea.

Almost as rare these days is the greatest of all idioms relating to *milkhiks: blaybn af der milkhiker bank*, "to be left on the dairy bench." The bench here is what we would call a counter, and someone who has been left there has been excluded from some activity or other on a transparently flimsy pretext. When Homer Simpson points out that the kids who formed the No Homers Club let Homer Glumplich join, the kids in the club tell him that the sign says "No Homers. We're allowed to have one." Homer has been left *af der milkhiker bank*.

The idea takes us back to the different waiting periods required for meat and dairy. There is no believable reason for leaving you out because you're *milkhik*; all it means is that they really don't like you. If a bunch of Jews of East European descent want to exclude someone of similar background from a social activity, they can claim that they're having an ice cream social right after he mentions having just finished a burger. Everybody's hands are tied; whatever the motive, the excuse has the appearance of legitimacy. "We're going for burgers and you're *milkhik*," doesn't make any sense at all; by the time you got there and ordered, it would no longer be an issue, even with people who insist on waiting.

The six-hour waiting period lends most idiomatic uses of *fleyshik* a sense of commitment and relatively long-term irreversibility. Since a single mouthful of meat leaves you irredeemably *fleyshik* for just as long as a thirty-two ounce steak, most figurative uses of *fleyshik* tend to have an underlying sense of "in for a penny, in for a pound."

Makhn zikh fleyshik, "to make yourself *fleyshik*," often has a sense of "take the plunge" in one metaphorical sense or another, most often with respect to business: "After months of deliberation, he finally made himself *fleyshik* and bought ten-thousand shares of stock." If buying the stock was going to tie his money up for too long and prevent him from making other potentially better deals, he might decide not to do so, on the grounds that *im loynt zikh nisht tsu farfleyshikn*, it doesn't pay for him to make himself *fleyshik*, it isn't worth the commitment. Making yourself *fleyshik* can also mean "to open or go into a business."

Similarly, you can ask someone who's been sitting on the fence about something if they're *milkhik* or *fleyshik*. It's the equivalent of "Yes or no; in or out?" or even, depending on context and tone of voice, "Shit or get off the pot."

The six hours of unsuitability for anything *milkhik* finds a nice reflection in a second, closely related sense of *makhn zikh fleyshik*—to take a drink or, latterly, other intoxicant. If you find someone you know with a bottle in front of them and they say *makh zikh fleyshik*, it means simply "Have a drink"—it's "wet your whistle" refracted through two millennia of looking at the world through a veil of food. Likewise, you can ask someone if they'd like to make themselves *fleyshik*; if you're pointing to a bottle or a barroom, it still refers to drink, but it also tends to be used by stoners who want to know if you'd like to get high. The old Ray Charles hit, "Let's Go Get Stoned," would be "Let's Go Get *Fleyshik*" in Yiddish, though the line that runs, "Ain't no harm to have a little taste," should not be rendered as "Eat something, already."

Food that is neither meat nor dairy plays a less prominent part in the speech of people notorious for their avoidance of green vegetables. Generally used as a synonym for *milkhik* in the sense of "bland, nothing special, of no determinate character," parve tends to be a bit more absolute. Someone or something *milkhik* might be bland, but has at least decided to be something; someone or something parve can't even make a commitment to blandness, a hesitancy that the linguist David L. Gold has allowed us to trace to the word's previously obscure origins. The West European Yiddish for such neutral food was once *minikh* or *minish*, from the German *Mönch*, which means monk (as in Munich, *München* in German). German and Yiddish both used the word as a slang term for a gelding, a horse that is neither male nor female, neither here nor there, not one thing and not the other.

Parve shifts the emphasis a bit. Gold compares it with two Slavic adjectives, the Czech *párový* and the Polish *parowy*, each of which is derived from a noun that means "pair" in its respective language. The phonology and semantics seem to work; as Gold puts it, "pareve foods, pots, etc., are pairable with meat or milk ones."

Once we start to think of parve as dual natured rather than neutral, it is easy to see where Yiddish gets an idiom like parve *lokshn*, parve noodles that can go with either dairy or meat. The phrase refers to an epicene or androgynous person—I've never heard it used of a woman—who does not have enough defining characteristics to be easily classified as either meat or dairy: Julia Sweeney's Pat, from *Saturday Night Live* in the '90s, as reviewed in the Yiddish papers.

THREE

If You Have to Ask, It's Treyf
More Dietary Laws

Jack Webb stated the basic idea on an episode of *Dragnet 1968*: "Marijuana is the flame, heroin is the fuse, LSD is the bomb." The dietary laws that we've seen thus far are gateway prohibitions designed to wean the Children of Israel from the mindless omnivorism that they might have envisioned as a perk of freedom. The rules of meat and dairy, along with the blessings said over the food that they affect, are also among the first commandments consciously observed by children too young to have encountered *treyf* but old enough to ask their mothers if there's any chance of ice cream for dessert. If supper were glazed Virginia ham, there would be no point to forbidding the ice cream, and that's where Webb has shown us the way: The sciatic nerve and suet are the flame, not mixing milk with meat is the fuse, forbidding hasenpfeffer, lobster, and pork is the bomb.

The laws concerning permitted and forbidden species are found in the eleventh chapter of Leviticus and are repeated, with slight shifts in emphasis and detail, in the fourteenth chapter of Deuteronomy. Animals must be ruminants with cloven hooves; most mammals don't qualify, nor do reptiles and amphibians. Deuteronomy lists the animals that do: "The ox, the sheep, and the goat; the deer, the gazelle, the roebuck, the wild goat, the ibex, the antelope, the mountain sheep, and any other animal that parts its hoof and has its hooves cloven in two and chews the cud" (Dt 14:4–6), a description that paves the way for buffalo, moose, elk, and giraffe.

47

Anything that lives in water has to have fins and scales. Insects are forbidden, with the exception of certain locusts, grasshoppers, and crickets. The grasshopper/locust aspect of this kosher surprise was explained to my third-grade class as a safeguard against starvation after the kind of locust plague we were learning about in preparation for Passover. According to our teacher, the only thing left to eat after such a disaster is the locusts themselves.

It looks as if we're allowed any birds we want except those on the Bible's forbidden list, one of which, the bat, is not a bird at all, and most of which—vulture, eagle, cormorant—are not terribly tantalizing. But no—the Bible tells us which birds we can't eat, but never bothers to specify which ones we can. And that's where the problems start. Since no positive criteria of avian kashrus are ever presented, generations of fowl-eating Jews have had to rely on generations of fowl-eating Jews to tell them which birds are kosher. This kind of tradition—which could only be invented by people who have never played broken telephone—is known as a *mesorah* in Hebrew, and no bird without one can be eaten. We know that a bird is kosher because a Jew of unquestionable piety has eaten it or seen it eaten by other equally reliable Jews, who all have their own Jews, and so on all the way back to the conquest of Canaan. When it comes to chicken, for example, those trustworthy Jews are probably your parents; the fact that chickens are mentioned in the Talmud (though not in the Bible) proves nothing. Names can change over time, and what was called a chicken in first-century Jerusalem might have nothing in common with what Colonel Sanders or your *bubbie* cooks up.

There is similar uncertainty about unclean birds; we are no longer sure of the meaning of some of the names and are therefore in danger of eating one if we rely solely on criteria extrapolated from the biblical list. Kashrus cannot be taken for granted, and the Torah, for once, isn't talking.

The Mishna tries to draw up some rules of thumb: "All raptors are unclean. All birds that have an extra toe, a crop, and a peelable gizzard are clean." (*Khulin* 3:6) The idea seems pretty clear: Check a bird's appearance and look at its feeding habits. It works for about three pages, until relying on physical signs alone leads Rov Papo, a prominent authority, to misjudge the moorhen as kosher. Hence the insistence of virtually all authorities that a bird that meets the Mishnaic requirements must still have a *mesorah* behind it. "A clean bird is eaten on the basis of tradition," says the Talmud (*Khulin* 63b), and *not* solely on the basis of the Talmud's own criteria. Poor Rov Papo didn't spend enough time watching the moorhen feed to realize that it's omnivorous and sometimes acts like a bird of prey (*Khulin* 62b).

This is not a purely academic matter, as any rabbi who has heard of turkey will tell you. The discovery of America threw a bit of a monkey wrench into the idea of tradition: There were no reliably Jewish Native American witnesses to vouch for the acceptability of this hitherto unknown species of bird, which left Old World Jews with no one to rely on. But, with Rov Papo in mind, once the turkey's feeding habits had been observed for a year and were judged to be in line with the Mishnaic requirements, most Jews in Europe were satisfied as to its kashrus. After a few generations, there was a bona fide tradition in place.

But some traditions are more traditional than others. Not a few authorities found it difficult to get behind a tradition that had no tradition behind it. Solomon Kluger, who fought so hard against machine-made matzoh, opposed the eating of any bird unique to the Americas, on the grounds that a place without Jews could not provide a valid *mesorah*. According to him, Jews who accepted turkey as kosher were proof of error, not tradition. And Kluger was hardly alone.

In practice, most contemporary rabbis with qualms about turkey are picky eaters. While rumors of people who won't eat it abound, documented descriptions of turkey rejecters tend to focus on prominent rabbis who saw their abstention as a personal matter, the kind of supererogatory precaution that helped make them prominent rabbis in the first place, and they made no attempt to impose it on others.

A *mesorah* is also required for insects. As soon as the Moroccans and Yemenites, who have one for grasshoppers, make a couple of YouTube videos, Friday night dinners will leave chicken behind and end with ice cream: Grasshoppers are parve—until you fry them in schmaltz.

The real place of insects in contemporary Jewish foodways, though, derives from a hitherto unsuspected ability to turn previously unremarkable fruits and vegetables into major sources of anxiety about "bugs," the unkosher enemy within all those green leafy things that our forebears were so right to avoid. The relatively commonsense, visible-to-the-naked-eye criterion of earlier generations has been abandoned. Suspect fruits and vegetables are often examined through a magnifying glass and have become subject to all kinds of strictures—washing strawberries with soap and water, for instance, is no longer considered safe enough by those rabbis who insist that they be immersed in boiling water prior to eating. The terror has led to the development of a market for "kosher" spinach, lettuce, broccoli, and asparagus, often produced with the help of massive doses of strictly kosher insecticides. God knows what will happen when yeshiva administrators learn that cruciferous means "carrying a cross"—just like the Hebrew term for crusader.

PIGS AND PARTICULARISM

Both Leviticus and Deuteronomy cite the same four mammals as examples of what Israelites are not to eat: the camel, the hyrax or rock badger, the hare, and the pig. Such unkosher animals as donkeys, foxes, and lions were considered so far from palatable as to need no mention at all. It's the false friends, the closet anti-Semites who conceal vital information or try to dazzle you with a superficial acceptability, against whom the Jews must guard themselves:

> But from those [animals] that chew cud or have cloven hooves, you shall not eat this: the camel. Because it chews cud but does not part its hoof, it is unclean for you. And the hyrax; because it chews cud but does not part its hoof, it is unclean for you. And the hare; because it chews cud and does not part its hoof, it is unclean for you. And the pig; because it parts its hoof and is cloven-hoofed but does not chew the cud, it is unclean for you. You shall neither eat their flesh nor touch their carcasses; they are unclean for you. (Lv 11:4–8)

Pet owners and 4-H club members might question the accuracy of some of these descriptions, but the errors don't affect the outcome. Each of these animals has or appears to have one defining characteristic of a kosher animal without the other, a distinction that might be overlooked by hungry or distracted Israelites, or those merely prone to jump to conclusions. God is letting us know that there's no such thing as a little bit kosher.

The pig is treated no differently from any of the other animals listed. Yet Jews do not recoil from hyrax the way they do from pork, possibly because the pig is the only animal named that has a cloven hoof but does not appear to chew cud, a fact sometimes adduced to cast the Jewish aversion in a moral light. A cursory look downwards is enough to show anyone that the camel, the hyrax, and the hare are not kosher, but the pig—as the Yiddish saying has it—sticks out its kosher little foot and hides its true nature behind an outward show of kashrus. A fifth-century midrash says that the pig lies on its back and waves its cloven hooves in the air, "As if to say, 'I'm kosher.'" It's the duplicity that rankles. Most living beings are *treyf,* but only the pig has the chutzpah to try to pass as kosher.

Less homiletically, the pig's real problem is its popularity. As virtually any historian of the Mediterranean region will tell you, pork accounted for most of the meat in a part of the world that can hardly be called ranch country. Shepherds were the closest thing to cowpokes, and sheep and goats were raised more for wool and milk than for flesh. To sacrifice a lamb or kid in the Temple was to deprive yourself of years' worth of clothing, dairy products, and potential income.

Pigs, on the other hand, were not really good for much except eating. Bristles, perhaps, maybe leather; in China, they often took the place of sewers. But their real importance was as a handy source of lard for cooking and baking, and of cheap and plentiful meat for eating—a fully grown pig yields many more bites per pound than a sheep or goat. The Jewish refusal to eat it was seen by many in the pork-eating world as a senseless and ultimately hostile gesture of contempt for established norms, as perverse as the Jews' refusal to work or cook on the Sabbath.

Indeed, the idea of abhorring rather than simply avoiding pork— at least in part, in reaction to its ubiquity—hardly went unnoticed, and led many in the classical world to misunderstand the nature of Judaism. Strabo, the Greek geographer who died around 24 CE and whose name means "cockeyed," seems to have taken Jewish absten- tion from pork as a sign of vegetarianism. In discussing the succes- sors of Moses (whom he describes as having led a small band of followers to Jerusalem), he writes that they declined into supersti- tion and tyranny, and that "from superstition arose abstinence from flesh, from which it is their custom to abstain even today."

This particular error seems to have been peculiar to Strabo. Jews were more commonly believed to abstain from pork because they considered the pig sacred and even worshipped it as a god. So Petro- nius, best known as author of the *Satyricon* (the Fellini version of which is alleged to feature a prefitness Richard Simmons in the role of "nymphomaniac's slave"), begins one of his fragments with the line, "Even if the Jew should worship his pig god . . . "

This is only incidentally insulting. It is clear from Petronius's Latin that pig is meant literally, as Plutarch bears out a generation later. One of the interlocutors in his *Quaestiones Convivales*, or *Table Talk*, written not long after the destruction of the Temple, refers to pork as "the most proper type of meat." Over the course of this work—a symposium that never dreams of becoming a seder—Plutarch's diners take up the question of whether Jews avoid pork out of reverence or aversion. One of the speakers says that Jews revere the pig for teaching them to plow and sow the ground; according to him, the pig "was the first to cut the soil with its projecting snout, thus producing a furrow and teaching man the function of a plough-share." As if this didn't have little enough to do with the Jews, a second symposiast, laughing off the idea that Jews don't eat hare because they consider it unclean, says that they avoid it "because of its very close resemblance to the ass, which they prize so highly." Go know.

The idea of pig worship was revived less comically in medieval Germany in the figure of the *Judensau*, "the Jews' sow." Sculptures, woodcuts, and paintings depicted Jews suckling at pigs, kissing their behinds, having sex with them, and so on. One painting in Frankfurt had a ritual murder thrown in for good measure.

The Roman historian Tacitus, who liked Christians even less than he liked Jews, describes Jewish rituals as "sinister and revolting," and says that the Jews "avoid eating pork in memory of their tribulations, as they themselves were once infected with the disease to which this creature is subject." The disease is leprosy, and Tacitus is referring to the widespread ancient rumor that Moses and his followers were lepers—not the nice Ben-Hur type, either, but nasty, resentful lepers who were thrown out of Egypt.

The association of pigs with leprosy has a venerable history. As another of Plutarch's diners explains:

> *The Jews apparently abominate pork because barbarians*
> *especially abhor skin diseases like lepra and white scale, and*

believe that human beings are ravaged by such maladies through
contagion. Now we observe that every pig is covered on the
underside by lepra and scaly eruptions, which, if there is general
weakness and emaciation, are thought to spread rapidly over
the body.

Here, if nowhere else, Plutarch agrees with the Talmud, which
warns that someone who encounters a pig right after being bled is
at risk of developing leprosy. (*Shabbos* 129b) As Rashi says, "Leprosy, which afflicts pigs, as it says in [tractate] *Kiddushin* [49b], 'Ten
portions of leprosy descended into the world; nine were taken by
pigs.'"

Shocking or laughable as these Greco-Roman beliefs might strike
us, the Greco-Romans themselves would have been even more
shocked had they troubled to ask a Jew and discovered that nobody,
ancient or modern, Jewish or gentile, has the vaguest idea of why
the forbidden species are forbidden. Theories have been advanced
and rationales adduced, but none is completely convincing: hygiene,
self-discipline, discomfort with creatures that challenge or defy the
demands of taxonomy. Popular as some of these beliefs have remained, they—or the first two, at least—might well be *effects* of
the dietary laws, but can hardly be seen as the reasons behind them.
As Isaac Abarbanel, a fifteenth-century philosopher, biblical commentator, and treasurer to the King of Portugal, puts it in his
remarks on Lv 11:13:

Many commentators have already considered that the Torah
forbids certain foods for the sake of bodily health and healing,
because these bad foods produce bad humors. Nachmanides
expresses this view in his comments on Leviticus 11:13. God
forbid that I should believe this, for if I did, then God's Torah
would be just another minor medical book, short on matter and
explanation. This is neither the way of God's Torah nor the

depth of its purpose. Do our eyes not see solid proof of this, in that the nations that eat the abominable pig and the mouse and the other unclean birds and animals and fish are strong, and none among them is tired or feeble?

The one justification for the food prohibitions that almost no one seems to want to accept is the one given by God Himself: "You shall be holy because I am holy." (Lv 11:45) He is telling us to do as He does, albeit in our own severely limited way. Theologians and biblical scholars have been saying for quite a while that one of the main senses of the word "holy" in the Old Testament is "separated, set apart, removed from the ordinary." In other words, the basic intent of these laws could well be to make sure that God's people remain separate, that they neither behave like others nor blend in with them.

Along with keeping the Sabbath and circumcising male infants, the dietary laws have traditionally been regarded by everybody, Jewish and otherwise, as the distinguishing sign of the Jew. Where English often uses supposedly typical foods as pejorative terms for members of different ethnic groups—beaner, rice-eater, frog, kraut, and even spaghetti—the equivalent for a Jew is simply "kosher." No anti-Semite ever called me a kugel, though I can remember walking by more than one alienated Canadian youth and hearing, "Look at that fuckin' kosher." In his novel, *The Grifters*, Jim Thompson has a character comment on a Jewish woman in a cafeteria, "Kosher kid can really put it away, can't she?" despite the fact that the kosher in question has a plateful of distinctly *treyfene* knockwurst. The reply leaves no doubt as to the friendliness of the epithet: "When she gets it for nothin', sure. That's how them kikes get ahead."

In a 1906 letter to his brother, Henry Adams complains that "there are said to be four-hundred-and-fifty thousand Jews now doing Kosher in New York alone"; as far as he was concerned, Jews who ate knockwurst on Yom Kippur were still doing kosher. Any group that can eat pork stuffed into a hog-gut casing and still be mocked as kosher can never complain that the dietary laws haven't kept it apart enough.

BLOODLESSNESS
Species aren't all that's forbidden:

> *If anyone of the house of Israel or of the strangers who reside among them partakes of any blood, I will set My face against the person who partakes of the blood, and I will cut him off from among his kin. For the life of the flesh is in the blood, and I have assigned it to you for making expiation for your lives upon the altar; it is the blood, as life, that effects expiation. (Lv 17:10–11)*

This extends even to eggs, and many people who have long since stopped keeping kosher never lose the habit of cracking every egg they use into a glass in order to check for the blood spots that would disqualify it from use. The glass has to be emptied after each egg, lest a single bloody yolk contaminate all the others.

The need to get rid of any blood is also the motivation behind the rules of kosher slaughter elaborated in the Talmud. An animal can be completely kosher, can even have the blood drained out of it, but if it has not been slaughtered in accordance with Jewish law, it might just as well be a pig.

Although the Mishna says that any acceptable animal killed according to the law by an adult Jew of sound mind is kosher, animal slaughter was professionalized a long time ago and women—whom the Mishna does not prohibit from slaughtering—were disqualified from the profession everywhere but Italy. The *shoykhet*, as the slaughterer is called, is the Jewish version of Caesar's wife: Not only is he expected to be a man of exceptional piety, he must also be seen to be a man of exceptional piety—the local rabbis have to feel comfortable eating the animals that he's dispatched. The job is a combination of attitude and technique. Thomas Mann, not often thought of as a source of Jewish folklore and practice, describes the ideal type of the *shoykhet* in *The Magic Mountain*:

> *Elia Naphta* [the shoykhet] *was himself filled with a quiet religiosity; there had been something priestly about him and his blue eyes, which, as his son described them, had glittered like stars and radiated a solemnity recalling ancient times when the slaughtering of animals had indeed been the duty of priests . . . [he would] flourish the large butcher knife and cut deep into the neck vertebrae of the bound and hobbled, but fully conscious animal.*

The Yiddish writer Joseph Opatoshu anticipates Mann's description in a novel published three years earlier: "A Jewish *shoykhet* is a model Jew, a Torah scholar, who would not hurt a fly. Soft eyes, a gentle gait, and when he slaughters a cow he does so with reverence, like the high priest."

A highly sharpened knife is drawn across the animal's neck, severing the trachea and esophagus (the "and" becomes "or" if the animal is a bird). The cut must be clean; the *shoykhet* cannot press the knife into the animal's neck or pause in mid cut. There must be no nicks or grooves in the blade; wool or feathers must be trimmed or moved away so that the *shoykhet* can always see it and the cut must be made in the proper area of the neck. Stunning the animal in any way is strictly forbidden. A proper cut severs the jugular veins and carotid arteries; the animal's blood pressure drops and it is said to lose consciousness and feel no pain.

After the carcass has been drained of the forbidden blood, the *shoykhet* checks the lungs of sheep and cattle for the punctures and adhesions mentioned in connection with *glatt*. If everything is kosher, the animal is chopped up and turned into meat. The hind part is usually separated from the forequarters and sold to nonkosher purveyors.

Blood removal continues after the meat leaves the slaughterhouse, when it is *kashered* (note the change of vowel): purged of any residual blood. These days, kosher butchers tend to do the *kashering* themselves, but up until the latter part of the twentieth century, well within memory of anyone who stayed up to watch Neil Armstrong's moonwalk, it was usually done at home (butchers charged extra) and almost always by the person then known as the lady of the house.

Kashering isn't terribly difficult, just messy and time-consuming. The meat—unless it's liver, which can only be *kashered* by broiling—is left to soak in a tub or other vessel for at least half an hour in order to soften it up and wash away the surface blood. Once the water has been sluiced off, the meat is covered with a nice dusting, more like a crust, of kosher salt, the rather large-grained salt that figures in many contemporary non-Jewish recipes, too. The "kosher" in the salt's name is better thought of as "*kashering*"; it isn't that the salt is kosher—any salt that doesn't contain ground-up animal bones or similar extralegal stretching agents already is—it's that this type of salt is most effective in drawing out blood and making other foods kosher.

The salted meat is placed on a slanted board for an hour to give the blood a chance to run off. After the salt has been shaken or washed off, the meat is rinsed in cold water three times to get rid of any remaining salt or blood. Only now can it be cooked and eaten. Blood left after the meat has been salted no longer counts as blood; the Jewish preference for well-done meat reflects mama's preferences or cooking skills—"Can Madam burn?" as Lester Young used to ask—and has nothing to do with halacha.

The tub, the board, and the box or shaker of kosher salt were probably the most immediately visible proofs of the kashrus of any given kitchen. Like matzoh, kosher meat is defined by what isn't in it even more than by what is, and removing blood from meat can be seen as analogous to keeping leaven out of the bread. Indeed, the word "matzoh" comes from a Hebrew root meaning "to squeeze, extract, drain out"—exactly what is done to the blood in the meat. Much kosher food is thus matzoh, in one form or another, and it's probably no coincidence that the Yiddish for "to squeeze, extract, drain out" is "kvetch."

All the more ironic, then, that the most pernicious of all anti-Semitic canards should be the so-called blood libel, according to which Jews need blood—the blood of juicy young Christians—for various ritual purposes, but especially for making matzoh. The accusation was so widespread, so widely believed, as to have been responsible for at least one major change in Jewish ritual and dining habits; according to the seventeenth-century scholar David ha-Levi Segal, fear of blood libels led the Polish Jews of his time to stop using red wine on Passover. The calumnies of anti-Semites are thus responsible for the miracle of turning Manischewitz and Mogen David, with their deep, rich, winey hue, into shimmering beacons of freedom.

MILK, BREAD, AND MARRIAGE

And that's not all. There are two or three further prohibitions that can have far-reaching effects, not only in the kitchen and dining room, but also on social relations with Jews and non-Jews alike. People unfamiliar with traditional Judaism or Orthodox shopping centers are often surprised to discover that dairy products, no less than meat, must also be kosher, and that an Orthodox coworker will avoid the Cheez Whiz or gourmet mozzarella at the office party no less assiduously than the frogs' legs.

The *Shulkhan Arukh* explains that "milk that has been milked by a gentile who has not been observed by a Jew is forbidden, lest it contain impure milk"—that is, milk from an unkosher animal, which is no more kosher than its meat. The only qualifications that the observing Jew need have are brains enough to tell the difference between a cow and a camel, and the ability to stay awake long enough to keep an eye on the milking. He need not even be present the whole time, only at the beginning and end and during an unpredictable interval or two during the milking, just to make sure that everything is kosher. Milk produced under Jewish eyes is called *cholov yisroel*, the milk of Israel, where Israel means Children, rather than State of.

Since the USDA definition of milk specifies that unless another animal is named on the package, it has to have come from a cow, Rabbi Moshe Feinstein, the rabbi with a taste for T-bones, ruled that all milk produced in the USA is permitted for Jewish consumption. Although *cholov yisroel* would be preferable, the milk available in any corner store is acceptable. There is no chance of its being *cholov akum*, "the milk of worshippers of stars and constellations," as unkosher milk is usually called; fear of punishment is enough to ensure that dairies comply with the law, but since this compliance has not been witnessed by a Jew, the milk is also not *cholov yisroel*. Rabbi Feinstein thus created a new, intermediate category, *cholov stam:* just plain milk, nondenominational milk that is neither Jewish nor gentile. The beauty of such an innovation is that *cholov stam* could not have been forbidden by our sages because it didn't exist for them to forbid. Feinstein's ruling essentially exonerated the overwhelming majority of American Jews from the sin of consuming unkosher milk and dairy products, even though most of those Jews neither noticed nor cared.

Although virtually no Conservative or Reform Jews worry about *cholov yisroel*, it has become a major status marker in the Orthodox community, a modern equivalent of the six-hour wait between meat and dairy in the days of Moses Isserles. People who "hold by" *cholov yisroel*—among whom we can include all Hasidim and ultra-Orthodox non-Hasidim—will generally not patronize otherwise kosher restaurants, bakeries, ice cream shops, and the like that do not serve *cholov yisroel*. They will generally also not eat in the homes of Orthodox Jews who use *cholov stam* and *cholov stam* dairy products, nor, more woundingly, will they allow their children to eat at the homes of friends and schoolmates whose parents use them. Many a Modern Orthodox paterfamilias with a fridge full of *cholov yisroel* is quick to let visitors know that "Personally, I don't go for this crap, but if I don't buy it, the kids' friends won't come to our house." Jewish isn't always Jewish enough.

Cheese is also cause for kosher concern, though not on account of the milk. Pigs' milk, donkeys' milk, camels' milk don't coagulate well and are not considered likely sources of cheese. The problem is rennet, the curdling agent found in the abomasum, the last chamber of a ruminant's stomach. The trouble has nothing to do with mixing meat and dairy—cheese is (or once was) started by putting a piece of salted and dried abomasum into some milk. But for technical reasons that we need not go into, rennet is not considered a meat product. Nevertheless, as a nonmeat product that *derives* from a meat product—just like milk, except the meat product there is still alive—it needs to come from a kosher animal that has been slaughtered by a *shoykhet* in accordance with the rules of *shekhita*. Where kosher milk is a matter of preventing contamination, kosher cheese is a response to an explicit prohibition.

The same passage of the Mishna that mentions non-Jewish milk (*Avoda Zoro* 2:6) also bans the consumption of oil and bread made by gentiles. The oil prohibition was rescinded in the third century by the grandson of the rabbi who compiled the Mishna, but bread has been a matter of debate ever since, becoming as much a locus of status definition and conspicuous kashrus as milk.

It's a little more complicated than milk, though, as the rules about bread baked by gentiles never even mention ingredients. Any kid can tell you that bread made with lard or other unkosher ingredients is off-limits, regardless of the baker's religion. The Talmud's worry is more adult, more exciting: "They [the members of the

School of Shammai who passed this ordinance] forbade gentile bread and oil on account of their wine; their wine on account of their daughters; their daughters on account of idolatry." (*Avoda Zoro* 36b)

It isn't what you're eating, it's who you might eat it with and where they might take you once you leave the table:

> *You shall not intermarry with them: do not give your daughters to their sons or take their daughters for your sons. For they will turn your children away from me to worship other gods, and the Lord's anger will blaze forth against you and He will promptly wipe you out. (Dt 7:3–4, JPS)*

And it all begins with breaking bread. The rabbis of the Talmud had the same nightmares as every subsequent Jewish parent. It's bad enough your kid "marries out"—just imagine where else the gentile who led them to bed might steer them: a cathedral, an idol fane, a free personality test, or some other anteroom of apostasy. Even if the kid doesn't actually convert—at which point you, like the Jazz Singer's father, will have no son or daughter—don't hold your breath for Jewish grandkids until you've been to the bar or bas mitzvah. If King Solomon could be seduced, it can happen to anyone.

And so the prohibition of *pas akum*—the bread of the same worshippers of heavenly bodies who appeared in *cholov akum*, and whom it would be more accurate and a lot more fun to call infidels—applies primarily to the bread of individuals, private householders whose bread you are eating because you've been invited to their home. As Joseph Karo says in the *Shulkhan Arukh:* "The main thrust of the prohibition is the weddings; if one eats the bread of private householders, he will come to dine in their houses." To put it more positively, Little Miss Sunbeam will never marry your son. Non-Jewish bakers, people from whom customers buy bread and then leave, are doing business, not forging friendships. As Karo also puts it, "In some places they are less stringent and will allow bread from a non-Jewish baker in places where there is no Jewish baker, as these are emergency conditions," but you can tell that he is not comfortable with such practices.

Most Ashkenazi authorities take a surprisingly relaxed attitude toward non-Jewish baked goods. As Isserles writes, "Most places permit *pas akum*, and I will therefore not dwell on differences of opinion about it, since the custom of permitting it and eating it is already a fait accompli, even when *pas yisroel*, bread baked by a Jew, is available." His student, Mordechai Yoffe, states explicitly that "The ban on gentile bread has made no headway in these countries [Poland, Lithuania, Bohemia]; not one person in a thousand takes any care about the bread of non-Jews, and they purchase all kinds of baked goods from [non-Jewish] bakers."

To transform a loaf of bread from *pas akum* to *pas yisroel*, a Jew has only to take part in making it. Not even the most stringent authorities demand that he do any real baking, so long as he turns the oven on, or puts the bread inside it, or merely adjusts the temperature of the oven at some point during the baking. The bakers can still be gentiles, but the Jew's participation, the idea that he is involved and has an eye on the proceedings, is enough to make the raw materials proof against *goyishe shtik*.

The safeguards for baking are closely related to those for cooking in general, and the prohibition of *bishul akum*, the cooking of you-know-who, which is forbidden for similar reasons. As Maimonides explains in a passage that Karo drew on for his comments about baked goods and marriage:

> *To what does this prohibition apply? To things that are served with bread [i.e., as part of a formal meal] on the tables of kings, such as meat, eggs, fish, and so on. But things that are not served thus—lupini, for instance, which have been cooked by gentiles— are still permitted, even though they are not eaten raw, and so are all similar foods. For the main point of the injunction has to*

do with marriage, and with preventing a gentile from inviting a Jew to dine with him—and no one invites another to eat at his house unless he is serving things that are served on the tables of kings.

These ideas, which can be traced back to a Talmudic tractate on levirate marriage (*Yevomos* 46a), are the bedrock of the kosher restaurant, catering, and factory-supervision businesses. Halachically speaking, *glatt* kosher meat cooked by a gentile in a pot in which nothing but *glatt* kosher meat has ever been cooked is as *treyf* as roast suckling pig with ice cream reduction served on the back of a lobster that walks into your mouth on Yom Kippur. Just as hot *treyf* communicates its impurity to any kosher food that it touches and hot gentiles do the same to your children, so can cooking in which the heat is provided by a gentile turn otherwise kosher food and utensils into their conceptual opposites.

Again, a Jew doesn't have to do any actual cooking to forestall problems of *bishul akum*. *Bishul yisroel* requires only that the Jew light or turn on the stove or burner after the food has been placed in position, or else that he light the pilot before anything is put into the oven. As long as the pilot stays on, anybody, Jew or gentile, can put food into the oven without compromising its kashrus.

While there is some small concern about forbidden ingredients or the mixing of meat and dairy, this prohibition is primarily social in nature. If we bear in mind the fact that no observant Jew will eat meat in the house of a gentile, the laws of *bishul akum* apply only to non-Jewish domestics or employees and in the circumstances described by Maimonides. Food that can be eaten raw, even if it has been cooked by a gentile, is OK; cabbage is never the food of love. Anything that would not be served at a royal table, or as Rabbi J.B. Soloveitchik recast the phrase, a state dinner, is likewise OK, provided all the ingredients are kosher: breakfast cereal, chips, popcorn, and, according to Soloveitchik, virtually any canned food.

Nor does the law apply to food that has been microwaved, which could give an enterprising Orthodox girl group—call them The Shangri-Latkes—a kosher version of "Leader of the Pack": "I met him at the microwave/He warmed my knish up, it wasn't *treyf*."

Virtually all Jews understood that food was a means of social control and Jewish continuity. Gefilte fish is more than a source of nourishment; it is the world's most elaborate prophylactic and is there to keep you from having sex with anyone whom your mother might reject for reasons of religion, a point made over and over again in the dining rooms of such once-flourishing kosher resorts as Grossinger's and the Concord. These Catskill hotels turned the two major clichés of mid twentieth-century maternal obstreperousness— "Eat, eat," and "When you getting married?"—into a socially responsible mode of doing business. As a history of Grossinger's describes it:

> *First they get the young couple to sit together, then they keep bringing additional foods: first waffles; then Danish pastries hot from the oven. They agreed to another cup of coffee and a nibble of pastry. Only who can stop at a nibble of Grossinger's hot Danish pastries?*

Irving Cohen, the maitre d' of the Concord, whom the *New York Times* called "King Cupid of the Catskills," kept a pegboard on which every table of his three-thousand-seat dining room "was represented by a circle. Around each circle was a set of holes, and as Mr. Cohen seated each diner, he stuck the appropriate hole with a color-coded peg—pink for single young women, blue for single young men." And what Cohen hath joined, let no *treyf* put asunder.

WINE AND WHISKEY

Food-borne contagion was not the only thing that worried our sages; there is also the potentially corrupting influence of drink, especially

wine or any other beverage derived from grapes. The rules for kosher wine make the rules for matzoh and kosher meat look like a
copy of *Highlights for Children*. Every step in the process must be
supervised, from harvesting the grapes to opening the bottle and
decanting its contents. The latter two acts have to be performed by
a Jew—and not just any Jew, either, but one who keeps the Sabbath—
otherwise even wine that was kosher when bottled turns suddenly
treyf.

But *a yid*, as the saying goes, *tut zikh an eytse*; if there's a way
around something, a Jew will find it, which is why non-Jewish wait-
ers, waitresses, and bartenders can be employed by kosher restaurants and caterers and your religious-fanatic cousins don't start
screaming when you pick up an open bottle of wine in their house.
The wine has been heated—cooked, in fact—at temperatures ranging from 165 to 194 degrees Fahrenheit. Perhaps because of the
taste that is lost, such wine is thought to be unfit for libations and
thus loses the ability to transmit metaphysical contagion.

Wine or grape juice that has not been made in accordance with
halacha is strictly off-limits. Although the libation wine forbidden
in the Talmud is no longer considered to exist, *stam yeynom*—regular
wine—is nonetheless forbidden for the expected reasons: fear of
smooching and what it might lead to.

Interestingly, these strictures apply only to wine and wine-based
liqueurs. Other alcoholic drinks—beer, whiskey, most other spirits
(as distinct from such liqueurs as Irish Cholov Akum, which have
ingredients that require supervision or certification)—are generally
acceptable, though the current mania for kosher certification usually guarantees that more religious topers will drink only brands that
have been certified as kosher. Whiskey aged in sherry casks has oc-
casioned considerable recent debate, centering on the question of
whether casks that have held unkosher wine can disqualify otherwise acceptable whisky. This controversy is a direct outgrowth of
the growing popularity of premium brand, single malt scotches in

the Orthodox community. These have almost completely supplanted Crown Royal, the classic post-World War II high-end *shul* shot; many a young man who came of age in Canada and the United States after 1939, when Crown Royal was first manufactured, received his starter set of tefillin in the purple velvet bag that came with the bottle that his father bought to mark the occasion.

KOSHER *TREYF*

Hard as it might be to believe, these prohibitions are not meant to deprive us of sensory pleasure. Not only are we not missing anything, we also experience the higher satisfaction of pleasing our Creator, who receives His own pleasure, as it were, from our efforts. Anyone who thinks Jews the poorer for not being able to have bacon with their eggs or shrimp in their cocktails is missing the point:

> *Yalso said to Rov Nachman: As a general rule, there is a permitted equivalent for everything that the Merciful One has forbidden us. He forbade us blood, but allowed us liver; forbade intercourse with a menstruating woman, but permitted the blood of purification [i.e., of virgins and postpartum mothers]; forbade us the* kheylev *of cattle and sheep, but permitted that of wild [non-treyf] animals; forbade us pork, but allowed the brain of the* shibuto *[a fish of indeterminate species]; forbade the* giruso *[an unclean bird of uncertain species], but permitted fish tongue . . . So what happens if I want to eat meat with dairy? Rov Nachman said to the butchers, Grill her an udder.*
> (Khulin *109b*)

The stuff about intercourse, including a couple of semihot clauses omitted here, can be ascribed to the fact that Yalso was not only a woman, she was Rov Nachman's wife and, so far as sex goes, is assumed to be speaking from their shared experience. Rov Nachman was the Babylonian Jewish counterpart to chief justice of the

Supreme Court; Yalso's father was the exilarch—the president, as it were, of all Babylonian Jewry—and Yalso was used to getting what she wanted and getting it now. One of the great spoiled brats of the Talmud, she goes around in a sedan chair (*Beytso* 25b) and once smashed four hundred jars of wine when she felt slighted by a sage named Ulla. (*Brokhos* 51b)

By attributing this speech to Yalso, the Talmud's editors are making the point that there is really no perceptible difference between the permitted and forbidden members of each pair: if *Yalso* isn't kvetching, there is nothing to kvetch about. If she wants milk with meat, she can have udder, which is kosher, and the rest of the discussion deals with the intricacies of its preparation.

The idea that there is a kosher counterpart to every unkosher food, dish, or sex partner (and that we therefore have no reason to envy other nations, who are like the kid down the block who gets to do whatever he wants) is fundamental to a legal system designed, at least in part, to keep meaningful contact between Jews and gentiles to an absolute minimum. Within the context of the biblical narrative, though, the Israelites are basically told, "You're free. You no longer have to eat what you're given. You can eat almost anything you want except for gross stuff like scorpions and vultures. And, uh, also pork, wine, and butter and milk with your meat." It was like finally getting cable and being told that you can watch anything except *Homeland*, *The Simpsons*, and this weekend's *Breaking Bad* marathon. Anything you want, except what you want—but someday you'll thank me for it.

Except . . . once again, the Jews find a way of eating the cake that they're not allowed to have. As Yalso's remarks indicate, fake *treyf* has been around since at least the third century; if we had better language skills or a proper *mesorah*, we would still be eating *shibuto* brain today. If Jews hadn't stopped eating it, we'd know what it was; the fact that we don't suggests that it wasn't very good, and as most

Hebrew-school teachers would be quick to tell us, if this proof of divine mercy wasn't very good, it can only be because *treyf* itself is no good, either.

If that were really the case, if Jews felt they had nothing to gain by eating it, we'd all keep kosher today. For a long time, most Jews don't seem to have had much interest in *treyf*, and those who did simply went out and ate it, though probably in secret. In Central and Eastern Europe, it was the food of the enemy; its gustatory attractions were neutralized by their association with a culture so bitterly opposed to everything Jewish. It is probably no accident that a Jewish veal dish called *chazarello*, which means piglet or little pig, picked up its ironically affectionate nickname in the Italian town of Pitigliano. It's a joke that could never have worked in Yiddish.

Full-blown attempts to counterfeit the forbidden and endow ritually pure foods with the taste, texture, and allure of the impure had to wait until Jewish immigrants in America were acclimatized enough to find kosher food that tasted "exactly" like bacon appealing instead of appalling. It took nearly half a century, and probably appealed a lot more to those who kept kosher only at home than to people who had never eaten *treyf* at all. Beef fry, seasoned strips of brisket or beef plate, made its first appearance in the mid-'30s, primarily as a means of allowing people who ate all their bacon in restaurants a chance to do so at home without discommoding themselves or their families. Their homes could stay kosher and they themselves could enjoy all the pleasures of *treyf* without having to worry about making their parents revolve in their graves. The notion that such food was aimed at the then-dwindling Orthodox community does not seem tenable; I never once saw beef fry or any similar product in the home of anyone at whose house I was allowed to eat. The idea flies in the face of Talmudic ideas about milk, bread, and intermarriage.

Such people—or such people's parents, at any rate—wouldn't

have known if beef fry was any good and didn't want to tempt themselves—bite by little bite, one package at a time—into a comparison test with the real thing. People who have never eaten real *treyf* are at the same disadvantage when it comes to the fake stuff as Joel Finkelstein, rabbi of Anshei Sphard-Beth El Emeth Congregation in Memphis, the Orthodox synagogue that is home to the World Kosher Barbeque Championship. "I don't know," he says, "what a real barbecue sandwich tastes like." People who look for proof of kashrus on Betty Crocker Bac-Os or McCormick Bac'n Pieces Bacon Flavored Bits are either much more observant than they used to be—and thus happy for anything that reminds them of what they gave up—or else have nothing with which to compare them.

The fact that people who have always been religious are involved enough with general American culture to want to *try* lobster- and crab-flavored chunks of Alaskan pollock, the active ingredient in McDonald's Filet-O-Fish, bears witness to a fundamental shift in the way that the Jewish community sees itself in relation to the larger society. Rather than dismiss other groups' food with the reflexive "Feh" of so many earlier generations, it has gone full circle to the attitude of Rov Nachman's wife: Anything they can have, we can have, too.

Ideally, fake *treyf* can only be judged for what it is, rather than what it fails to be. Rather than fake, think of it as virtual *treyf*, the gastrointestinal forerunner of internet sex; it might not be real, but it packs a consequence- and guilt-free punch nonetheless.

IT REALLY BELONGS TO GOD

Real *treyf*, fake *treyf*, kosher—the good Lord made them all, and it's up to us to make sure that He knows that we know. Blessings must be said—before eating, after eating, sometimes even during eating, though never with food in your mouth—and it isn't a simple matter of saying grace. Judaism has three basic kinds of blessing:

the ones that announce our intention of fulfilling one of God's commandments; the ones that acknowledge His power and might, usually made on seeing, hearing, or otherwise experiencing some aspect of these (hearing thunder, seeing a king, going to the washroom); and the ones that serve as notice that we are about to use something—food, for instance—that really belongs to Him.

There is no easier way to see the difference between Jewish and Christian attitudes to God and the world than to compare their approaches to the act of eating. "*Tibi deo gratias agimus*," "For what we are about to receive," and "Bless us, O Lord, and these Thy gifts" make no sense in a traditional Jewish environment, even if we ignore the shadow of Jesus hovering overhead. Jews do not thank God until *after* they have eaten; only He knows what could go wrong between the blessing and the act, and making wasted blessings, as they are known, is a major Jewish faux pas.

If Jews can't thank Him before they eat, all they can do is bless Him, offer praise in minutely specific terms for His wisdom and foresight in creating the food before them. Different types of food require different types of blessing. There is one for bread; another for grain products whose ingredients or manner of preparation take them out of the category of bread; a third for wine and grape juice; a fourth for fruit that grows on trees; yet another for vegetables and fruits that grow straight from the ground; and a sixth for everything else, including meat and fish, fruit and vegetable juices, and all other liquids not made from grapes.

Confronted with a complicated or unfamiliar delicacy, observant Jews will ask, "What is this?" They don't want to know the name of the dish; they're trying to figure out what blessing to say, and the proper answer consists of the name of that blessing, not a list of ingredients. In the traditional Jewish world, recipes are a prescription for prayer and those who do the praying thus need to be hyperaware of the contents and composition of whatever goes into their mouths.

A snack of French fries, an apple, and a milkshake would require three separate blessings, each uttered immediately before the first bite or sip of the food to which it applies—technically, the apple is supposed to be eaten first, as its blessing outranks those of the other two, but most authorities allow for individual preference in such cases. A further all-inclusive final blessing must be said once you've finished eating. A single vegetable—an onion, for instance—can be subject to different blessings, depending on how it is usually eaten (and your particular take on the meaning of "usually") and whether it is served raw or cooked.

If you're going to eat anything that qualifies as bread, the rules change slightly. *Hamoytse*, the blessing over bread, is the big cheese of food blessings; once you've made it, you needn't make any more blessings during the meal proper. Unlike any of the other blessings, though, *hamoytse* can only be made following a ritual washing of the hands, which is accompanied by a special blessing of its own.

At the close of such a meal, *birkas ha-mazon*—"The Food Blessing," usually translated as "Grace After Meals"—is recited. This is a four-blessing postprandial prayer, with a few supplications tossed in for good measure, along with special additions for the Sabbath and various holidays. It is to be distinguished from the blessings that follow food unaccompanied by bread, which vary according to what has been eaten.

Blessings fore, aft, and in between endow even the most commonplace foods with an air of difference that can turn a slice of apple pie with ice cream into an adventure in anthropology. These ritualized expressions of submission and gratitude can certainly become a little rote, but they are never taken lightly by anyone who makes them of his own volition; many a fugitive from orthodoxy still feels an occasional twinge halfway through a meal, *treyf* though it be, when doctrinal muscle memory kicks in and reminds her that she's forgotten to make a blessing.

The Talmud leaves no room for doubt about the importance of these and all other blessings:

> *A person is forbidden from enjoying the things of this world without making a blessing, and anyone who does so has abused that which has been consecrated to the Lord . . . as it is written, "The earth is the Lord's, and the fullness thereof." (Ps 24:1)*
> (Brokhos 35a-b)

It's God's world; we just live in it. The food belongs to Him; He only lets us use it. And just as you don't grab the keys and take off in the car without asking Dad if it's okay, so you don't tuck into any comestibles without first confirming the formalities of usufruct: The blessing acknowledges God as sole creator and owner, a declaration that deconsecrates the food just enough to let you use something that is His without running the risk of punishment. If food were your father's car, the blessing would elicit the grunt of assent from behind Dad's paper; it's the cue for him to say, "Don't be too late." God's food is also like Dad's car in one other way: You won't be using it long. Between elimination—which comes with a blessing of its own—and the decay of the body after death, you'll be giving it back before you know it.

Like virtually all other Jewish blessings, those over food can be seen as an acknowledgment of God's copyright on earthly phenomena and activities. The earth is the Lord's, and so are your guts. Where Christian preprandial graces are essentially spoken thank-you cards, Jews—who have been depending on the cruelty of strangers since the days when these blessings were formulated—know that there's no such thing as a free lunch: Fair use tends to come with a price. Christians want God to *give* them food; Jews are happy to negotiate a lease.

Whatever these blessings are, they are intended for use only with food that is worthy of blessing; uttering them over food that is not kosher—save in cases of dire emergency—is as dangerous a mockery of God and His laws as blessing a loaf of bread previously consecrated to Thor, Apollo, or any other nonexistent deity. Try to imagine the look on the face of a first-century Roman who has just been forbidden to offer a prayer to Jupiter to complement his Jewish host's invocation of the Hebrew god, and is given an explanation that makes no sense. The Jews have their deity, sure, but so do the Romans. Good manners, good taste, consist in acknowledging both, especially when the Jew is in Rome. The failure of an ancient traveler to make a pro forma offering to the tutelary deity of the place he was visiting was seen as just as ill bred, just as a classless, as a Canadian refusing to stand for the "The Star-Spangled Banner" before a game in Yankee Stadium. People can't help but take it personally.

The Jews had no choice, though; as far as they were concerned, if they didn't act this way, they would be ignoring their obligations as Jews. This feeling of obligation became even more intense after the destruction of the Second Temple in 70 CE. The Temple sacrifices had been the backbone of the religion; once they vanished, observance of more private mitzvahs became the only way of being Jewish. Without the Temple as symbol and focal point, without the forgiveness effected by the sacrifices, the mitzvahs could no longer be overlooked by anyone who wished to remain Jewish, especially now that the Jews had been definitively exiled. Prayers and blessings and laws about everything from diet to doing business had to take the place of what they had, at best, once complemented, and they will have to go on doing so until the advent of the Messiah.

Until then, it's all exile. Jews took this idea seriously, remaining resolutely apart from the peoples among whom they were living. Only relatively recently did fate, as Lord Buckley used to say, take its cut. Just as noticeable numbers of Jews were beginning to abandon strict obedience to religious law, along comes "scientific" anti-Semitism to set all their efforts at naught. Anyone born a Jew had no choice but to stay a Jew, regardless of practice or belief— regardless, indeed, of religion. Heinrich Heine could convert to Protestantism, however cynically, and continue to be seen as a Jew.

Karl Marx, baptized at the age of six, is still thought of as one of the Jews who helped shape the modern world. Disraeli was baptized when he was twelve for reasons that sound like a Jewish joke: His father got into a fight with the board members of his synagogue and decided to teach them a lesson by converting his children and depriving the synagogue of their Hebrew-school fees. Isaac, the father, remained Jewish himself; otherwise, he'd have had nowhere to go to gloat.

Modernity allowed Jews to throw off the yoke of the mitzvahs and still be excluded from the larger society. For the past couple of centuries, Jews haven't needed to *do* anything in order to be seen as Jews; they haven't even needed to be Jewish. Once conversion to Christianity could no longer erase the inexpungible stigma of being Jewish, Jews no longer needed religious rules to keep them apart; they had gentiles to do it for them. Attempts to redefine and destroy us made us *unable* to disappear. And as generations of Jews could tell you, it's better to be in exile than not to be at all.

Exile in Jewish terms means everlasting unassimilability, *staying* a stranger instead of just being one. And this eternal strangeness is expressed in terms of food:

> *And gentiles are never exiled? Even in exile, though, they're gentiles and their exile is no exile: they will eat the bread and drink the wine of the people among whom they are exiled. But the Jews won't eat their bread and won't drink their wine—the Jews' exile is* Exile.

The same passage goes on to say that the verse, "Judah has been exiled because of affliction," (Lam 1:3) is meant to let us know that the Jews were exiled "because they ate leavened food on Passover" instead of matzoh. We can't get away from it: Matzoh got us out of Egypt and it got us out of our own land, too. What the rest of the world sees as bread of affliction is really the bread of relief from affliction, the bread of a prosperity that we're always too stupid to notice. The dishes that we have been cooking up since the fall of the Second Temple are the aliments of exile, the food we have to eat until the really good stuff comes along. The dishes we're about to look at are those that we'll be telling the Messiah that we miss.

FOUR

Fat of the Land
The Fundamentals of Yiddish Cuisine

It all comes down to schmaltz. One of the consequences of the dietary laws is to make food preparation somewhat more complicated for Jews than for other people. Cooking fat must be made from kosher ingredients, and if not parve can only be used with like kinds of food. Butter works wonderfully, but only in dishes that will never be served with meat. Oil works better; not only is it parve, but, unlike butter, it needs no supervision, no special processing or Jewish involvement. Still prominent in Sephardi and Mizrachi cooking, oil was far from abundant in the lands where the Ashkenazim settled and in which the primary animal fat was lard. Anthropologists speak of two types of culture, at least when it comes to cooking: butter and oil, each of which is said to have distinctive characteristics that extend beyond the pan. Once again, the Jews—perhaps only Ashkenazim in this instance—are outside: In the midst of all those Central and East European butter cultures, ours was a culture of schmaltz.

Although *shmalts* in Yiddish can mean any kind of edible animal fat, it is inevitably assumed to refer to the fat of poultry, especially of chickens, who claimed total victory over geese in the centuries-long struggle for the title of Jewish National Bird only in the twentieth century. Domesticated geese were much more widespread in Western and Central Europe than in the less prosperous

77

East, where the goose was to the chicken as the successful entrepreneur is to the peddler: less numerous and more respected. Yiddish-speaking Jews certainly raised and bought plenty of geese; they just raised and bought a lot more chickens.

The goose retained its prestige for a very long time, in part because of its schmaltzy moistness, but economics and convenience—and the fact that no one has ever lost a fight with a chicken—eventually turned the latter into the default Jewish bird, the inexhaustible mine of those who moil for edible gold. Goose fat became a treat, and plenty of shoppers would save up for the occasional goose. *Dos Familiyen Kokh-Bukh* (*The Family Cookbook*) published in New York in 1914, gives us both the how and the why:

> *The stuffed goose is killed, as usual, in winter. After it has been singed, it should be well cleaned and trimmed and, if possible, hung outside in the cold, unopened, until it is not only chilled but frozen. Once it is back inside, the goose should be skinned completely (except for the mid-backbone) and the skin should be removed wherever it joins the fat. Then, when it has been opened up, the fat should be removed. In a word, the fat should be separated from the flesh. The fat should be* kashered *and then fried. . . . Many geese can have as much as seven or eight pounds of pure schmaltz.*

Seven or eight pounds will fry an awful lot of latkes, and since geese were usually slaughtered at the tail end of fall in order to lay in a supply of meat and schmaltz for the winter, it is no coincidence that once cheese latkes were replaced by potato in the mid-nineteenth century, when potatoes were introduced to Eastern Europe, the smell of smoking goose fat became the traditional scent of Chanukah. Costly as goose might have been, the sheer amount of meat and schmaltz—which can keep for months and months without refrigeration—made it reasonably economical.

Goose fat is generally thought of as the tastier, more full-bodied schmaltz, the Jayne Mansfield of kosher cooking, as compared with the Audrey Hepburn that is chicken schmaltz. But taste in schmaltz, as in Hollywood stars, varies from person to person. And taste it they did. No mere shortening or lubricant, schmaltz—the WD-40 of the kosher kitchen—is also condiment, dip, and spread: ketchup, butter, salsa, humus, and relish all rolled into one. Sammy's Roumanian Steakhouse on New York's Lower East Side makes something of a shtick out of having a syrup dispenser filled with schmaltz on every table so that your waiter can lubricate your chopped liver while you watch. What you do with the schmaltz once he leaves is entirely up to you.

With the closing long ago of the other East Side Romanian-Jewish restaurants, Sammy's, like all sole survivors, has become unique. Calvin Trillin's description of the Parkway, where Marvin Hamlisch's father used to play the accordion, provides us with some context: "Following the Jewish tradition, a dispenser of schmaltz (liquid chicken fat) is kept on the table to give the vampires heartburn if they get through the garlic defense." This is schmaltz for people who use it like pepper. A couple of recently established delicatessens in New York feature schmaltz at every table, too, but as an earnest of authenticity rather than an inducement to shtick.

Latkes are far from the only dish in which schmaltz has played a historic role. Traditional recipes for chopped liver, kugel, kishka, *cholent*, kasha, matzoh balls, mashed potatoes, and chopped eggs—with onions and without—all call for liberal doses of schmaltz. There are Hasidic tales about its centrality that read like the work of the young Woody Allen:

> *The holy Rebbe of Sanz [1793–1876] was very particular about mixing his eggs with onions and chicken schmaltz. It is told that once, when he had no schmaltz in the house, he sent around to his neighbors until someone brought him some schmaltz.*

There is a miniseries in there somewhere. The volume in which this story appears was published in Brooklyn in the year 2000; on the very next page, the author goes on to warn against trying to substitute mayonnaise for schmaltz on the Sabbath: "It should not be mixed with the traditional Sabbath foods, which have the sanctity of the Sabbath within themselves." For such radical traditionalists, mayonnaise smacks of intermarriage; schmaltz, on the other hand, provides the defining taste of both the Sabbath and the whole of Jewish life in Eastern Europe, the taste through which all others were filtered.

As a staple of the Jewish diet, schmaltz could appear almost anywhere, any time. The breakfasts that my father remembered best from his childhood in Poland in the 1920s—the *good* ones, that is—consisted of either a radish ("Not the kind you get here, but big ones, black"); a piece of bread; or, when neither of these was available, an onion dipped in schmaltz. Lacking any of these, they'd eat their schmaltz off a clove of garlic. The washing and blessings before and after the piece of bread would have taken longer than the actual eating. The protein in these breakfasts must have given him and millions of other children the quick energy that they needed to sit over the Torah for ten hours a day. Supper was often breakfast, but with a potato as the bearer of schmaltz.

Schmaltz for breakfast does not seem to have been quite as common in Lithuania and White Russia, where dairy dishes were more popular than in Poland. A breakfast of schmaltz meant that unless lunch were parve or *fleyshik*—which is like saying parve or gold—it would have to be late. Since the standard midday meal in Lithuania often involved some form of sour dairy, the local Jews seem to have considered it prudent to keep away from any breakfast that might provoke a delay. If they took a piece of bread, they'd have it with garlic. Both communities, Polack and Litvak as they are known in Yiddish, were getting by with what they had, which was not necessarily what they wanted: Asked at the end of Y. L. Peretz's short story to choose a heavenly reward as recompense for a lifetime of silent suffering, Bontche Shvayg, whose name gives the story its title, replies, "A hot roll with fresh butter every morning." But he wouldn't say no to a little schmaltz at night.

Gelatinous fat on a raw vegetable or hunk of bread doesn't sound like much of a treat, but schmaltz, real Jewish schmaltz, is the champagne of animal fat. Here's a standard recipe, taken from Leah W. Leonard's *Jewish Cookery*, first published in 1949:

> *Cut fatty skin and other fat clusters into small pieces. Cover with cold water and cook in a heavy kettle or frying pan, uncovered, until the water has almost entirely evaporated. Reduce heat and add diced onions, allowing one onion to each cupful of fat. A clove of garlic adds flavor . . . The fat is done when the onion is nicely browned . . . and the cracklings are dry and crisp.*

The cracklings are known as *grivn* or *gribenes*, the bacon—or better, the bacon bits—or better than that, the pork rinds—of the traditional Jewish diet. Their German counterpart and likely inspiration, *griebenschmalz*, gets its *grieben* and schmaltz from a pig. Leah Leonard calls *gribenes* "Jewish popcorn," though I never saw anyone eat them at the Yiddish movies and have never been able to find out if the *gribenes* eaten in Yiddish theaters were purchased on-site or brought from home. *Gribenes* can be mixed into mashed potatoes, chopped liver or eggs, potato kugel, matzoh balls and other dumplings, or else eaten as a snack on their own, preferably with a bit of whiskey on the side. We know that the Maharil was eating them in the late fourteenth century, and they have been well-loved ever since. No longer as common as they were even half a century ago, *gribenes* are due for a revival, if only to counter disturbing trends toward schmaltz-free eating.

Gribenes are so closely associated with schmaltz that there was a German-Jewish saying, "to add schmaltz to the *grivn*," that meant to carry coals to Newcastle or ice to the Eskimos. In the late 1960s, teenagers in Bathurst Manor, an overwhelmingly Jewish Toronto neighborhood with a substantial population of Holocaust survivors, used to refer to zits as "greebs," a term adapted from *gribenes*, which can not only look blotchy, but are also small, roundish, and encrusted. Such a sentence as, "He's a nice guy, but he's got a face full of poultry cracklings," was in no danger of being misunderstood.

GARLIC

With or without the *gribenes*, Leonard's recipe not only yields a fine traditional schmaltz, it is also a compact encyclopedia of Jewish food basics. The onions and garlic that figured so prominently at breakfast were so much more prominent elsewhere as to constitute a defining feature of Jewish cuisine and the Jews themselves. In *Eat and Be Satisfied*, John Cooper cites "a sixteenth century account of the Jews of Prague [that] mentioned that 'they feed continually on onions and garlic.'" Despite a general aversion to uncooked vegetables that persisted among Jews of East European descent until their children or grandchildren decided to get back to the garden, onions and garlic, the real Jewish vegetables, were both consumed avidly—raw, cooked, or somewhere in between. The Mishna actually refers to Jews as "garlic eaters" (*Nedorim* 3:10), while the *gemore* extols the virtues of garlic in order to explain why Ezra, who gets a book of the Bible all to himself, decreed that Jews have to eat it on Fridays:

> *Five things are said about garlic: it is filling; it is warming; it makes the face glow; it increases semen; and it kills intestinal lice. Some say that it encourages love and eliminates jealousy.* (Bovo Komo, *82a*)

The same passage is not at all coy about letting us know that Ezra prescribed garlic for its aphrodisiac effect: "They are to eat garlic on the eve of the Sabbath on account of marital duty, as it is written,

'It gives fruit at its appointed time.'" [Ps 1:3] While the rabbis are ostensibly talking about the preferred time for marital intercourse, the real point of the biblical verse is found in the clause that follows it, which you're expected to fill in for yourself: "Its leaf does not wither." As we'll see when we come to talk about chala, Sabbath nights were made for love, and Jewish law lays the burden of that lovin' squarely on the male. Anything that keeps the sap flowing has to be good for the Jews.

Ordering Jews to eat garlic is like forcing them to complain; the problem is making them stop. No one knows why, but Jews like garlic; they cried for it in the desert, and the original Ashkenazim thought so highly of it that they gave its name to their brand-new home. The standard acronym for the three leading communities of early German Jewry—Speyer, Worms, and Mainz, the cradles, as it were, of Ashkenazi civilization—is *shum* (rhymes with "room"), which also happens to be Hebrew for garlic. All that early talk about "the bylaws of *shum*, the *shum* communities" could just as easily mean "laws of garlic" or "garlic assemblies."

Conjugal obligations aside, it has long been traditional to make a point of eating onions and garlic at the Friday-night Sabbath table. While this custom undoubtedly has its economic aspects, the official reason has to do with the idea that the manna contained all the flavors in the world and could taste like anything you liked. Tasting all the flavors in the world is one of the things we are supposed to do to fulfill the commandment of "Call the Sabbath a delight." (Is 58:13) Impossible on the face of things, but once again the Jews find a way. The traditional Sabbath foods are supposed to contain the taste of the manna (which mayonnaise, as we have seen, most emphatically does not), and hence every pleasant taste on earth—except those of onion and garlic. Their tastes were excluded from the manna out of consideration for nursing mothers and the babies who would have refused such adult-flavored milk. It is therefore obligatory to eat onions and garlic on the Sabbath in order to redress this slight and complete the full complement of pleasant tastes. Failure to do so would be failure to honor the Sabbath, a violation of the fourth commandment.

The tradition is being kept alive today at Yiddish Farm, a community in upstate New York dedicated to speaking Yiddish and farming organically. An autumn 2012 ad for one of its programs reads: "Learn Yiddish. Celebrate Shabbos. Plant Garlic."

This fondness for garlic hardly went unnoticed by the nations of the world. Even in so allium-friendly a land as Spain, Jews who converted to Christianity were accused of continuing to smell of onions and garlic. The association of Jews with garlic took particular root in Germany and became a fancier, slightly more urbane way of saying "dirty, stinking Jew" without using any of those words. Heine was assailed for his metaphorical garlic breath (i.e., his inescapable Jewishness) and a former colleague accused Karl Marx of sweating democratic garlic. Some Nazis wore lapel buttons with pictures of garlic bulbs that would have a diagonal line running through them today: No Jews. It is no wonder that as early as the nineteenth century, German-Jewish cookbooks began to omit garlic from their recipes.

The association with garlic merges almost imperceptibly into the idea of the *foetor judaicus*, the Jewish stench, that gained currency in late antiquity and the Middle Ages. Jews are supposed to smell bad, probably because they were supposed to have killed Jesus, but possibly because they were Jews and would have smelt bad anyway. The latter idea was picked up in modern times by the Nazis; the former led many Christians to believe that the *foetor* disappeared as soon as a Jew was baptized. Sometimes the smell was blamed on religious practices rather than the inherent nature of the Jewish people. A fifteenth century *Judensau* woodcut features an inscription that reads, "Because we do not roast pork to eat/We are yellow and our breath stinks." It was all a matter of diet and exercise.

The joke wears off rather quickly once we discover that many

Christians believed that Jews thought Christian blood to be the only acceptably Jewish way of ridding themselves of the stench, a belief that even Martin Luther found ludicrous. In this kind of cultural context, garlic turns into the devil's deodorant.

Its medicinal uses were pretty much the same among Jews as among everyone else. As the Talmud implies, garlic, usually roasted, was seen as a specific against impotence and erectile dysfunction. Raw, it worked well against airborne afflictions; my father claimed to have spent much of his childhood with a lump of garlic knotted around his neck in a sock. Visitors to cemeteries would scatter garlic and salt to ward off evil spirits, and bad as life could be, no evidence has ever surfaced of a single Jewish community with any kind of vampire problem.

ONIONS

The onion, hardly less ubiquitous, does not seem to have aroused quite as much opprobrium, possibly because it was overpowered by the scent of the garlic. As biological relatives, onions and garlic tended to go hand in hand, the Abbott and Costello or Mary-Kate and Ashley of the traditional Jewish kitchen. As the saying has it, *tsibele mit knobl zenen layblekhe brider*, they're brothers from one mother. Standard accompaniments of the onion included schmaltz, radishes, eggs, herring, chopped liver, kasha, and *gribenes*. And these are only the compulsory uses. Note that with the exception of herring, garlic is either part of these dishes or else wouldn't do them any harm.

Sliced, diced, chopped; raw, boiled, fried, or baked, it's entirely possible to eat a full-course Ashkenazi meal in which onions figure in every course, starting with a *pletzl*—an onion flatbread—then moving on to eggs and onions, a little herring with rings of raw onion, then a chicken stuffed for the roasting with half an onion, a few cloves of garlic, and a chopped carrot. Those who didn't start the meal with an onion *pletzl* might like to end it with an onion *kichel*, literally, a cookie, but with the look and much of the texture of a giant potato chip. Or—lest they be overcome by goodness—a simple poppy-seed *kichel*, since it, too, is made with onion. Sophisticates or fashion victims aspiring to a certain retro chic might like to start things off with a Gibson: gin, vermouth—kosher, of course—and onion. Rimming the glass with garlic is strictly for Friday nights.

When Jews were not eating onions, they were talking about them. The onion figures quite prominently in Yiddish sayings and idioms, whereas garlic—which seems to have spoken for itself—really comes up only once in the well-known piece of folk wisdom, "If you don't eat garlic, your breath won't stink," that is, a truly innocent person has nothing to hide. This saying is obliquely related to a rhetorical question posed in the Talmud: "If someone eats garlic and then smells of it, is he going to eat another clove and smell of *it*?" (*Shabbos* 31b)—just because you've committed one stupid sin, you are not obliged to commit a second.

Otherwise, though, onions get all the good expressions. *A bitere tsibele*, "a bitter onion," is the kind of person you'd call a buzzkill in English, someone haunted by the fear "that someone, somewhere," as H.L. Mencken put it, "may be happy." Imagine the face of someone who has just taken a bite of bitter onion, then think of Edna May Oliver harrumphing indignantly in dozens of old Hollywood movies. As a corollary saying has it, "All onions are bitter"; with a personality like that, what can you expect?

Tsibele trern, "onion tears," are the Yiddish version of crocodile tears, the tears that you don't really mean. Although these can be cried, it's even better when someone is described as *pishn mit tsibele trern*, "pissing onion tears"; they might be flowing in streams, but they're so far from real that they're not even coming from the proper place.

The use of onions in folk medicine is hinted at in the damned-if-you-do, damned-if-you-don't resignation of "When a Jew has a boil he doesn't have an onion, and when has an onion, he's got no boil" (rubbing a boil with onion was a common means of reducing it). But probably the best—certainly the best-known—onion idiom in the language is a curse rooted in simple biology: *zolst vaksn vi a tsibele*—may you grow like an onion, *mitn kop in dr'erd*—with your head in the ground. When this curse was first uttered, the first half would have sounded like a blessing. Like garlic, onions were thought of as an aid to virility, in part because there's virtually nowhere where they won't spring up. Like the Jews, they are rather lowly during the week, but are exalted and made a bit of a fuss of every Sabbath. Just count a silent beat between "onion" and "with," and the curse will regain something of its initial effect.

ANGLO-SAXON SCHMALTZ

The onions, the garlic, the *gribenes*, important though they are, are but satellites of schmaltz, the sun of this culinary cosmos. Unusually for something found so often in Yiddish-speaking mouths, schmaltz—which we respect too much to mention promiscuously—figures in only one really popular idiomatic expression. *Araynfaln in shmalts-gribl*, to fall into a schmaltz mine, means either to strike it rich (as Jan and Dean did in "Surf City," where there's "two girls for every boy"), or to stumble into an unexpected stroke of good luck: "I was looking for Archie comics at the swap meet and found a Gutenberg Bible for fifty cents—*bin ikh arayngefaln in shmalts-gribl*, I fell into the mother lode of chicken fat." Ironically, someone who does so is often described as having *treyfene mazl*, unkosher luck, the Yiddish version of "the luck of the Irish."

English, on the other hand, has been using schmaltz for at least eighty years in a sense undreamed of in Yiddish. The earliest metaphorical use given by the OED is from a 1935 article in *Vanity Fair* that describes schmaltz as "a derogatory term used to describe straight jazz." Straight jazz in this context means people like Ted Lewis, Guy Lombardo, or Horace Heidt and his Musical Knights (with vocals by Art Carney)—big but far from swinging bands at a time when jazz was still a loose catchall term that included what would now be classed as easy-listening or adult-oriented pop music. Schmaltz was the rendered essence of square, and soon came to be applied to any artistic production, musical or not, that was overly sentimental, excessively sweet, and never, ever subtle. If the emotion in sentimentality is unearned, that in schmaltz is indigestible. Nat King Cole, superhip in his heyday, used the pseudonym Sam Schmaltz to get around restrictions in his recording contract; Charlie Shavers, the trumpet player and composer of the standard "Undecided," is called Joe Schmaltz on similar off-the-books recordings done for the same label.

The term caught on fairly quickly and has never fallen completely out of use. Frank McHugh invokes it beautifully in 1944's *Going My Way*, when he has to tell Bing Crosby that the movie's title song, which Crosby's character is supposed to have written, has been turned down by a music publisher on the grounds that, "Schmaltz isn't selling this season." Both Crosby and McHugh play Catholic priests.

The full meaning of this sense of schmaltz comes out with unusual force in the last place anyone would think to look for either Yiddish influence or dictionary definitions, AC/DC's "Let There Be Rock," written by Bon Scott and the Young brothers in 1977. In outlining the state of music in 1955, they tell us that "The white man had the schmaltz/The black man had the blues." And after schmaltz met blues on a tabletop in the Romanian-Jewish dining room of the muses, the blues had a baby and they named it rock 'n' roll, spawn of systemic injustice and distillate of chicken.

PSEUDO-SCHMALTZ

Most fans of Ivory soap have no idea that this ever-popular personal hygiene product owes at least part of its long-term survival to schmaltz, another animal fat product that floats. Around the beginning of the twentieth century, Procter & Gamble, the maker of

Ivory, found itself in a difficult situation: The meatpacking companies that had already forced P & G out of the kitchen-lard business were well on the way to gaining control of the market in cottonseed oil, an important component of the lard compounds sold for commercial use. Two packing houses alone were buying almost half the cottonseed oil produced in the United States, and Procter & Gamble was beginning to worry about rising prices and future supply; cottonseed oil was a crucial ingredient in Ivory, the company's core product since 1879. In order to fend off the meat packers, it bought a couple of mills, started a cottonseed oil company of its own, proceeded to build even more mills, and ended up with more oil than the soap business could use.

Once supply was assured, it was time for a little payback. After five years of lab work, Procter & Gamble applied for a patent on "a food product consisting of a vegetable oil, preferably cottonseed oil, partially hydrogenated, and hardened to a homogenous white or yellowish semi-solid closely resembling lard. The special object of the invention is to provide a new food product for a shortening in cooking." Crisco came into the world on Martin Luther's 427th birthday, November 10, 1910; it hit the stores in 1911, and, with the help of a famously vigorous advertising campaign, didn't take long to become a success.

Things might have been otherwise. The look of cooking-supply aisles in supermarkets and the nature of the food we eat—or the food that we grew up eating—might have been vastly different if P & G had marketed Crisco under the name originally proposed. People like my mother would have avoided any aisle where it was stacked and no Jew who wasn't ashamed to be Jewish would have let it into her mouth, let alone her kitchen. Anyone who has ever read a Yiddish newspaper knows that the people of the book are surprisingly lax about spelling, and "Cryst" would have been as hard to promote in the Yiddish press as kosher-for-Passover communion wafers.

The name we all know is the result of a compromise between Cryst and the second choice, Krispo, which turned out to be unavailable. Whether or not the name change was motivated by the fact that someone at P & G realized that a neutral-tasting shortening with no dairy or meat ingredients might strike a chord with the growing Jewish market, the result was the same: Along with a head-on challenge to butter and lard—an early salvo in the eight-decade "trans fats are better than animal fats" campaign only recently scuttled by science—Procter & Gamble also went straight for the Jewish market, which was still defined by religion rather than ethnicity:

> Crisco is Kosher. Rabbi Margolies of New York, said that the Hebrew Race had been waiting 4,000 years for Crisco. It conforms to the strict Dietary Laws of the Jews. It is what is known in the Hebrew language as a "parava," or neutral fat. Crisco can be used with both "milchig" and "fleichig" (milk and flesh) foods. Special Kosher packages, bearing the seals of Rabbi Margolies of New York, and Rabbi Lifsitz of Cincinnati, are sold the Jewish trade. But all Crisco is Kosher and all of the same purity.

Rabbi Margolies's line about the four thousand years is often quoted by writers on Jewish food, and almost as often attributed to P & G's copywriters, a misreading that sucks the life from his blurb. The man for whom New York's Ramaz School, the Modern Orthodox answer to Horace Mann or the Dalton School, has been named, Rabbi Moyshe Zvulun Margolies held the most visible Orthodox pulpit in the United States and can be fairly described as the most prominent Orthodox rabbi in the country. His seal on the package meant more than kosher; it meant classy. He might have rounded the chronology up a bit—according to the traditional reckoning, 1912 marked only 3,725 years since the birth of Abraham, who was seventy years old when God made His covenant with him—

but anyone interested enough in kashrus to care about such things would have got the point: Crisco was that rare new thing, one that is good for the Jews.

Parve or not, Procter & Gamble had fallen into a schmaltz mine and was not about to stop digging. It was hardly the first major concern to try to pitch its products to a Jewish market, or even to advertise in Yiddish newspapers. The National Biscuit Company (Nabisco), Quaker Oats, and Borden's Condensed Milk had all preceded P & G in a field pioneered by manufacturers of patent medicines, including Fletcher's Castoria, the children's laxative that strained many a parent-child relationship and is still available under the name Fletcher's Laxative for Kids. These pharmaceutical companies evinced a precocious understanding of the ongoing Jewish need for digestive help and had begun to reach out to the straining Yiddish masses by the late 1880s.

Procter & Gamble was also not the first non-Jewish company to claim that its products were kosher; Quaker Oats and Old Dutch Cleanser had already done so, and a Borden's ad from 1910 let consumers know that Moses had been right: "Pure Means Kosher— Kosher Means Pure," which apparently also meant that milk products, *pure* milk products, didn't need kosher certification. While Borden's and the other companies might have glossed over or even ignored religious law, Crisco gloried in it, going so far as to use three Yiddish terms in the passage quoted above, which was included in every edition of the 231-page *Story of Crisco*. Already in 1911, two years before the first edition of the product's biography, Crisco was being advertised in the Yiddish press in terms virtually identical to those in the book. By 1914, it was being name-checked in Yiddish-language cookbooks that had no connection with Procter & Gamble: "Put a fair amount of schmaltz or Crisco into a pan"; "Each croquette should be dipped into the egg white, then into the bread crumbs. Then fry it in chicken fat or Crisco."

A landmark in the history of American advertising, the 1911–12

Crisco campaign marked a revolution in Jewish marketing. Earlier campaigns aimed at Jews were either Yiddish versions of ads that ran elsewhere, or else appealed to the vague sense of "Jewishness" evoked by Borden's attempt to equate kashrus with nonritual purity. Crisco was the first "non-Jewish" product to move beyond simple lip service to Jewish ideas and values. By identifying a niche that no other product had thought to fill—the need for a cooking fat that was both kosher and parve, religiously acceptable and appropriate to any situation—and then linking age-old traditions of ritual purity with modern American concerns for health and hygiene, Procter & Gamble made Crisco into a "Jewish" product, a vehicle through which consumers could demonstrate their loyalty to both halacha and American ideas of progress, even if P & G's much larger gentile clientele was utterly unaware of the fact.

By 1933, when the first edition of "Crisco Recipes for the Jewish Housewife" was published, P & G's copywriters had become even more overt in their attempt to transform modernity into a natural expression of Jewish law. As folklorist Barbara Kirshenblatt-Gimblett puts it: "By placing Yiddish and English versions of a recipe on a single page, the cookbook's aim was to encourage Yiddish-speaking mothers and their English-speaking daughters to cook traditional dishes together—with Crisco. The suggestion was that Crisco conserved culture."

Conserved might not be a strong enough term; Procter & Gamble wasn't shy about claiming that Crisco was *improving* culture:

> *Ever since it was put on the market, Crisco has been the princi-*
> *pal cooking fat in many Jewish homes. It fills a great need, taking*
> *the place of heavy fats and oils which have been used in Jewish*
> *foods for hundreds of years.* Goose-fat, chicken-fat, and olive oil
> were good enough when there was nothing to take their
> place, *but when it became possible to obtain a strictly Kosher*
> *and Parve fat in the form of Crisco, Jewish women quickly*

appreciated its merits. In Crisco they find a pure, sweet-flavored fat which they can use for meat, dairy and parve foods. They find in Crisco a fat which is so easily digested that it makes everything in which it is used more digestible.

Al Jolson expressed the same sentiment six years earlier in *The Jazz Singer*: "Tradition is all right, but this is another day." Schmaltz might have been good enough in Europe, but if Europe was so great, you wouldn't be here. We've got something that is as kosher as schmaltz, tastes better than schmaltz, is cleaner and more versatile than schmaltz, and is much, much better than schmaltz at keeping heartburn and other forms of gastric distress at bay. It really is another day: Crisco leavens Jewish tradition with American know-how to create a new, improved tradition that is no less American than it is Jewish.

THE MATZOH FACTOR

Crisco is to the Jewish market as Chaucer is to English lit or Elvis to rock 'n' roll: not necessarily the first, but the first to have a lasting impact. Crisco's influence on a market that it might not have created but certainly brought to maturity can be seen as a textbook case of the happy accident. The product was not developed with Jews in mind; P & G wanted cottonseed oil for its soap. In the course of developing a product that could use enough of it to justify the company's expenditure on cottonseed mills, someone made the wholly unanticipated discovery that the ersatz lard that they were working on satisfied certain urgent Jewish religious requirements that would not have meant diddly to the company's deeply religious Christian founders. No one seems to know quite when this brainstorm struck, but it is hard to believe that it had nothing to do with the location of the company's head office.

By the beginning of the twentieth century, Cincinnati had long been home to a prosperous and influential Jewish community. The oldest such community west of the Alleghenies, by 1872 it could boast nine working *shokhtim* (ritual slaughterers), "five Jewish restaurants, sixteen abattoirs for kosher meat, and three matzoh bakeries," according to Jewish food authority Joan Nathan. It was also home to a large and influential community of German Jews, most of whom regarded themselves as Reform and would rarely, if ever, have patronized any of these businesses. Cincinnati was the spiritual and administrative headquarters of organized Reform Judaism in the United States. The Union of American Hebrew Congregations, now known as the Union for Reform Judaism, was established there in 1873; Hebrew Union College, the Reform rabbinical seminary, opened two years later and attained widespread notoriety within the Jewish world for the so-called "trefa banquet" held in 1883 to celebrate the ordination of its first graduates. The menu featured soft-shell clams, crabs, and frogs' legs.

Cincinnati was also home to the Bloch Publishing Company, the oldest Jewish publisher in the United States. Established by the brother-in-law of Isaac Mayer Wise, the founder of Hebrew Union College, Bloch, which is still in business, scored a major hit in 1889 with the publication of *Aunt Babette's Cookbook*. Though not the first Jewish cookbook published in America—an honor that goes to Mrs. Esther Levy's 1871 *Jewish Cookery Book*, which does not seem to have been widely read—*Aunt Babette's* was one of the most successful, despite the fact that it was so indifferent to the dietary laws as to include recipes for ham, oyster, shrimp, rabbit, squirrel, and prairie chicken. There are even instructions on "How to Make a Bacon Bandage for Sore Throat," which take the presence of bacon in the home for granted.

Still, there is a Star of David on the title page and many of the recipes reflect the "central European bourgeois cuisine" common to Jews and gentiles in that part of the world. *Treyf* aside, there are plenty of other recipes, especially for poultry and pastries, that would have been familiar to observant Jews. Non-Jewish readers might have been slightly put off by the fact that the section on "Easter Dishes" opens with a short chapter entitled "How to Set the Table for the Service of the 'Sedar' [*sic*] on the Eve of Pesach or Passover" in which the word *charoses* is printed in Hebrew characters without any transliteration. The recipes that follow include such Easter favorites as "Matzo Kloesse" (matzoh balls), "Matzo Kugel," "Chrimsel" (matzoh meal pancakes), and "Matzo-Mehl Cake." The appearances are saved, but only barely, when the author, whose real name was Bertha Kramer, remarks, "In some families hard-boiled eggs are distributed after the sedar (Easter eggs)." All that's missing are hotcross matzohs.

Nonetheless, with nine *shokhtim* and sixteen slaughterhouses, Cincinnati also had a sizable population of more traditionally minded Jews, whose numbers increased even further with the influx of East European Jews after 1881. In 1886, Isaac Oscherwitz, an Orthodox Jew from Germany, opened the kosher butcher shop that developed into Best's Kosher Sausage Company, a major national brand until its recent demise. Two years later, Behr Manischewitz, an immigrant from Lithuania who had come to Cincinnati as a *shoykhet*, opened a matzoh bakery in his home and soon came up with the revolutionary idea of keeping it running after the Passover season had ended.

Like bock beer or Beaujolais nouveau, matzoh had always been a seasonal product and would probably have stayed so had Manischewitz settled in one of the larger Jewish centers on the east coast. In the Midwest and beyond, where Jews were fewer and distances farther, traveling Jews had no guarantee of being able to find kosher food on the road—many peddlers subsisted on hard-boiled eggs cooked in pots that they shlepped with them. Gentiles heading west had equally long journeys, especially if they were going by horse, and Manischewitz quickly identified a dual market: Jews, whether travelers or not, who would buy matzoh for religious reasons, and non-Jews who would buy his crackers for convenience. Matzoh has something for everybody: It is kosher and portable, slow to go stale, and meets halachic requirements for bread on the Sabbath. Pesach comes but once a year, but if Manischewitz was to stay in business, he had to figure out a way of bringing Christmas to July. Year-round availability of matzoh was an innovation, but without contra deals with laxative makers, matzoh was unlikely to attract enough customers to keep a large business afloat.

By 1900 the basement bakery had grown into a factory capable of producing upwards of fifty thousand pounds of matzoh a day, and Manischewitz was shipping the stuff all over the world, though not to those areas of the Russian, Austrian, and German empires where most of the world's Jews were living. The company branched out: A 1912 invoice to a store called Brochin's lists egg matzohs, matzoh meal, cake meal, farfel, potato flour, and loaf sugar, along with regular matzohs.

Egg matzohs and matzoh meal were the major early innovations. The former, which still turn up once in a while in lieu of bread or even pastry at the morning kiddush in cash-strapped or gastronomically traditional synagogues, was a favorite Passover treat that many people hadn't eaten in decades. It is made with apple cider and eggs, and even though Joseph Karo says that matzoh made with fruit juice or "egg water" is acceptable on Passover, though not at the seder, Moses Isserles demurs: "In these [i.e., these here] countries it is not the custom to knead [dough for matzoh] with fruit juice. . . . The only exceptions are for the elderly or infirm," and children, who would be given it to eat during the transitional time on Passover eve when both leaven and "real" matzoh are forbidden. As a child, I associated egg matzoh with the well-yellowed pages of the *Lethbridge Herald* in which we wrapped our Pesach dishes for storage, but egg matzoh tastes much better than the plain stuff, having a bit of flavor and a certain give that the flour-and-water type can never attain.

Egg matzoh is *nisht ahin un nisht aher*, neither one thing nor the other. It certainly isn't *chometz*, or you couldn't have it in the house on Pesach; but it isn't, loosely speaking, quite kosher for Passover either. It was only really there if you were too old, too young, or too toothless to able to chew or digest regular matzoh. Its year-round availability was one of Manischewitz's earlier Christmas-in-July innovations.

An even bigger innovation was the packaging of matzoh meal—flour made of ground or soaked matzohs. Although this indispensable flour substitute had existed for centuries, it had been available only during matzoh season and was generally homemade, usually by women who would wrap matzohs in a cloth and pulverize them with rolling pins, mallets, the bottoms of heavy pots, in a Yiddish-speaking take on barefoot grape stomping. The alternate method of leaving the matzoh to soak until it was pliable and then crumbling it was avoided by some people—and all Hasidim—out of fear, however unwarranted, of making the matzoh *chometz* (even though normative Jewish law declares this to be impossible). Matzoh meal (and its cousin, cake meal) is essential to any Passover baking and is also the active ingredient in that most emblematic of Ashkenazi dishes, the matzoh ball, which began as the food of dreams, as much an object of Jewish anticipation as the Christmas goose for otherwise gooseless Christians, only to end in the depressing ubiquity that has made it the main ingredient of too many lousy jokes.

"Deck the halls with matzoh balls"; "Do you eat any other part of the matzoh?"; "LSD, matzoh balls, trip to Israel"—we'd have been spared them all if the matzoh ball had remained a Pesach treat, "the main Passover dish," as one writer called it. Of course, we would also have been deprived of Sol Weinstein's *Matzohball*, featuring Israel Bond, Agent Oy-Oy-7; and latter-day hipsters would be unable to groove to Slim Gaillard's "Matzo Balls." Gaillard, who is best remembered for "Flat Foot Floogie (With the Floy Floy)," also recorded with Charlie Parker and Dizzy Gillespie when he was famous and they were not. He knew what he was singing about and let his listeners know that "a little horseradish on the side" will "make it very mellow."

The standard Yiddish word for matzoh ball is *kneydl*, which really means dumpling, and dumplings of every sort were once a standard Yiddish dish. The oldest recipes we have specify that they be made from *zeml*, white-bread rolls usually made of chala dough; centuries later, the first Yiddish cookbook ever published gives a recipe for *zeml-kneydlekh*, as well as recipes for *kneydlekh* made with yeast, cabbage, liver, apples, cottage cheese, and potatoes. Year-round availability of matzoh meal seems to have led to mass abandonment of virtually all other forms of *kneydlekh*, though. It's been a long time since the others were widespread, and many Jews living today have never seen one.

Once eaten, matzoh balls are not quickly forgotten, as the following pre-Manischewitz recipe, from the Yiddish cookbook just mentioned, makes clear:

> *Thoroughly soak two matzohs, press them in a linen cloth or let the water run off through a strainer. Pour schmaltz into a pan; once it is hot, put the matzohs in, pressing them with a spoon, and mix until nothing sticks to the pan. Now put it into a bowl and mix in a reasonable amount of salt, a little pepper, and a diced onion. Once this has cooled, mix two eggs in thoroughly. Then add as much ground matzoh [i.e., matzoh meal] as needed for the [number of] kneydlekh, making sure that the dough is not sticky. The soup must be simmering when the kneydlekh are thrown in. This takes place a half hour before serving.*

This recipe yields bland, rather doughy matzoh balls that look a lot like kettle bells and lie, as they say in Yiddish, like a rock in your gut, the way they are supposed to. Yiddish cuisine, especially the late nineteenth/early twentieth century versions that have come down to us, was developed by people who often considered themselves lucky to have one real meal a week, and it was designed to keep these people from forgetting that they had eaten. The old joke that claims that the only thing wrong with Jewish food is that seventy-two hours later you're hungry again reflects a truth that most of the jokers had either forgotten or never knew: East European Jewish food is heavy because so many of the people eating it were already worrying about when they might get to eat it again. Most of the dishes discussed in this book were originally associated with the Sabbath and holidays, when people did whatever they could to fill themselves up and arm their innards against a privation that was soon to resume. Upset stomach, indigestion, heartburn are less painful, less annoying, and finally less shameful than the pangs of hunger—your stomach might be upset, but at least you've already eaten.

Jewish immigrants from Europe who found themselves able to eat like it was *shabbes* seven days a week did what they knew how to do: they ate like it was *shabbes* seven days a week—one of those lucky Sabbaths when they'd managed to buy or scrounge as much as they needed, as much as they and their families could hold.

They didn't care about being fat. More than a sign of prosperity, heftiness was a visible sign of health: Weight loss is among the earliest signs of tuberculosis, and a chubby kid was felt to have a better chance of becoming an adult. *Es, es, mayn kind*, "Eat, my child, eat," is about theurgy, not nutrition; preventing weight loss was a charm against contracting TB.

To return to the matzoh ball, the same Yiddish cookbook gives an alternate recipe, titled "Another kind of *kneydlekh*," that more closely approximates the taste and preparation that most of us are used to:

> *Beat four eggs with a wooden spoon, pour in one small glass of water and mix well. Add three spoons of schmaltz and mix again. Then add matzoh meal until the dough is thick. Add salt,*

ground pepper, and cinnamon and knead well with the spoon until the dough is smooth. Then roll them into dumplings by hand and put them into the simmering soup for twenty minutes, taking care to press them down with the spoon when they float to the top. . . . If you want the kneydlekh *fried dry, remove them from the soup and put them into a pan of melted fat or schmaltz. Turn them over frequently.*

Such recipes would have been used considerably less often were it not for the unprecedented changes that Manischewitz brought to the world of Jewish food. By the time Behr Manischewitz died in 1914, the size of the West Sixth Street factory that he moved into in 1905, and where he was now producing somewhere in the vicinity of seventy-five thousand pounds of matzoh a day, would have let any passerby know that whatever this "matzos bakery" was making, it must have been doing all right.

When Procter & Gamble was developing Crisco, Manischewitz was located at 838 West Sixth Street, while P & G was about a mile and a half away at West Fourth and Main, in the old Citizens National Bank building. No one living in Cincinnati could have failed to be aware of Procter & Gamble; both companies were located on streets with major streetcar lines, and somehow, somewhere, someone at P & G must have found out about Manischewitz. Whether it was a Jewish employee who realized what could be done with a parve schmaltz substitute, or a gentile who did some research and made the same discovery, is immaterial. As we have seen, companies that targeted the Jewish market before P & G did no more than point out that their products contained nothing explicitly forbidden by Jewish law; their kashrus was a matter of chance. Procter & Gamble gave every impression of having gone out of their way to make Crisco kosher. No one whose product just "happened" to be kosher would have the chutzpah to seek certification, let alone a separate statement of endorsement, from a religious celebrity like

Rabbi Margolies; no company that was not aiming for kashrus would talk about *milkhik, fleyshik,* and parve in elaborate publications that were also directed to gentile customers. According to a 1910 business directory, there were eighteen rabbis in Cincinnati on the eve of Crisco's launch; even though at least a third of them were Reform rabbis associated with Hebrew Union College, it still seems more than mere coincidence that Crisco's second certifying rabbi, the one there on the ground in Cincinnati, Rabbi S. Lifsitz, was also the *rov ha-hamakhshir,* the certifying rabbi, of the Manischewitz Matzos Bakery a little over a mile away.

The details about how all of this took place—P & G's discovery of dietary laws and schmaltz, its quest for kashrus and what active role, if any, Manischewitz or Rabbi Lifsitz might have played in its education—is the stuff of a Thomas Pynchon novel. Two companies that had only Cincinnati in common unwittingly came together to transform kosher food in America from a scattering of local butchers, bakers, and grocery stores into an industry that could turn ethnic particularity into a national brand and religious need into all-American product preference.

Crisco was an entirely new product, not a common food item that had been certified as kosher or adapted to meet the requirements of kashrus. There had been earlier stabs at making vegetable shortening, but none had been good enough for the product to stay on the market, and it is unlikely that many, if any, of Crisco's first Jewish customers would have known of them. Crisco had no history to overcome or update; Rabbi Margolies could not have said that we'd been waiting four thousand years for "new, improved X" without being laughed at even then. In 1912, a matzoh ball made for Thanksgiving with Crisco instead of schmaltz would have been a miracle, not a novelty. It would also have been a powerful advertisement for Manischewitz, Procter & Gamble, and the Jewish way of life; a statement, however unplanned, that being Jewish *added* something to the matzoh-ballers' Americanism, and that being

American added something to their Jewishness. For the first time in the experience of any Jew who had come from Eastern Europe, citizenship and religion were no longer at odds. It might have taken longer to convince certain non-Jews of the fact—there are some who are still not convinced—but as far as acculturation without assimilation goes, we owe it all to the discovery of parve schmaltz.

SHORTENING WARS

The problem is, Crisco isn't schmaltz. Love it or hate it, no one would ever describe real chicken or goose schmaltz as light or neutral tasting. Crisco and other such schmaltztitutes (its major competitor, Spry, didn't come along until 1936) might be godsends with respect to cookies, pastries, and desserts; they certainly allowed Chanukah, with its emphasis on latkes, to regain the *milkhike* associations it had had for centuries before the potato came to Eastern Europe, but they brought about a fundamental change in the taste of traditional Jewish cooking, in which butter, schmaltz, and, less frequently, oil furnished the base notes. The only reason to make matzoh balls without real schmaltz is lack of real schmaltz—they are usually served in chicken soup and have no need to be parve. Matzoh balls made with vegetable shortening strike most people accustomed to the real thing as insipid, lacking precisely that je ne sais quoi that only schmaltz can provide.

Still, not all women who were discontented with Crisco's lack of *fleyshike* zing had the time or inclination to make schmaltz of their own. But after four millennia of waiting for Crisco, the term of a single bar mitzvah is nothing: in 1924, I. Rokeach and Sons gave the world Nyafat, a schmaltz substitute by design. By the time Nyafat was released, Rokeach was a well-established kosher company, second only to Manischewitz in terms of name recognition and geographical reach. Opening in Brooklyn in 1890, the company had actually been founded in Lithuania in 1870 by Isaac Rokeach, whose surname means "pharmacist" or "chemist," to manufacture the coconut oil-based kosher kitchen soap he had invented and which is still manufactured under the Rokeach name. The soap, which is marked with a red dot to denote *milkhiks* and a blue one for *fleyshiks*, became well known enough to be mentioned by Lenny Bruce: "I'm in the kitchen, I'm washing with the Rokeach soap," which gets a big laugh because everybody knows that it's not for cleaning yourself. It's like saying that you took a shower with Ajax Triple Action.

Rokeach had an arrangement with a man named Aaron Proser, who granted the company the right to manufacture and distribute a product he had come up with called Parev Schmaltz (*parev* is a variant of parve) in return for a royalty on each bottle sold. Rokeach changed the name to the catchier and slightly less Jewish-sounding Nyafat, which is simply the Yiddish for "new" joined to the English "fat" (in Yiddish it would have been *Nyafets*). The main differences between Nyafat and Crisco are that Nyafat was made with coconut oil—the same thing that went into Rokeach soap—and, much more significantly, was flavored with onion, an innovation that brought it a lot closer to schmaltz. Where Crisco could be seen as schmaltz-like chiefly because it was also kosher, Nyafat was a deliberate attempt to recreate the taste of schmaltz in a parve form that had none of the original's side effects: "Foods prepared with Nyafat are easy to digest and cause no heartburn." It was immensely popular for decades and had a taste not easily forgotten.

Nyafat also made its mark on the American legal system and is familiar, if only by name, to virtually anyone who studied contracts in a US law school. Aaron Proser, the inventor of Parev Schmaltz, sued Rokeach in a 1941 case that has become the classic example of an implied negative contract. Rokeach had started to distribute a vegetable shortening called Kea (which was actually made by another company) and Proser felt that its sales were cutting into those of Nyafat, depriving him of royalties while Rokeach benefitted from sales of the competing product. The judge's opinion sums up the difference between the two products, which is essentially the difference between Nyafat and Crisco:

> *The basic ingredient of Nyafat is cocoanut oil 95 per cent, the balance hardened cottonseed oil, coloring and onion material, all cooked, stirred and strained before packing . . . The basic ingredient of Kea is straight cottonseed oil hydrogenated and deodorized. No other oil is added, nor is there any onion material or coloring and there is no cooking.*

The first sentence, with its "cocoanut oil 95 per cent," seems to indicate that the judge, whose name was Campbell, had spent an inordinate amount of time listening to Yiddish-inflected English. He goes on to say that "because of the onion flavor [Nyafat] was not attractive to non-Jews," and that Rokeach had taken on the distribution of Kea in an effort to compete more successfully with Crisco and Spry. In other words, not even Jews with some concern for kashrus wanted to bake their birthday cakes with onion-flavored shortening. The judge ruled for Rokeach.

Proser need not have worried. Kea didn't do very well and soon disappeared without a trace. In view of the market that it reached, its failure represents a miscalculation on a par with General Motors's attempt to sell a car called the Nova in Spanish-speaking countries, and indicates the influence that religious practice continued to have on the Jewish market. Whether K-E-A was supposed to be pronounced *ki*, like the thing that opens a lock, *ki-a*, or *keye* (to rhyme with "may a"), the product was in trouble as soon as the first label went on. The Hebrew word *ki* comes up in a verse of Isaiah that is quoted in the Mishnaic tractate known in English as "The Ethics of the Fathers." A different chapter of this tractate is studied each Saturday afternoon during the spring and summer, making it familiar to most immigrant Jewish males who gave any thought to kashrus. "Three who have eaten together and not spoken words of Torah are considered to have eaten from sacrifices to idols, as it is written, [Is 28:8] 'All the tables are full of vomit [*ki*] and excrement.'" (*Ovos* 3:4) Yes, *ki* means vomit in Hebrew. *Kee-a* or *kia* is another form of the same word, which explains why I drive a Hyundai: It comes into standard Yiddish as *keye*, the polite word for vomit.

After all this time, it's hard to be sure how the name was meant to be pronounced and whether the product was supposed to be called Barf or Barfo. One wonders what Rokeach's founder, who died in 1925, would have said.

FIVE

The Mother of Us All
Cholent *and Its Children*

Here is a shopping list for poor people, with prices:

A pound of meat, 15 kopecks
Barley kasha, 3 kopecks
A marrow bone for *ptche*, 2 kopecks
A kugel from a sheet of noodles, 3 kopecks
Poultry fat for heft, 2 kopecks

Place in sealed pot, put pot into oven two and a half hours before lighting Sabbath candles on Friday afternoon. Remove at lunchtime the next day. In the depths of a north-European winter, it will have cooked for nearly twenty-three hours.

There are a hundred kopecks to a ruble; the whole thing—this recipe yielded three distinct courses—cost the equivalent of a quarter and helped feed God knows how many people. Often, there would also be beans, lots and lots of beans, with or instead of the kasha.

This is *cholent*, the ground zero—the big bang, if you ask those who eat it—of East European Jewish food, the primal ooze from which many of the best-known, most-characteristic Yiddish dishes emerged. The kugel, the kishka, the stuffed neck of poultry known as a *heldzl*, all came out of *cholent*; calf's-foot jelly and the fruit or vegetable stew known as *tsimmes* were intimate associates. As the womb in which so many Sabbath and holiday foods were nurtured, *cholent* has been shaping tastes and eating habits for centuries. Second only to matzoh in antiquity, *cholent* is the only other Jewish food that might have originated with the Jews themselves. Where matzoh balls, for example, owe their existence to the German and Slavic fondness for dumplings, *cholent* was inspired by a couple of seemingly contradictory divine commandments and a healthy Jewish appetite for acting *aftselokhis*, to piss the other guy off. It was developed more to deal with disagreement than to stave off hunger; *cholent* originated as the slow-cooked analogue of a gay wedding held in front of an Orthodox synagogue or fundamentalist church.

More than a meal, *cholent* was an attempt to reconcile the prohibition against cooking on the Sabbath with the Pharisaic interpretation of the commandment to call the Sabbath a delight, which the rabbis of the Talmud—Pharisees, in standard English—read as an injunction to supplement Friday night's hot meal with a second one on Saturday.

This additional meal was meant as a slap in the face to the Sadducees, the Pharisees' chief rivals for power within the Jewish community, who rejected any number of the Pharisaic doctrines and beliefs that have come to define Judaism as we understand it; indeed, they rejected the whole notion of an Oral Law that complements the written Torah. Centered among the religious and administrative aristocracy and very much oriented toward the Temple in Jerusalem—the New Testament Book of Acts tells us that "The high priest rose up, and all they that were with him (which is the sect of the Sadducees)" (Acts 5:17)—Sadducees tended to a more linear, literal-minded reading of the Torah than the Pharisees.

Among other things, the two factions disagreed over the interpretation of Exodus 35:3. The standard translation—"Do not kindle a fire in any of your settlements on the Sabbath"—reflects the Pharisaic reading, but Hebrew grammar can always provide a fertile field for contention, especially when there is nothing else to argue about. The Pharisees took the verse to mean "Do not cause a fire to burn;" making new fires was thus forbidden, but benefitting from old ones, within carefully prescribed limits, was all right. The Sadducees, on the other hand, read the verb simply as "burn" and took the verse to mean that no fire at all was to be allowed in those settlements. They spent the Sabbath in the dark, eating cold food and doing nothing else to heat things up: They also forbade sex on *shabbes*—lest it light their fires—along with leaving the house (unless they were priests on duty in the Temple). For all we know, they might even have banned garlic.

The Sadducees disappeared soon after the destruction of the Temple. While their influence might never have been as far reaching as the Pharisees', it seems to have spread widely enough to contribute to the not-uncommon Roman idea of the Sabbath as a fast day. While not accurate even for Sadducees (the Talmud does cite a couple of isolated cases of Pharisaic rabbis—the only kind there was—who found nothing wrong with fasting then), it could very well be based on a mistaken interpretation of the abstention from cooked food.

Some Sadduccean ideas were revived centuries later by the Karaites, a breakaway Jewish sect that accepts the Written Law but not the Talmud or any of the laws or traditions derived from it. Like the Sadducees before them, Karaites ban any use of fire on the Sabbath. Karaism attracted alarming numbers of adherents between the ninth and twelfth centuries, and considerable time, effort, and rabbinic ink were devoted to combating its influence. As late as the mid-fourteenth century, David Abudarham, the Spanish author of a standard commentary on the liturgy, quotes the twelfth-century Provençal sage Zerachya ha-Levi on the importance of eating *khamin*, hot food: "Anyone who does not eat *khamin* on the Sabbath should be investigated, lest he be a *min* [heretic; here, Karaite]; should he die, let him be looked after by *amamin* [non-Jews]." It's those *mins* at the end of every word that make the joke funny.

Four hundred years later Moses Isserles expresses the same idea, but in an entirely serious context: "Anyone who does not trust the words of the sages and forbids the eating of *khamin* on the Sabbath is suspected of heresy." A hot lunch on Saturday started out as a protest, a way of defying the Sadducees who controlled the Temple and sought to impose their ideas on the masses whose tithes and offerings had helped to enrich them; in the Middle Ages, it turned into a pledge and outward sign of orthodox practice and belief, an intra-Jewish version of the role that kashrus plays in the outside world. From day one, though, it also provided a definitive solution to an apparently contradictory demand: Eat well, but do not dare to cook.

Aside from matzoh, a hot meal on Saturday—more accurately, a meal that has been kept warm for anywhere between sixteen and twenty-four hours—is the Jewish dish with the longest uninterrupted history, possibly because, like matzoh, it arose in response to ritual rather than physical needs. The fourth chapter of tractate *Shabbos* deals with how food cooked before Sabbath is to be "hidden"—i.e., wrapped—so that it retains its heat. The wrapping cannot add any heat or cause the food's temperature to rise; if you were allowed to raise the temperature, you might be tempted to cover the food with ashes which you might then stoke, an action that constitutes burning, which is forbidden on the Sabbath.

The prohibition of cooking allows for food eaten then to be kept warm or, within certain limits, reheated, but not actually cooked. It must be prepared, put into the oven or over a fire and, if necessary, removed for wrapping before the Sabbath begins; it must be more than half cooked before the onset of the Sabbath—edible, if not quite appetizing—so that the completion of the process can be ascribed to prevention of heat loss rather than active cooking. This is why the Mishna forbids any wrapping that might raise the food's temperature.

We have evidence of wrapping that actually predates the Mishna but cannot be understood without it. The Roman poet Juvenal, who died over half a century before the Mishna was compiled, makes a couple of unflattering references to Jews and food wrap that are unique in Latin literature. In his third "Satire," Juvenal, whose own talent for kvetching lends his complaints about Jews a certain un-intentional irony, is grousing about how the Jews, whose household utensils consist of hay and a basket, are renting all the good groves and shrines—Roman vacation properties, in modern parlance—and lowering the tone of the neighborhoods. The basket and hay have puzzled commentators on his work, few of whom seem to have studied in yeshiva. Such scholars have been equally baffled by his description of a Jewish fortune teller: "With her basket and hay left behind, the trembling Jewess, interpreter of the laws of Jerusalem, high priestess of a tree, and faithful messenger of high heaven, whispers into the secret ear."

Rome had a substantial Jewish population by Juvenal's time, but no one else makes any mention of Jews carrying baskets of hay. Someone would have been sure to notice if they wandered around with them habitually; the Talmud would be sure to discuss the materials that made for a valid basket, what type of hay, how much of it an individual could carry, and so on. In light of the Mishnaic rules for keeping food hot, we can only assume that Juvenal must at some time or other have seen enough Jews on their way to or from a local baker or communal oven with hay-wrapped pots of *khamin* in the baskets to conclude, however erroneously, that the baskets them-selves had some religious significance. Keeping food warm in this way persisted for a very long time. According to John Cooper, some late nineteenth-century German Jews would sometimes place their *cholent* "in a hay box (*Kochkiste*) to cook overnight, instead of [taking it] to the communal bakery." Such *Kochkisten* were a recent development and were aimed at the poor or those struggling not to become the poor. They were the forerunners of the electric Crock-Pot—you had to bring your own pot, though—and were not marketed to the members of any particular ethnic or religious group.

We don't know what Roman Jews or their contemporaries in Palestine used in their *khamin*. Given the popularity of the broad bean in Mediterranean and Near Eastern cuisines, these dishes might very well have resembled the *cholent* eaten today, but we have no actual evidence. Certain themes, however, recur universally in such Sabbath stew recipes as have come down to us: A base of grains, beans, or chickpeas is embellished with locally available meats, vegetables, and spices. The earliest mention of the Ashkenazi *cholent* is found in the popular halachic work, *Or Zarua*, which was written around 1260. Its author, Isaac ben Moses of Vienna, usually known as Isaac (or Yitzkhok) Or Zarua (which means "light is sown [for the righteous]"), was a Bohemian—Czech, not beatnik—who studied in France and Germany. Toward the end of a rather involved discussion of permitted and forbidden ways of keeping food warm, he mentions being in the home of his teacher, the eminent Tosafist Judah Sir Leon, in Paris, and seeing Rabbi Judah's non-Jewish servants light a fire and place the pots near it to make sure that "their *cholent*, that is, the food that had been kept warm" would be warm enough. Rabbi Isaac explains the reasons for allowing the servants to do so on *shabbes*—the Germans and Bohemians were much stricter about such things and did not accept this line of reasoning—but falls short of recommending such a procedure himself. He is not really concerned with the *cholent's* ingredients and never mentions if it was grain- or bean-based; he does, however, say that it contained chicken and eggs, and also mentions that apples were included in *cholents* in Champagne, which gives us some idea of how long Jews have been eating baked apples.

Judah Sir Leon died in 1224; Isaac is thought to have studied with him before 1220 and the *Or Zarua*, as mentioned above, was written around 1260. The term *cholent* was well established, at least

in France, by the early thirteenth century and had entered the halachic literature—generally a sign of widely extensive use—by its
middle.

There are a few folk etymologies for the name: it comes from *shul
ende*, because it is eaten after shul, synagogue, has let out; that it's a
combination of the French *chaud et lent*, hot and slow; and my
favorite, that it's onomatopoeic, meant to echo the thud of the *cholent* as it storms your empty stomach five hours after you've got out
of bed on a Saturday: *tshulnt* (as it's pronounced in many dialects of
Yiddish)—the *tsh* is the sound of its descent, the *ulnt* of the crash.

The truth, as usual, isn't quite so much fun. "*Cholent*" is a simple
translation of *khamin*, and comes ultimately from the Latin *calentem*,
the present participle of a verb meaning "to be warm," as filtered
through Jewish versions of Old French that predate Yiddish. Less
scientifically, imagine the Spanish *caliente* with a ^ over the *c*.

As the name indicates, the dish that we know seems to have originated in France, with the fava beans at its base suggesting a Spanish, and ultimately Arab, influence. No one is sure if *cholent* was
adapted from cassoulet—unnecessary, in view of *cholent's* Sephardi
forebears—or if cassoulet developed from *cholent*, in which case its
porkocentricity and relentlessly nonfestive associations would imply one hell of a psychic journey; or if they developed independently.
Stumbling upon the secret of slow-simmering beans with meat is
not quite the same as discovering the circulation of the blood and—
especially when we recall the importance of porridges, paps, gruels,
and stews in medieval European cuisine—there is no reason to
assume that different communities could not have come up with
the same idea independently.

Both dishes were originally made with fava beans, the broad
beans that have been cultivated in Europe for at least eight thousand years. These were so thoroughly replaced in the sixteenth
century by haricots brought over from the Americas—kidney beans,
French beans, and the like—that the Latin term for beans of this

type, *phaseolus vulgaris*, is the ultimate source of *fasolye*, the standard Yiddish word for such standard Yiddish foods as green beans, white beans, kidney beans, and lima beans (a broad bean is called a *bob*). The Sephardi *adafina*, thought by many to be the immediate ancestor of *cholent*, is still made with fava beans and chickpeas, but uses oil instead of schmaltz.

Beans are the most common base; in some areas, though, barley kasha was preferred. Unmodified kashas in Yiddish are generally assumed to be made from toasted buckwheat, but the word can refer to virtually any kind of porridge or cooked cereal. Barley was quite cheap and tended to be used to bulk out soups, stews, and *cholent*. The barley soup called *krupnik* (also known in some areas as *kolish* or *kulish*) was as widely consumed among East European Jews—to call it popular might suggest that they thought they had a choice—as similar dishes were in Scotland. During winter, it was sometimes eaten every day. Adapted from a similar Polish dish, the Jewish *krupnik* dispensed with the bacon that was often added for flavor and made do with mushrooms, the inevitable onions and garlic, and schmaltz for those who weren't planning to garnish it with sour cream. A potato could lend extra bulk. Although there are recipes for *krupnik* with meat, the reality seems to have been that such meat as wound up in it tended to be scraps. As people used to say, "If we could afford meat, we wouldn't be eating *krupnik*." It was a humble food for humble folk, most of whom didn't seem to have much good to say about it. As the proverb has it, "If *krupnik* is food, there's a synagogue in Handrivke;" substitute Coutts, Alberta, for Handrivke and you'll get the general idea.

The basis of the beef-and-barley soup that still looms large in kosher and Jewish-style restaurants, *krupnik* isn't mentioned much these days. It pops up, though, in the "W. A. Mozart, Superhero" section of Daniel M. Pinkwater's *Young Adults* in "the ancient formula by which the mild-mannered genius composer is transformed into the greatest crime fighter and champion of justice the 18th century has ever known . . . *Kakamun und pishdertzee und mach a krupnik in der früh"*; that is, "Shit on him and also pee and make a *krupnik* in the morning." Mozart then turns into—Beethoven.

Barley is arguably even less exciting than beans, especially if you have to eat it the rest of the week. In his story, "Shabbes," Mendele Moykher Sforim, sometimes called the grandfather of modern Yiddish and Hebrew literature, offers an approving description of a basic *cholent* that makes the shopping list at the beginning of this chapter look like an all-you-can-eat buffet: "Well-stewed [barley] kasha with a fat marrow bone and a nicely browned noodle kugel." Assuming that there was also some schmaltz in there, the total cost of the meal, according to the prices cited above (which date from about twenty years later and were higher than those that Mendele's characters would have paid), is ten kopecks: a dime. Beans might have taken it to eleven. In Romania, which was under Ottoman rule for three hundred years, chickpeas had a presence in *cholent* that they never enjoyed in Poland, Russia, or Lithuania, thanks to the powerful Sephardi influence on Turkish Jewry: They came straight from the *adafina*.

A recipe from the Yiddish cookbook published in Vilna in 1896 gives us a picture of a basic, no frills, bean-based *cholent*. It calls for white beans, shards of marrow bone, fatty meat, "the usual amount of salt," cold water, an onion, ground pepper, and "if you like . . . the thickest barley." This, again, is a bare-bones *cholent*; the fat from the meat does duty for schmaltz, thus saving the chef two kopecks. The fatty meat would have consisted of trimmings that would have been unsalable had *cholent* not existed.

The next *cholent* recipe in the same cookbook is much more elaborate and might well betray Romanian influence in its inclusion of chickpeas. While these were quite popular in Lithuania, where they were known as *nahit*, they weren't usually associated with *cholent*.

As the editorially inserted capitals in the word "OR" make clear, this is *cholent* for people with a choice:

> *Take flour, chopped bits of schmaltz, a chopped onion, salt, and water and mix into a dough. Put a piece of schmaltz or marrow on the bottom of the pot. Make the dough into a dumpling for kugel and lay it on top of the schmaltz. Put beans or barley or both on top of the dough, along with a few marrowbones or some fatty meat and add salt.*
>
> *OR instead of the meat add chopped garlic sausage which has been soaked in hot water, and instead of beans add sorted and soaked chickpeas. Some people mix syrup into the kugel. If you have a raw goose or chicken back[bone], you can stuff it with the kugel dough.*

Ample as this recipe might seem, especially after it has stewed for the better part of a day, it wasn't enough for some. Potatoes found their way into the *cholent*, especially in Poland, in the mid-nineteenth century, after Czar Nicholas I, more mindful of the potato's superior yield and short growing season than of the recent disaster in Ireland, introduced its mass cultivation to his empire and transformed the East European diet. If potatoes could find their way into vodka and be used as Chanukah menorahs (which they sometimes were), it would be unseemly to exclude them from the one Jewish food capable of absorbing anything that isn't dairy.

Modern times have seen the birth of commercially packaged *cholent* bases. One of the more widely distributed brands, Unger's Chulent [sic] Mix—the spelling reflects the usual Yiddish pronunciation—contains pinto, red kidney, and navy beans, and comes with a warning on the package:

> *This is a natural product of the earth. Even with diligent processing using the most modern equipment available,*

we suggest you examine the contents carefully. Sort out any
foreign substances (small stones, particles of soil, metal, etc.)
Rinse with drinkable water before cooking to assure maximum
wholesomeness.

It is no accident that the Anglo-Saxon dish that most closely resembles *cholent* is called hotchpotch, a heavy stew of potatoes, other
vegetables, and meat which also gives us the word hodgepodge: a
bunch of things with no intrinsic connection jumbled together in
no discernible order—much like the informal weekly gathering
aimed at bohemian Hasidim and ex-Hasidim in New York that both
serves and calls itself Chulent. While beef might have been the *cholent* meat of choice, people made do with whatever they could find
and afford; as we have already seen, this was often nothing more
than a bone. Over here, where prosperity has produced leftovers and
the refrigerator has made it possible to keep them for days on end,
cholent is often a nourishing alternative to the compost bin. When
I read that Calvin Trillin's mother served nothing but leftovers for
thirty years, I knew that his family could not have been Orthodox:
a weekly *cholent* makes nondairy leftovers unlikely.

To most of us, *cholent* appears as a barely differentiated mass, a
turgid swamp of beans, barley, or what-not from which a chicken
neck or piece of stuffed intestine occasionally protrudes. As *cholent*
grows more popular, though, this sludge of ingredients becomes a
bit of a problem for more observant eaters. As part of one of the man-
dated Saturday meals, a *shabbes cholent* is by definition preceded by
hamoytse, the blessing over bread that covers anything else eaten at
the same meal. But once *cholent* began to be featured on the menus of
kosher restaurants, some of which serve it every day; once it became
a yeshiva practice to serve it as a fortifying snack at the weekly
Thursday night *mishmar*, or Torah-study vigil, it turned into a treat
that you have to crawl through a minefield to get to. Without the
protection afforded by bread, a *cholent* has to be analyzed according

to its constituent elements so that the proper blessings can be said. As one handbook puts it, "Before you sit down to eat it, you have to know what is in it." If it's an all-bean *cholent*, you say "Who has created the fruits of the earth." If there's meat, you add—not substitute, add—"By whose will everything has been created." If, however, the pieces are small enough to be mixed together in every spoonful, you make only the blessing that applies to the ingredient that comprises the better part of the *cholent*.

This continues for another half page, during which the correct blessings for *cholents* featuring kishka, barley, or really big pieces of meat or potato are listed, as well as which blessing to choose should you be eating the *cholent* only for the sake of one of the main ingredients rather than the whole hodgepodge: "I came for the kishka, but got stuck with the beans." The blessings to be said *after* eating the *cholent* are also indicated.

This kind of minute, if not obsessive, analysis of the contents of every plate, pot, and bowl as if they were elements of a vast system in urgent need of interpretation is the source of the frequently noted concern with food and digestion so often displayed by even completely irreligious Jews. Although the ritual or religious motivation for such worries might have vanished, the behavioral reflex remains and is passed from one generation to the next as just that: a reflex, a way of dealing with food that is often assumed to be universal. You can stop keeping kosher or making blessings; it isn't as easy to stop looking deeply into everything that you eat, even if you no longer know why you're doing so.

As the simmering embodiment of the Yiddish principle of uncertainty, *cholent* certainly repays close analysis, if only because people like to know what they're eating. There are, however, those who feel that well enough is best left alone. "Don't look too closely," the Yiddish proverb tells us, "at a *cholent* or an offer of marriage;" if you knew what was in either one, you probably wouldn't touch it. Another proverb that links *cholent* to marriage says simply that "A son-in-law is like a *cholent*"—you don't know what's really inside until it's already too late.

In old-country Yiddish, *cholent* was never said to be cooked. Instead, it was slid. Since most private homes did not have ovens big enough to hold the Friday-night meal and the *cholent* pot at the same time, women would take their pot of *cholent* makings to the local baker, who would then slide the pots into his oven with the help of the big paddles usually used for baked goods. The pots were often personalized in some way—a sign, a mark, a family name—and were sealed with dough to keep the vapor inside. The baker's oven was sealed with clay after all the pots had been put in, the better to contain its warmth once the fire burned itself out. The pots were picked up after the Saturday morning services, usually by kids, and carried home wrapped in bedding, coats, defringed prayer shawls, or whatever else was thought to provide decent insulation.

Cholent wasn't all that went into the baker's oven. Mayer Kirshenblatt describes Friday afternoons when he would go to the baker in Apt (Opatòw), Poland, in the early 1920s with:

> . . . *the food to be cooked for the Saturday meals: coffee and milk for breakfast, and soup and* tshulnt *for the midday dinner . . . The baker would put the dairy dishes on the left side of the oven and the meat dishes on the right side. Everything cooked slowly overnight in the baker's oven, which retained the heat from Friday's baking. . . . [The baker] was paid a few cents for his services, but not on the Sabbath itself."*

The less indelicate effects of a good, weighty *cholent* are best hinted at in the Yiddish idiom, *shnarn vi der hunt nokh tsholnt*, "to snore like a dog after *cholent*." Beloved as the traditional *shabbes* afternoon nap might be, *cholent* makes sure that it is not a matter of choice. The first solid food eaten on Saturday, anywhere between three and five hours after awakening and usually preceded by a shot of whiskey or vodka, *cholent* induces a weighty languor that fades irresistibly into windy slumber. When the Kotzker Rebbe, the last of the great figures of classical Hasidism, was asked why he had never written a book, he replied by asking, "Who would read a book by someone like me? The big-shot rabbis—who am I that they should read me? The only people who would even buy my book would be regular householders, merchants and craftsmen, who fight to make a living from the minute they get up until the minute they go to bed. When does someone like this have time to read? *Shabbes* in the afternoon, after the *cholent*. And what's going to happen? He's going to pick up my book, lie down on the couch with it, and fall asleep with the book on his chest. For this, I don't need to write a book. He can sleep just as well without me."

Literary composition isn't all that *cholent* can interfere with. Husband and wife traditionally fulfill the first commandment in the Bible, "Be fruitful and multiply," on the Sabbath. As one of the few recreational activities permitted and even recommended, as we saw in our discussion of garlic, sex—or conjugal duty, at any rate—is closely associated with the Sabbath. Although it is usually thought of as a Friday-night activity, Saturday afternoon became the preferred time in many homes. A woman who has been cleaning, shopping, cooking, and fretting since Thursday night is often too tired to do anything more than collapse into bed on Friday. On Saturday, though, the *cholent* is there to sap everyone's élan vital. But a commandment is a commandment, and people can do no more than their best. "Snoring like a dog after *cholent*" calls up the image of a domestic satiety so profoundly multifaceted that even the dog has been affected. Some cultures equate food with sex; with us, it's the nap that matters.

Cholent enters European high culture in Heinrich Heine's *Prinzessin Sabbath*, where it is presented, not entirely seriously, as a consolation for not being able to smoke on *shabbes*: the steaming *cholent* is there as a divine tobacco substitute, a metaphysical Nicorette that can also be used to make fun of the relentlessly high-minded Schiller. "*Schalet, schöner Götterfunken/Tochter aus Elysium/*That's how Schiller's anthem would have sounded/Had he ever tasted *schalet.*" *Schalet* is the Western Yiddish form of *cholent.* Heine goes on to say that God gave the recipe to Moses on Mount Sinai, along with the Ten Commandments; that *cholent* is kosher ambrosia, beside which the false ambrosia of the heathen Greek deities is nothing but devil's dung. Elsewhere he says that "It is deeply to be regretted that the Christian Church, which borrowed so much that was good from ancient Judaism, should have failed to adopt *schalet* as its own."

Heine's comrade in apostasy, Moritz Gottlieb Saphir, was a lesser writer but had a far better Jewish education than Heine, whose comments on the religion, even when he's trying to be serious, occasionally betray a shocking lack of basic knowledge. Saphir, on the other hand, came from a much more religious family and even spent some time at Rabbi Sofer's Pressburger yeshiva in what is now Bratislava, one of the main bastions of Central European Orthodoxy. His first play, written when he was twenty-five, was in Yiddish. Years later, well after his conversion, Saphir came up with what is almost the last word on the subject of *cholent*; he calls it *scholet*, just to bug Heine and everybody else (and also because he came from a different dialect area):

> In order to fully enjoy it one has first to rid oneself of all prejudices and emancipate one's stomach of all preconceptions; the tongue must be free of all anti-Jewish feeling, and the palate must be elevated. . . . The German has his pumpernickel, the Englishman has pudding, the Italian has macaroni, and the Jew has his scholet. It is just like the fate of the Jew: it is neither cooked nor roasted, is accorded no rights of citizenship in the cookbook, and is not allowed even in the same guild with other foods.

Saphir also describes a variant of *cholent* that calls Isaac Or Zarua to mind, the *scholet* egg, eggs prepared as if they were *cholent*
and likewise eaten at Saturday noon. You put ashes in an earthen
pot, then put some eggs into the ashes. "Then you put a cover on
the pot and close it hermetically, but if you cannot make it airtight,
you take some soft dough instead and you close up all the chinks
between the cover and the pot." The pot goes into the oven on
Friday afternoon and comes out the next day full of *scholet* eggs.
According to Saphir, "It is reflectively brown and full of wisdom-
wrinkles. . . . Usually the egg becomes very small, reduced at least
to a half of its size when it is only boiled. This *scholet* egg makes one
think of a trill by Mlle. Lind, or better yet, of a pirouette by Elssler,"
one of the major ballet stars of the day.

Of course, simply by virtue of their conversion to Christianity,
Heine's and Saphir's slightly ironic sentimentalities about the foods
they left behind places them in the vanguard of what Yiddish calls
tsholnt yidishkayt, "*cholent* Judaism," the earliest manifestation of
what later came to be called gastronomic, or bagels-and-lox, Judaism. While its practitioners rarely go quite so far as Heine and Saphir,
the deli-every-week-synagogue-twice-a-year members of the Jewish
community have been roundly condemned by leaders of every major stream in modern Judaism, most especially by the outreach
groups that try to entice young adults into the Orthodox fold. The
men who supervise the kosher restaurants and certify the kosher
food products, who spend a large part of their lives studying and
thinking about the laws of kashrus, seem unable to see the bagels-
and-lox Judaism that they so deplore as the logical secular counterpart of a religion that manifests itself most clearly at mealtimes. It
might not be Judaism, but that doesn't mean that it isn't Jewish: That
weekly deli is little *shabbes* of the mouth.

For Jews today no less than for apostates like Heine and Saphir,
a *cholent* or kugel is a way of reminding themselves and everyone
else that no matter how they present themselves to the rest of the

world, they know that there is still a *pintele yid*, an inextinguishable spark of Jewishness—whatever that might actually be—somewhere inside them. For people like Heine, who made no secret of having converted to Christianity for reasons that had little to do with accepting Jesus as his personal savior, *cholent* was what Rosebud was to Charles Foster Kane; when Heine talks about watching Jewish girls go past the cafe where he is sitting on *shabbes* and says that they smelled of *cholent*, his facetiousness is tempered with a sigh.

Outside of the Orthodox world, where *cholent* has recently undergone a resurgence that parallels the renewed secular popularity of various comfort foods, *cholent* fell out of favor decades ago, in part because of declining Sabbath observance—*cholent* loses its raison d'être once you turn on the oven and stop going to shul—and partly as a consequence of an increasingly Americanized Jewish palate. Leah Leonard's *Jewish Cookery*, Gertrude Berg's *The Molly Goldberg Jewish Cookbook*, and Sara Kasdan's *Love and Knishes*, published, respectively, in 1949, 1955, and 1956, all give lima beans—and lima beans alone—as the main ingredient in their basic *cholent* recipes; Leonard's inclusion of navy or kidney beans in an alternate recipe lets us know that the latter would have been readily available in Jewish neighborhoods. Since lima beans were rarely, if ever, seen in the parts of Europe where Jews were allowed to live, their presence in these recipes seems to reflect a concession to American taste.

ENTER THE KUGEL

Earlier references to *cholent* as the matrix—or better, the incubator—of a number of other archetypal Ashkenazi foods were neither purely rhetorical nor even vaguely hyperbolic. Some of the most typical and popular Yiddish dishes came quite literally out of the *cholent*; others developed in the way that they did only because *cholent* allowed them to. The word itself became Yiddish shorthand for any kind of slow cooking, and the *tsholnt-top*, the *cholent* pot, was once a conspicuous feature of every Ashkenazi kitchen. Ranging from simple clay pots to elaborately inscribed vessels of bronze and other metals, some with built-in feet, the *cholent* pot is so firmly fixed in the Yiddish-speaking imagination that when Mordkhe Schaechter, the late Yiddish linguist, set himself the task of coining a Yiddish word for Crock-Pot, he came up with *elektrisher tsholnt-top*, electric *cholent* pot, which would have been an even better name for a swinging psychedelic disco. Heads of all nations could have said things like, "Far out, man, I'll dig you at the Cholent Pot," while self-important poseurs would have insisted on pronouncing the *ch* as if *cholent* were Chanukah and not cheese-free.

The *cholent* pot began to expand its repertoire not long after it acquired its name. Somewhere around the time that Isaac Or Zarua was watching his teacher's servants heat *cholent* on the Sabbath in France, Jews in German-speaking areas who were tired of eating the same old thing every week or just wanted to do something constructive with the dough left over from their Sabbath chalas began to add some of that dough to the *cholent*.

They didn't just dump it in, though. The dough was put into a round pot that Germans called a *Kugeltopf. Kugel*, still widely used in contemporary German, means "ball, sphere, bullet"—something round. Street signs all over Germany advertise *Kugel Eis*, a *kugel* of ice cream that comes in a cone; a *Kugelschreiber*—kugel writer—is a ball point pen. The earth is sometimes called the *Erdkugel*, the globe, a term that even made its way into the fancy, highfalutin Yiddish of speakers and writers who wanted to sound refined and *epes* continental. The forward to the Yiddish half of *Tempting Kosher Dishes*, a promotional cookbook that Manischewitz started publishing in the 1930s, talks about "*balebustes* [housewives] from every part of the *erdkugel*." In regular Yiddish, though, kugel means nothing but pudding. Where Germans and Scandinavians see the earth as a ball, Yiddish-speakers familiar with the term *erdkugel* begin to conceive of Spaceship Earth as Planet Pudding. A gentile with excellent prospects of success is said to have the world as his oyster; for a Jew in a similar position, it's one big mass of noodles.

The roundness of the kugel has long ceased to be a matter of any particular interest or concern; the photo on the Streit's Potato Kugel Mix box shows a potato kugel in a rectangular foil baking pan, while the kugel slices on the Manischewitz mix's box betray no rounded edges anywhere. Originally, though, the ingredients went into the round pot known as a *Kugeltopf* which was then lowered into the preloaded *cholent* pot, allowing the dough to luxuriate in a warm *cholent* bath for anywhere from half to three-quarters of a day, by the end of which it had turned into a—dumpling is the only word that comes to mind—that was called either *Weck-schalet* or, more commonly, *Schalet-kugel*.

The use of the term *kugel* to refer to baked dough has led commentators to link this early kugel—think of it as the acoustic version—with the south German and Austrian cake still known as a *Gugelhupf*. *Gugel* is just an alternate form of *kugel*, and the *Gugelhupf* gives us a good idea of what they meant by round in the twelfth or thirteenth century. Still popular today, the *Gugelhupf* is a Bundt cake made with raisins, almonds, cherry brandy, and whatever other fruits or nuts the baker thinks will work. Turn one sideways and it resembles the kind of hood that was part of many robes and coats in the Middle Ages; the word *kugel* derives from the same Latin word—*cucullus*, a hood—that gives us the English "cowl." *Gugelhupf*, then, equals something along the lines of "hoody yeast" in modern English (though "yeast ring" is probably closer to what it really means), and is clearly the kind of *gugel* or *kugel* that the visionary who first introduced chala dough into *cholent* was aiming for.

Kugel probably started out as a post-*cholent* dessert; we don't know when it came to be thought of as one of the main components of the Sabbath lunch, a sort of sop to help absorb the *cholent* in which it was cooked. Hence the name *Schalet-kugel*, to indicate that *cholent* was a mechanism as much as a meal. With a trencher made of bread, you finished the meal by eating the plate; with a *cholent*-cooked kugel, you got to eat the stove.

Where *Schalet-kugel* indicates the where and the how, *Weck-schalet* also adds the what. *Weck* is a south-German word for a bread roll of the type that Yiddish now calls a *bulke* or *zeml*. Beef on *weck*—roast beef on a caraway *weck*, garnished with horseradish, with a kosher dill on the side—is still a popular snack in the Buffalo area of western New York and is thought by some to be an even greater contribution to the American menu than the now-ubiquitous Buffalo hot wings, if for no other reason than that you have to go to Buffalo to get one.

The 1896 Yiddish cookbook from Vilna gives a recipe for a kugel of this type under the Yiddish rubric *tsholnt-kugel*, which the author himself translates into German as *Schalet-kugel*:

> *Take well-soaked rolls, flour, ½ pound of schmaltz in small pieces, ½ pound of syrup, ground cinnamon, a little ground pepper, a couple of ground bitter almonds, grated lemon peel, and salt. Drain the rolls through a strainer, mix everything thoroughly until it forms a paste. Smear the* kugel-*pot well with schmaltz, put everything inside and cover tightly. The next day, on* shabbes, *it is a beautiful golden kugel. You can also add boiled millet or chopped apples, but the rolls will need a more thorough wringing out.*

Note that the special kugel pot is still being used. As the author never mentions putting the pot into the oven, we have to assume that if it was not going directly into the *cholent* pot, it was at least going into the local baker's oven alongside it. Even after ovens in private homes became more common in the nineteenth century, they were far from universal and were rarely either large enough to hold the number of pots, pans, and roasting tins needed for a proper *shabbes,* or powerful enough to retain the kind of heat that a baker's oven could generate for the better part of a day after being turned off.

Schalet-kugel of this type is rarely, if ever, encountered anymore. Although the recipe gives no indication of how many people it is meant to feed, the amount of bread, syrup, and schmaltz suggests something that would never be described as featherlight. Saphir, who was raised on precisely this type of kugel, makes the same point when he puns on the difference between the German and Yiddish meanings of the word and says that "many Jews go through battle practice every Sabbath by advancing in the face of the kugel with serenity and bravery."

The kugel has increased and multiplied since its days as a fresh-bread pudding. Sholem Aleichem lists ten different types; Nahum Stutchkoff gives fourteen in his Yiddish thesaurus, but offers no explanations. One, at least, has produced a fantastic idiom. I. J. Linetzky, a nineteenth-century Yiddish writer, gives us: "*Creatio e nihilo,* making something out of nothing—in plain Yiddish, to make a nutmeg kugel from a fart." Usually, though, if you say the word kugel to anyone familiar with the dish, they're going to think immediately of one of two kinds, noodle and potato, and noodle almost always comes first.

The noodle kugel is far older, of course, and enjoys all the privileges of pudding primogeniture. Noodles—specifically egg noodles—are among the oldest Ashkenazi dishes and have occupied a prominent place in Ashkenazi cookery since at least the eleventh century, when they were mentioned under the name *frimsls* in the High Holiday prayer book of Simcha ben Shmuel of Vitry, who died in 1105. Isaac Or Zarua also mentions *frimsls,* which he calls *grimsls* and defines as "crumbs of dough." These West Yiddish forms are versions of "vermicelli" and remained in active use among German Jews until comparatively recently, even though noodles have been called *nudeln* in standard German for centuries. Mrs. Esther Levy's

Jewish Cookery Book, the first Jewish cookbook published in the United States (1871), has a recipe for "A Good Frimsel (Or Noodle) Soup," which begins with a commandment followed by millions of cooks who have probably never heard Mrs. Levy's name in their lives: "Take a piece of thick brisket."

Brisket or not, *frimsls* had become identified with *shabbes* and *cholent* no later than the twelfth century, when they are described as being added to the *cholent*, a process mentioned again in the following century. Isaac Or Zarua mentions how "Rabbi Kalonymus and the elders" would eat noodles immediately after making kiddush on the wine, before they said the *hamoytse* blessing over the chala, and the Maharil mentions that the noodles were made with schmaltz or nut oil.

In Eastern Europe these *frimsls* were known as *lokshn* (singular, *loksh*), a word that came into Yiddish from Polish. *Lokshn* were so closely associated with *cholent* that Moses Isserles actually slipped up in his comments on the *Shulkhan Arukh* and wrote "*cholent*, which is called *frimslekh*," long since corrected in all printings to "*lokshn*, which are called *frimslekh*," thanks to a note by one of his students.

Whether you called them *frimsls* or *lokshn*, noodles were not packaged until relatively recently and had to be made at home, a process that took a lot more effort than opening a package. *Aunt Babette's Cookbook*, which remained in print until 1914, gives us a good idea of just how much effort so humble a dish required:

> *Sift about one pint of flour into a bowl, make a cavity in the center of the flour, break four eggs into it, and add a pinch of salt and two tablespoonfuls of water. Now take the handle of a knife and commence to stir the eggs slowly, and in one direction, doing so until you can not [sic] work it any more in this way, then flour a baking board and put the contents of your bowl on it and work the dough with the palm of your hands, always kneading toward*

*you. Work a long time until perfectly smooth, then divide the
dough into four equal parts and work each piece separately. Now
roll out as thin as possible and lay on a table to dry. When dry
cut into strips half an inch wide. Have a kettle of boiling water
on the stove ready to receive the noodles; add salt and let them
boil about five minutes, stirring occasionally to prevent the
noodles from sticking to one another. Then put them into a
colander and let cold water run through them.*

And do it all without running water. It is no wonder that the
author of a Yiddish cookbook published in Warsaw in 1930 described
lokshn as "the touchstone of a woman's ability as a cook." Aside from
their close association with *cholent* and chicken soup, noodles were
also popular as a cheap and relatively filling day-to-day food and
were prepared quite often, usually in dairy form, with butter or
cheese. Since every housewife was expected to make *lokshn* at least
once a week, the ability to do so was one of the virtues ascribed to
the good *balebuste*, the crackerjack homemaker; a compulsive liar
is said to *brokn ligns vi a yidene lokshn*, "to hack out lies like a
housewife hacks out *lokshn*"—so often and so skillfully that it's
become second nature. A good housewife is said to be able "to
make *lokshn* out of nothing." The *lokshn-bret* or *lokshn* board on
which the sheets of dough are chopped into noodles was as much
an emblem of the Jewish kitchen and the women who ran it as the
salt board used for *kashering* meat.

Lokshn, sometimes used in the old country as a way of referring
to paper—and especially American—money, also served as a bench-
mark of popularity or desirability. Popular items are snapped up
like *lokshn* on the eve of a Jewish holiday, and people, especially kids,
who grab for something instead of asking nicely or waiting their
turn are told, *khap nisht*, "Don't grab," *s'iz nisht ken lokshn*, "it isn't
noodles." A couple who are all over each other after the first look
are said to *tsukhapn zikh vi tsu heyse lokshn*, "throw themselves at

each other as if at hot *lokshn*," a uniquely Yiddish way of describing unbridled lust.

Sheets of *lokshn* that have been chopped into small pellets, dried and, if desired, toasted, are known as farfel. Just as *lokshn* have been said to be the touchstone of a woman's ability in the kitchen, so, according to Mordecai Kosover, cooking farfel is "the ABC of Jewish home economy in the kitchen." It can be boiled, baked, added to soup; it can be a side dish, a stuffing, or a meal on its own. Our farfel is made of wheat; earlier generations knew a very different dish:

> *The farfel was made from a dark flour called* privarok, *which was a ground mixture of chick peas, barley, rye, and buckwheat. It had a taste all its own and was used primarily in summer, when there was plenty of sweet milk. When potatoes were available, they would be peeled and added to the farfel.*

Farfel is also a Yiddish nickname for a small, undergrown person, rather like Shorty in English. There was once a well-known New York mobster named Philip "Little Farfel" Kovolick whose corpse turned up in a steel drum in Florida. Farfel—the word if not the food—is familiar to every baby boomer in America, thanks to the old Nestlé's Quik commercials featuring ventriloquist Jimmy Nelson and a dummy in doggy form called Farfel, who would yawn the word "chocolate" as the climax to Nelson's singing, "N-E-S-T-L-E-S, Nestlé's makes the very best" at the close of every commercial.

If farfel can be thought of as a sort of *lokshn* reduction, the kugel represents *lokshn* in their highest form. Beloved today as a Friday-night delicacy, the kugel spent most of its life being eaten with the *cholent* around midday on Saturday. Not until the spread of home ovens large enough to accommodate more than a chicken or a joint of beef did the kugel make the transition from *cholent* sponge to freestanding dish.

Different kugel recipes reflected larger cultural and linguistic differences between the various East European Jewish communities, which were usually divided in the popular mind between Polish and Litvish (Lithuanian), designations that reflect the sixteenth-century borders of these countries rather than anything resembling the boundaries of today. Lithuania was a much larger country at the time and included areas that are now part of Belarus and Ukraine. The Litvaks who lived there—the Lithuanian Jews—were widely famed for their love of sharp, salt-and-pepper dishes, a preference also reflected in their gefilte fish and peppered chickpeas. A typical bare-noodles Litvish *lokshn* kugel consists of noodles, eggs, and schmaltz baked in a well-greased pan, then seasoned with pepper and a little salt.

The Litvish kugel lacks the superficial allure of the sweet kugel, a cross between a side dish and a dessert that can get quite elaborate. The second part of the recipe quoted from *Aunt Babette's Cookbook* gives us a good picture of what goes into one that is baked at home. The noodles are boiled for five minutes in salt water, put into a colander and doused with cold water:

> When all the water has been drained off, beat up eight or ten eggs and stir the noodles into the beaten egg. Now line a flat-bottomed iron kettle . . . with nice drippings or goose fat, put in a layer of the noodles, sprinkle with a handful of sugar, and some pounded almonds, the grated peel of one lemon and a few raisins, sprinkle some melted fat over this, then add another layer of noodles, some sugar, and proceed as you did until all are used up. Bake two hours. . . . You ought to have a kugeltopf [kugel pot] for this noodelockschen [sic]. You may make this pudding out of very finely-cut noodles, which make it still better.

I would quarrel with Mrs. Kramer's call for only a few raisins and "some" sugar, but otherwise her recipe is so accurate a reflection of the typical Polish sweet kugel that it was taken over almost verbatim in the *Kokhbukh far Yudishe Froyen*, the Yiddish cookbook published in Vilna seven years later. A good moist kugel, gleaming with schmaltz, was considered by many to be as good as cooking could get. Sholem Aleichem quotes a folk song in one of his novels:

Kugl heyste	Your name is kugel
In oyvn shteyste	You go into the oven
In moyl tsegeyste	You melt in the mouth

Even non-Jews considered kugel the Jewish food par excellence. In 1728, Jesuits in Vilna threatened to excommunicate Catholics who ate "Jewish kugel and other Jewish dishes." Hasidim were even more partial to it than other Jews. Mayerl Premishlaner, a nineteenth-century rebbe, declared unequivocally that "*Lokshn* kugel is from Mount Sinai," and other *rebbeyim* had no trouble finding mystical meanings in the kugel that might have eluded the casual observer. A disciple of a rebbe called Aaron of Kaidonov explains how his master associated the kugel with one of the divine *sefiros*, the ten spheres, corresponding to parts of the human body, through which the divine makes itself felt in both the visible and invisible worlds:

> *I once asked him why he eats all the* shabbes *foods with his hands, except for the kugel, which he eats with a fork. He replied that it is said in the name of Rebbe Israel of Rizhin that all of the* shabbes *foods correspond to the upper* sefiros *. . . Since kugel is the main food that is added in honor of the Sabbath, it contains the secret of increase. Increase corresponds to the* sefirah *of yesod [foundation, which is believed to correspond to the male member], and thus the Hebrew letters of kugel—KGL—correspond to those of* dereḥ, *the word for "way"—DRḤ—as in,* dereḥ gever, *"the way of a man with a maid." [Prv 30:19] In the Psalms it is written, "I will guard my way [DRḤ]" [Ps 39:2]; therefore it*

is forbidden to touch this dish with the hands, because it is
forbidden to touch your yesod, *your penis.*

Martin Buber is probably spinning in his grave, longing for a slice of a schmaltzfree, non-*shabbes*, dessert-type kugel made with cottage cheese or sour cream or some other invertebrate breed of dairy. These *milkhike* kugels are a fitting gastronomic counterpart to Buber's sanitized but highly influential version of Hasidism. Both are legitimate rethinkings that dispense with some of the less palatable aspects of the original—schmaltz, say, or the idea that noodles made with it and eaten on the Sabbath are somehow a form of penis (and if they are, why do Hasidim let women eat it—and make it by hand, yet?). Joan Nathan gives a recipe for a kugel that includes chopped spinach, as well as Parmesan, Swiss, and cottage cheese. But the daddy of 'em all, the kugel that traded its yarmulke for a toupee and its long black coat for a burgundy Nehru jacket, is the one I stumbled across in a kosher dairy restaurant in what used to be East Berlin sometime in the 1990s. It started out promisingly enough; the *Speisekarte* listed *kigel* as one of the items on offer, and the use of the Polish-Yiddish form of the word raised hopes of a nice *lokshn* kugel, gleaming with Nyafat, its raisins and currants winking out from egg-noodle shutters; a kugel that reminds you that you're not alone in the world, that somewhere there are people who understand your insides. I ordered a double portion, one for me and one for the friend who had taken me there, a German student of Yiddish who had never before come face-to-face with the dish that she had read so much about.

Thirty minutes later, our waiter emerged from the kitchen with two of the most heavily laden plates I have ever seen. *"Kigel, zwei Mal,"* he proclaimed.

Three large scoops of rapidly melting vanilla ice cream were trying to flatten the pile of cinnamon-flecked egg noodles on which they were resting. There were layers of soft cheese or sour cream—or maybe bits of both—between the noodles, a few raisins, no longer really supported by the damp and drooping *lokshn*, scattered here and there about the plates. And on top, at the crest of the ice cream's middle peak, a cocktail umbrella straight out of a tiki bar.

I must have looked like I'd found a cache of matzoh in the Berchtesgaden pantry. "And this," asked my friend, "is this how your family ate kugel on the Sabbath?"

I bit my lip; no member of my family would have gone *near* an umbrella on the Sabbath. I bit it again and thought of the Yiddish saying, *shabbes on kigl iz vi a foygl on fligl*, "*Shabbes* without kugel is like a bird without wings," then imagined the look on my father's face were such a *milkhike* beast to come within a dozen yards of his *cholent*. I bit my tongue very lightly and opened my mouth. "Only," I told her, "if we'd been to Communion."

THE OTHER SIDE OF THE NOODLES

Almost as popular as the *lokshn* kugel, the potato kugel, its much younger cousin, gives aficionados and self-styled guardians of authenticity the opportunity to fight kugel wars on two simultaneous fronts: sweet versus salt and pepper when it comes to *lokshn*, and—less vehemently—noodle versus potato on the Friday-night table. No sides will be taken here, save to mention that the potato kugel has a hefty piquancy that is particularly welcome on a cold winter weekend. A mixture of grated potatoes, eggs, onion, and schmaltz, with salt and pepper to taste, the potato kugel is basically a baked potato latke—all the goodness, none of the grease; a tuber-sourced birthday cake, but with the candles moved to the middle of the table.

A Mendel-come-lately to the kugel world, the potato kugel has never been as closely associated with Saturday lunches as the *lokshn*, and many a traditional home with a large-enough oven will serve potato kugel on Friday night and *lokshn* kugel on Saturday, especially if there is a potato or two in the *cholent*. Others reverse the order, still others serve both at both meals, in order to fulfill the mitzvah of eating as much kugel as possible. Although Rebbe Itsikl of Przeworsk has been quoted as saying that "*Lokshn* kugel is the principal kugel, while potato kugel is just another *shabbes* food," it must be borne in mind that Reb Itsikl, for all his manifold virtues, was a relatively modern man (he died in 1976) and a native of Galicia; his pronouncements on such matters must be taken with a grain of schmaltz.

The last of the three major kugels, the Yerushalmi or Jerusalem kugel, has spread beyond its country of origin only in the last few decades. A noodle kugel—but with the thin noodles characteristic of the Litvish salt-and-pepper pudding—the Yerushalmi is distinguished from other *lokshn* kugels by the caramelized sugar poured over the noodles before they are baked, and the black pepper that is added to the mix. It's a cross between Polish and Litvish *lokshn* kugels that also has the soothing mahogany richness of a well-baked potato kugel. Its origins are sometimes traced to disciples of the Gaon of Vilna, a group of ultrapious Lithuanians who moved to Jerusalem in the eighteenth century. The Yerushalmi is particularly associated with the post-synagogue lunch on Saturday; I have never seen it served on Friday night.

Lokshn, potato, and Yerushalmi make up the ruling kugel triumvirate, but they are far from the only kugels around. There are almond kugels, raisin kugels, apple kugels, *krepl* (as in kreplach) kugels, molasses kugels, cabbage kugels, nutmeg kugels, kugels in layers like lasagna (with raisins, according to Sholem Aleichem, between the sheets of *loskhn*), rice kugels, farfel kugels, eggplant kugels, cauliflower kugels, matzoh kugels, and many types of kugel known to no one but the family and friends of those who have made them.

The will to kugel is strong and draws other foods along with it. When a *heldzl* or *megele*—a goose or chicken neck stuffed with flour, schmaltz, salt, pepper, ground beef if you're lucky and paprika if you're Hungarian, and then sewn up—when such a neck is baked inside the kugel it is known as a *ganef* or thief—some say because it steals the flavor of the kugel for itself, others—more convincingly—because it lurks within the kugel (or sometimes the *tsimmes*) like someone who's up to no good. In old-fashioned cooking environments, *heldzl* was thought of as a grandchild of the *cholent*.

Saphir, who holds by the flavor-theft derivation of the name, mentions a different type of *ganef*: "a coarse, doughy mess filled in the middle with rice, beans, breast of goose, goose livers, and other delicacies" that is left inside a sealed oven for a full twenty-four hours, a hybrid of kugel and *cholent*. "In order to be able to eat and digest a ganef," he says, "one has to have the stomach of a Jew who grew up in Russia, and then, as a grown man, traded with oil of roses in Turkey, and finally spent six weeks as an invited guest in Berlin." This type of *ganef* seems to have been a West- or Central-European specialty; I have never run across one.

Folklorically, kugel is thought to produce a powerful thirst in the adult male; kugel eating was traditionally accompanied by whiskey drinking during *shabbes* lunch, when most East Europeans prefer to make kiddush over hard liquor instead of wine. As the Yiddish proverb has it, "Whoever eats a lot of kugel has to drink a lot of hooch," or in a less positive German-Jewish version, "If you didn't eat kugel, you wouldn't need booze."

Just as folklorically, kugel outdoes even *cholent* in being thought of as the quintessential Jewish food—so Jewish that it is sometimes used to symbolize Judaism and Jewish identity. Someone who is said to have a face full of kugel (*der kugl ligt im afn ponim*) is someone who cannot disguise his Jewish origins no matter how hard he tries; his face is shining with all the kugel that he has eaten in his life—and it's the schmaltz that gives it that sheen. The phrase is usually used of someone who is extremely Jewish in appearance and general demeanor, but doing his utmost to play down, if not completely deny, this Jewishness.

Similarly, you can say that someone is good to eat kugel with, the implication being that he is no good for anything else: business, friendship, personal relations, repayment of debts, and so on. The expression is often used—in Yiddish only—of the Jewish people itself. *Mit yidn iz gut kugl tsu esn*, "Jews are okay to eat kugel with," is a culinary version of such self-deprecating folk expressions as "May God save us from gentile muscles and Jewish brains," or *Vos mer yidn, alts mer ganovim*, "The more Jews, the more thieves." Less cynically, "A hometown marriage is a *lokshn* kugel": if the kugel doesn't come out very well, you've still got *lokshn*; if the marriage should fail, at least everyone's still at home.

The kugel is so closely identified with the whole notion of Judaism that "kugel with lard"—*kugl mit khazer-shmalts*—is used in Yiddish to describe un-Jewish ideas that have been given a superficial coat of Jewishness. Opponents of the Jewish labor movement would have characterized it as such; if Jewish liberals still spoke Yiddish, they'd be using it on Jewish Republicans who use their religious background to justify their social and political ideas; at one time, most religious Jews would have used the phrase to characterize Zionism.

A recent article in *The New York Times* exemplifies a more modern version of the same phenomenon, even though nothing unkosher is involved in the recipes. Martha Rose Shulman, the *Times'* "Recipes for Health" columnist, was asked to provide a recipe for a quinoa and carrot kugel, a concept that calls a number of Yiddish phrases—none of them terribly polite—to mind. Ms. Shulman not only did so, she also provided recipes for a quinoa and cauliflower kugel with cumin; a sweet millet kugel with dried apricots and raisins; a cabbage, onion, and millet kugel; and, skewing closer to traditional ingredients, a sweet potato and apple kugel. Interesting and tasty as such kugels might be—apple kugels, incidentally, are a popular Passover substitute for sweet *lokshn* kugel—none but the last brings *shabbes* to mind. While millet was not uncommon as a substitute for unaffordable or unavailable wheat or rye—*me' baganvet di hiner*,

we're taking food from the chickens' mouths, they used to say—
quinoa is of far too recent vintage to have penetrated at all deeply into
Jewish ceremonial life. All other factors being equal, though, it is
Passover-safe for Ashkenazim and Sephardim alike, and it is hardly
impossible that quinoa, like sushi, will eventually become fairly common in Jewish cuisine. At the moment, though, the quinoa kugel
is like matzoh-meal muesli: a non-Jewish idea still trying to fit in.

We get a glimpse of the Yiddish senses of humor and propriety
working together in the egg kugel, which is sometimes known as
a *zokher kugl*, "a male kugel." In Yiddish, as in many other languages, the word "eggs" (*eyer*) can also refer to testicles; the Hebrew
beytsim—eggs—has the same meanings, but comes into Yiddish
only as testicles. So close is the association of *beytsim* with balls that
religious people who are studying or discussing the Talmudic tractate *Beytso* (which means egg) habitually avoid its name and call it
Beyo instead. Thus, the egg kugel becomes a man-kugel because it's
a kugel made from the *beytsim* or *eyer* that we shouldn't mention in
public. The Kaidonover Rebbe, who thought that kugel represented
the human penis, was working within a well-established tradition.

We'll leave the final word on what kugel once meant in Jewish
domestic and culinary life to a Yiddish folk song that was once very
widely known. Its first line is also its title:

Hot a yid a vaybele,	A Jew has a wife
Hot er fin ir tsures.	Who gives him trouble.
Kon zi nisht kayn kigel makhn,	She can't make a kugel,
Toyg zi af kapures.	And is good for nothing at all.

A good kugel covers a multitude of faults.

INNARDS, OUTARDS, AND A GREAT BIG *TSIMMES*
Kishka today is usually thought of as one of those dishes loosely
classed as deli, and is often served à la carte in restaurants that spe-

cialize in corned beef, pastrami, smoked meat, and the like, generally in gravy, with rye bread on the side. While restaurant kishka is either baked or, less frequently, boiled, kishka was originally another *shabbes* dish that was left to cook in a *cholent* or in the fruit or vegetable stew known as *tsimmes*.

As its unapologetically Slavic name makes clear, the Jewish kishka is an adaptation of a non-Jewish dish; kishka means intestine, and the standard Polish kishka is made of pigs' blood and grains (usually barley or buckwheat) encased in a pig's intestine. Its Jewish problem needs no comment. Both kosher and kosher-style cooks replace blood with schmaltz, a substitution on which you could almost found a religion. They use bread crumbs, cracker crumbs, or matzoh meal instead of barley or buckwheat, toss in a chopped onion for tang, and shove it all into a casing that tends nowadays to be made of cellulose—sometimes edible, sometimes not—but was originally a well-cleaned beef intestine.

After the better part of a day inside a simmering *cholent*, the kishka would have absorbed flavor and, more importantly, moisture from the surrounding mess, while imparting some of its own taste to the *cholent*. It was a bit of a pain to make, especially because the casings needed to be cleaned. The kishka recipe in 1956's *Love and Knishes* starts off with "9 feet of clean beef casings"—that's a lot of scrubbing.

Popular as kishka has always been, it doesn't seem to have captured the popular imagination in the same way as kugel, *cholent,* or *tsimmes*. Yiddish is full of proverbs and idioms about *kishkes*, but the guts in question belong to people. Walter Solek's "Who Stole the Keeshka," which charted in the early '50s and was revived by Frankie Yankovic in the early '60s, concerns the pigs' blood variety—a technicality that didn't keep it from the Hebrew-school hit parade. The Jewish kishka, sometimes "translated" into English as "stuffed derma," surfaced briefly and covertly in the mid-'60s, when one of the supporting cartoons on *The Milton the Monster*

Show featured a hobo named Stuffy Derma. Earlier, during and immediately after World War II, entertainers working in the Catskills borscht belt sometimes referred to it as the "Derma Road."

Such legend as kishka still has lives on on every box of Manisch-ewitz Tam Tams crackers, all of which feature a widely popular recipe for mock kishka. Tam Tams, which date back to 1941, were Manischewitz's first non-Passover product. The company's Web site describes them as "addictively crispy, unbelievably tasty, and cholesterol and trans-fat free"; pros know that Tam Tam is really pronounced Tum Tum, *tum*—usually transliterated confusingly as *tam*—being the Yiddish word for taste, and there are rumors that the name was dreamed up by a well-known Yiddish writer whom the company had hired for just that purpose.

Mock kishka has become so widespread that I have encountered people who feel no need to move on to the real thing; some fear that it might disappoint, others simply fear. The recipe tells you to grind a box of Tam Tams, a large onion, two carrots, and three stalks of celery in a food processor, add margarine, salt, and pepper, roll into kishka-like strips and bake for half an hour. It ain't really kishka, but it's certainly something.

What it isn't is something you'd want to find in a *cholent* or a *tsimmes* or even a calf's-foot jelly. Although calf's-foot jelly is not, strictly speaking, a *cholent* or even part of a *cholent*, it was a surpris-ingly popular Sabbath treat, one version of which—a sort of mock calf's-foot jelly—was prepared *after* the Friday-night meal by pour-ing the leftover soup onto the chopped-up chicken offal—head, feet, comb, and neck—and leaving the whole thing to stand overnight while the schmaltz in the soup helped it all to congeal.

A real calf's foot was depilated, scraped, and cut into small pieces. The bones were left in, but sliced very thin. Thus prepared, the foot was cooked with eggs, vinegar, pepper, sugar, garlic, and onions until the mixture was nice and thick, then poured out to cool and set. In Lithuania, the foot was often seasoned with nothing but onions and garlic and left to simmer overnight so it could be eaten hot for *shabbes* lunch, or cold at the late-afternoon third meal.

There is a not entirely serious Hasidic tradition that claims that we eat a foot on *shabbes* because *shabbes* is truth, and falsehood, according to our sages, has no legs. We thus eat the foot to demonstrate our faith in the Sabbath and its Creator.

Ashkenazim have displayed a fondness for aspics and jellies for as long as Ashkenazim have existed—just open a jar of gefilte fish. I have seen old men, beguiled by slime, come nearly to blows over who got to slurp up the gel once all the fish was gone. Known colloquially as *smarkatch*, or snot, when I was a kid, the gel in gefilte fish runs the gamut from see-through to cloudily translucent; a good calf's-foot jelly, flecked with added extras that scream "Don't ask," even when you've made it yourself, has the off-white, greenish-yellow pallor more commonly associated with motion sickness and hospital walls.

Unlike kugel or *tsimmes*, which come in many varieties but have only one name, calf's-foot jelly has all kinds of names, depending on where the eaters or their forebears originated. Sometimes called simply a *fus* or *fis*—Yiddish for foot—it was known as *fisnoga* (accent on the *no*) to Lithuanians. *Noga* means foot in Polish and Russian; since Lithuanian Yiddish did not distinguish between *sh* and *s*, *fis* from a Litvak could mean either feet or fish, and no one would know the difference until it was way too late. So fish became *fisribe*, "*fis*-fish," and the jelly *fisnoga*, "*fis*-foot." In Poland, it was called *gale* or *galerete*—from the German *galrat*, which means the same thing—but the best-known names, *ptcha* and *ptche*, come from Turkish, and of them all only *ptche* rhymes with *feh*.

In some places cold *ptche* was known as *kholodets*, from the Russian for cold. In Germany, it was called *Sulze* and figures under this name in *Aunt Babette's Cookbook*. The recipe begins with "Take one calf's head and four calf's feet," and is careful to let us know when to "add the boiled brains." Aunt Babette also provides details that the Yiddish cookbooks lack. "Strain through a flannel bag. Tie the bag on a door knob with a bowl underneath to catch the juice or jelly. Do not squeeze or shake it until the jelly ceases to run freely."

It takes a lot of work to produce so efficiently neutral a medium of garlic delivery. I last ate one on Labor Day 2012, and was tasting it at intervals until the end of the month. Still, *ptche* has its partisans, and they are a hearty, if generally older bunch, half in love with childhood memories, half with a food that needs no teeth to be enjoyed.

Tsimmes didn't develop from *cholent* either, but the two are closely enough associated to be thought of as cousins, if not quite siblings. A fruit or vegetable stew generally associated with the Sabbath and Rosh Hashana, *tsimmes* is limited only by the fruits or vegetables available and the cook's imagination. Its name comes from the Middle High German *zuomuese*, which means side dish. There are *tsimessn* made of apricots, raisins, apples, plums, and pears. *Tsimessn* to scare your kids with: parsnip, garbanzo, green bean, farfel, lima bean, rutabaga, prune, and turnip. These can be mixed and matched in any way you please—raisin-and-rutabaga, farfel-and-prune—so long as you make sure to slice the ingredients up, add the right amounts of sugar or honey and schmaltz (some people prefer molasses to honey; this is acceptable, but only if you know how to say molasses in Yiddish) and let it simmer for a nice long time.

The concept is so all embracing that some of the *tsimessn* just mentioned—rutabaga, lima bean, turnip—were originally jotted down as jokes, the kinds of *tsimmes* that you *could* make if you were crazy enough to be bothered. Not only did I find recipes for all of these in popular and reputable Jewish cookbooks, but I also discovered that the first *tsimmesn* might even have been made with turnips or parsnips rather than the carrots that usually stand for *tsimmes* in its purest form. *Le Ménagier de Paris*, a non-Jewish guide to proper housewifery that dates to 1393, gives recipes for chopped turnips, carrots, and gourds cooked in honey, suggesting that the dish, prepared as it was by women who were either literate themselves or had someone around who could read to them, probably had some upper-class cachet.

The recipe for turnip *tsimmes* in the 1896 Yiddish cookbook gives us some idea of how the first *tsimessn* might have looked and tasted. Pieces of peeled, chopped turnip are covered with sugar that has been browned in schmaltz; they are then sprinkled with flour and steamed. Some broth is added and it is all left to cook. The author recommends "adorning" it with fried, breaded calf's spleen. After bathing so long in a tub full of sugar (a medieval version would probably have used honey), the turnip loses its bitterness and turns quite tasty. The spleen—*milts* in Yiddish—is not to be argued about: You'll either love it or you'll hate it.

While the spleen in this *tsimmes* is merely an ornament, many cooks make their *tsimessn* with meat, usually brisket, as an integral part of the dish. The lengthy cooking time helps to soften this otherwise tough cut and transforms the *tsimmes* from a vegetable side dish into a sweet, beanless *cholent*. Some cooks even add potatoes to the mix.

Versatile as the dish might be, the first thing to come into the mind of any native eater of Yiddish food who hears the word *tsimmes* is likely to be a carrot. The carrot *tsimmes* is to *tsimmesn* what the gin martini is to martinis: the standard to which all others must aspire. Sliced carrots—preferably, but not necessarily round—or, now that they are easily available, baby carrots; honey; and a nice, luminous roux made of flour, schmaltz, and the liquid from the carrots and honey—for most Ashkenazim, this spells *shabbes*; it spells Rosh Hashana for all of them.

Whether anchoring a *tsimmes*, floating in chicken soup, or crowning a piece of gefilte fish, the carrot is among the preeminent Yiddish vegetables, in part because its Yiddish plural form, *mern*, is identical to the Yiddish verb that means "to increase." Along with apples and honey and various other foods, it is eaten on the night of Rosh Hashana as part of a tasting ritual that presents our hopes for the new year in edible forms. The apples and honey are eaten for the sake of a sweet year; a sheep's head (often replaced by a fish head) is supposed to be eaten when we ask the Lord to make us like a head and not like a tail, despite the fact that Juvenal calls a sheep's head "a feast fit for a shoemaker." Carrots are eaten to go along with a supplication that our merits might increase.

While commentator after commentator has pointed out that the pun on *mern* as carrots and *mern zikh*, the reflexive form of the verb "to increase," is clear to any Yiddish speaker, fewer deign to mention that the supplication is in Hebrew, not Yiddish, and that we ask the Lord not that our merits might *mern zikh*, but rather that they *yirbu*, the third-person plural of the Hebrew verb for increase, which sounds nothing like the Hebrew word for carrot; the Yiddish pun is reserved for explanations of something that most of the folk doing the explaining no longer really understand.

In a nod to the power of sympathetic magic, the Talmud (*Krisos* 6a) recommends that five foods be eaten on Rosh Hashana as punning warrants of a good new year: pumpkin, fenugreek, leek, beet, and dates. The Aramaic for fenugreek is *rubyo* (the same word means black-eyed peas in modern Hebrew). At one time, people ate *rubyo* and said *she-yirbu*, "might increase." But fenugreek, widely grown in India, Africa, and the Near East, was only slightly less important than lard in the diet of European Ashkenazim; it was unavailable and almost universally unknown. *Rubyo*, though, sounds a lot like *Rübe*, a German word that still means carrot in the south German dialects from which Yiddish developed (in standard Modern German it usually means turnip). As most Yiddish speakers could not understand the connection between fenugreek and increase, and couldn't get any fenugreek even if they did, they began to replace *rubyo* with *Rübe*. As fewer and fewer Yiddish speakers were able to understand *Rübe*, it was translated once again to the more common *mer* (compare the standard Modern German *Mohrrübe*, carrot), which made it necessary to translate the Hebrew *yirbu*, increase, to the Yiddish *mern* in order to preserve the pun. The Yiddish is there because of the carrot, not the other way round.

The carrot also figures in a variant version of the onion curse that we saw earlier. *Zolst vaksn vi a mer*, you should grow like a carrot, *mitn kop in dr'erd*, with your head in the ground. The real sting lies in the use of something that has nothing but positive connotations everywhere else in the culture. Even more than with the onion, "you should grow like a carrot" must originally have sounded like the introduction to a blessing for increase and prosperity; the carrots in the Rosh Hashana chicken soup are often cut to resemble coins, just to reinforce the association with the verb *mern*.

This *tsimmes* of record is so popular at other times of year—in many households, every Friday night—that, like kugel and *cholent*, it tends to be associated with general notions of warmth, festivity, and good company, rather than anything specific to Rosh Hashana; it tastes just as sweet in January. And if there's a kishka inside to impart a bit of meaty goodness to all that sweet—hog heaven isn't really a Jewish concept, but that's as close as a kosher meal can come.

The modern *tsimmes* often features pineapple alongside the carrots, chunks of canned pineapple that assure us of a *dolce sabato* and a sweet new year and make us long for a deliverer who will lead us to Hawaii. Generations of North American Jews already think of canned pineapple—Dole, Del Monte, Gefen brand, or Festive—as a thoroughly Jewish food; the can might be new but the pineapple, though hardly an everyday item in the Pale of Settlement, was not quite unheard of, either. It was introduced into Russia in the eighteenth century, where it was grown in hothouses, usually by members of the aristocracy, and quickly became "a symbol of luxury and Western culture." It pops up in Pushkin's *Eugene Onegin,* Tolstoy's *War and Peace*, and Dostoyevsky's *Brothers Karamazov*, where Liza Khokhlakova, a wealthy and not-very-bright young woman, describes her fantasy of committing a "Jewish" ritual murder while eating a pineapple compote, possibly—depending on the nature of the compote—the first reference to pineapple *tsimmes* on record.

Elena Molokhovets, whom Julia Child described as "the Fanny [sic] Farmer and Isabella Beeton of Russia's 19th century" and whose *A Gift to Young Housewives* went through twenty editions between 1861 and 1917, gives four recipes featuring pineapple, all of them in the nature of special treats (ices, preserves, syrup, and jelly). It was expensive and hard to come by, to be sure, and while most Polish and Russian Jews were desperately poor, there were a tiny few wealthy enough to have had access to such luxuries. Similarly, sauerkraut with pineapple has long been traditional in Austria, which ruled vast swathes of Jewish Eastern Europe from the early nineteenth century until the end of World War I.

None of this proves that Jews were eating any noticeable quantity of pineapple or even that they were eating it at all, let alone in a *tsimmes*. Norman Salsitz, born in a Polish shtetl in 1920, describes how his aunt went to Berlin and came back with a pineapple: "No one in our house had ever eaten a pineapple, or probably ever seen one;" the knowledge that they were out there and available to a lucky few helps to explain the alacrity with which Jews embraced the pineapple once they arrived in America. And not only in America; Salsitz was "so entranced" by the aroma that he decided to put it to work for him. He started "to charge people to enjoy the smell of the pineapple. Each day I would rub the pineapple skin on my hand, and for a fee would let my friends inhale near my hand ten times." That's what they mean by symbol of "luxury and Western culture." The speed with which the pineapple found its way into one of the most traditional Jewish dishes can be traced to precisely this aura of wealth and western sophistication; rather than embracing American habits, pineapple-happy Jewish immigrants were putting American abundance into the service of a hitherto unrealizable European ideal.

As we have already noted, there is almost nothing from which a *tsimmes* cannot be made. Dried fruit, with or without rice, was popular among Jews from Romania and Hungary and has caught on to a degree in North America. Leah W. Leonard gives four different recipes for prune *tsimmes* (not to mention one each for lima bean and rutabaga), leading one to suspect that such *tsimessn* must have been more popular in the immediate postwar period than some of us can recall. "Eat your prune and farfel *tsimmes* or no *Howdy Doody* for you, mister," is not a threat that I ever heard; such a *tsimmes*, with or without meat, was as unknown to me as the prune-and-potato or prune-and-rice *tsimmes*. I have, however, experimented with a south-of-the-border fresh-fruit *tsimmes* of pineapple and banana. You wouldn't think that they'd take so well to schmaltz, but "*Tsimmes* Carmen Miranda" turned Friday night into a tropical paradise, especially after it was adorned with fried, breaded chicken livers.

Like most things worth having, a *tsimmes* takes a fair bit of effort to prepare. The ingredients have to be chopped, the roux has to be made, and—traditionally, at any rate—the whole thing has to be left to cook for hours and hours on end. In his *Encyclopedia of Jewish Food*, Gil Marks points out that *tsimmes* was "originally simmered over a flame or more likely the embers of a fire" and did not become a baked dish until home ovens became common in the nineteenth century. In conjunction with all the pain of preparation, these earlier methods of cooking help explain the real thrust of the popular Yiddish phrase *makhn a tsimmes*, "to make a *tsimmes*"—a fuss, a big deal—out of something. *Vus makhstu a tsimmes?* "Why are you spending all of your time—and mine—cutting whatever it is into little pieces, seasoning it, making a sauce, letting it monopolize your fire or your oven for hours at a time, arranging an attractive service and maybe even an adornment at the end? Whatever it is, it isn't that important. *Tsimmes* is a side dish; you're making a big deal out of small potatoes." *Tsimessn*, the plural, can also mean extraneous details, subplots that don't have much to do with the main story.

You can also talk about *a moyd vi a tsimmes*, "a maiden like a fruit or vegetable stew": a robust young woman, someone along the lines of the late Anna Nicole Smith, a girl with plenty of pineapple ripe for the plucking. Her male counterpart is disappointingly characterized as being like an oak; acorns are among the few things that cannot go into a *tsimmes*.

An upper-class person, one to the manor born, can likewise be described as *tsimmes*, rather as you'd call the same person a member of the upper crust in English. In Yiddish, as in English, you could also say that he or she is from the *same smetene*, the very cream of society, but only Yiddish can portray Caroline Kennedy as a glittering vegetable stew.

SIX

As the Cholent Cooks
The Rest of Friday Night,
Appetizers and Soup

The proof, like so much else, is in the *cholent*: Saturday is the most important ingredient in Ashkenazi cuisine. If not for the Sabbath, we'd have little more than matzoh, bitter herbs, and whole roasted sheep to call our own. Throw in some matzoh balls, maybe blintzes on Shavuos, latkes on Chanukah and hamantaschen on Purim. Does the Rosh Hashana apple in honey count? Take away *shabbes*, and most Ashkenazi food, kosher though it be, doesn't differ significantly from that of gentiles in Central and Eastern Europe and has no more to do with Judaism or Jewish identity than a Caesar salad or an easily kosherable plate of moo goo gai pan; Jews might eat them, but they're unlikely to be thought of as Jewish unless they are linked to a Jewish holiday or take on Jewish associations through quirks of immigration—no one in Romania thinks of pastrami as Jewish. As mentioned earlier, the greater part of this book is concerned with Sabbath and holiday food, and much of the holiday fare is merely Sabbath food that's been moved to the middle of the week. Most signature Ashkenazi dishes are closely associated with observing and celebrating the Sabbath, and the cuisine itself can almost be said to have developed from the union of *shabbes* and schmaltz. Little of the traditional Jewish menu that doesn't depend upon at least one of them would seem out of place at a church picnic in the proper part of Europe.

If the dietary laws determine the boundaries of the Jewish menu, the Sabbath provides most of its more elaborate content. Indeed, the Sabbath can be said to furnish all Jewish practice and belief with a great deal of their content, too. According to God Himself, it is the sole component of the natural world accessible only to Jews, "an everlasting sign between Me and the people of Israel that the Lord made heaven and earth in six days, and on the seventh day He rested and was refreshed." (Ex 31:17) So central is it to the religion, so essential to the work of creation, that it sometimes seems as if God created the universe only for the sake of the divine endorphin rush that He experienced after creating human beings on day six. *Shabbes* makes nondoing into a cosmic principle that the Jews have been chosen to uphold on earth; it is an incontrovertible declaration of freedom, the apotheosis of the nonslave time discussed in Chapter One: "Do what you will, I still won't work on Saturday." The commandment to keep the Sabbath is the only one of the Ten Commandments that cannot be assimilated to any other system of belief, and only liberal capitalism and Soviet-style Communism have challenged it successfully.

The Bible tells us that "God blessed the seventh day and made it holy" (Gen 2:3), made it different from the other days; to sanctify something is to set it apart from other members of its class. Abraham Ibn Ezra, the twelfth century poet, biblical commentator, and philosopher tells us that the Sabbath has been set apart because "unlike its fellows, no work is done on it," which is why the day is so blessed. "Blessing," he says, "means increase of good things, and on this day the reproductive strength of the body and the soul's powers of discernment and intelligence are renewed." As God was refreshed by resting, so are we. The Hebrew verb translated as refreshed derives from a root that also gives us the noun *nefesh*—vital spirit or soul— and is the ultimate source of the oft-cited Talmudic idea that each Jew receives a second soul at the beginning of the Sabbath (*Beytso* 16a), as transcendent an increase as anyone can get.

Just as the blessing and sanctification of the Sabbath are mentioned long before it is ever observed, God uses the manna to explain it to the Israelites before they are commanded to keep it. From Sunday to Thursday, they were to gather only as much as was needed for each day, lest the leftovers turn rancid and rot, but:

> On the sixth day they gathered double the amount of food . . . and when all the chieftains of the community came and told Moses, he said to them . . . "Tomorrow is a day of rest, a holy Sabbath unto the Lord; Bake what you would bake and boil what you would boil; and all that is left put aside to be kept until morning." So they put it aside until morning, as Moses had ordered; and it did not turn foul, and there were no maggots in it. Then Moses said, "Eat it today, for today is a Sabbath of the Lord; you will not find it today on the plain. Six days you shall gather it; on the seventh day, the Sabbath, there will be none. (Ex 16:16, 19–20, 22–26)

As Rashi points out in his comments to Genesis 2:3, the blessing and sanctification of the Sabbath are made manifest in the manna-fall: blessing in the double portion that appeared on Friday, sanctification in relief from gathering it on Saturday. As far as the Israelites were probably concerned, the term Sabbath—used here for the very first time—must have been another one of Moses's crazy neologisms, like the Passover mentioned four chapters earlier: "Who knows what he means? Just do what he says." And since no manna appeared on the Sabbath, they had no choice but to obey. Much as it sustains them in the desert, the manna also serves as training for the Sabbath observance that looms so large in the Ten Commandments that they were about to receive.

And loom it does. Sabbath observance is the most prominent outward sign of Jewish difference and, as one of the few ritual commandments incumbent on every Jew, can fairly be described as the centerpiece of the entire religion: Orthodox vegetarians don't need to think about the dietary laws, but there's no getting around the

Sabbath, which becomes, as it were, the linchpin of any form of Jewish practice and observance. As the resolutely secular cultural philosopher Ahad Ha'Am put it in one of his Hebrew essays, "More than Jews have kept the Sabbath, the Sabbath has kept the Jews." Without some form of Sabbath observance, whether in strict accord with religious law or not, Judaism withers rather quickly, and Jewish identity along with it. The history of the Jews in the modern west is a chronicle of declining Sabbath observance that bears out the domino theory of religious decay so popular in the Orthodox world: Once you stop keeping *shabbes*, insurmountable anti-Semitism becomes the only certain barrier to total assimilation. Shallow as an obligatory but ritual-free Friday night family dinner might appear to those who consider the food more Jewish than the people eating it, such a dinner is proof that the *pintele yid*, that supposedly inextinguishable spark of Jewishness, continues to glow in the hearts of people who rarely, if ever, set foot inside a synagogue. The meal might be a little light on blessings, but the chicken and brisket and gefilte fish have lost none of their sectarian oomph.

SKIP THE BREAD AND IT'S JUST A BIG SNACK

The structure of the traditional Friday night dinner is as rigidly fixed as that of the Catholic Mass that owes so much to it. The meal opens with an aperitif, a glass of kosher wine over which a special, Sabbath-only blessing is pronounced. The blessing over bread is then made on a double portion, two whole loaves, and pieces of the bottom loaf are distributed to all the participants.

Since the presence of bread makes the simplest Jewish collation into a formal meal, the rules for eating it can turn a humble peanut-butter sandwich into a bit of a *tsimmes*. Before observant Jews can make the *hamoytse* blessing, they must first wash their hands in a precise ritual manner and make the blessing that goes along with it. Water has to be poured over the hands from a vessel which has been filled from a tap or natural source specifically for the sake of this mitzvah (two pours per hand, dominant hand first), which means, of course, that there has to be a source of water and a secondary vessel of some sort nearby (hence the paper cups that keep popping up in the water fountains of buildings where Orthodox Jews are employed). After drying their hands, they have to make their way to wherever the bread happens to be—and there are myriad rules about how much time is allowed to elapse in case, say, the eater is in the woods and the nearest stream is a mile or more away from the site of the meal—and only then can they say *hamoytse*. Once they've swallowed an olive's worth of bread (often helpfully described as equal to either a third or a half of an egg—olives come in different sizes, after all, and the issue is highly contentious), they are obliged to finish the meal with the "Grace after Meals," which runs to two or three pages in the average prayer book, not counting additions for the Sabbath and various holidays, or three of the four sides of the printed, laminated cards found in kosher restaurants. All but the most newly Orthodox Jews can rattle it off in their sleep, but most authorities frown on the idea of praying from memory, holding that the sight of the words helps to focus the mind and increase the reciter's insight into the meaning of the prayer.

Unless you're in a military unit on combat duty or out in the wild—somewhere where water for washing might not be immediately available (in tractate *Pesokhim* 46a, the Talmud lets us know that if you're more than four Roman miles—about seventy-two minutes' walk—from the water, you don't have to wash)—all this washing and praying isn't really as disruptive as it might appear. Eating bread forces a pause that no other food demands and leads ideally to a form of mindful eating that is supposed to be the final stage in a process that also includes mindful shopping for acceptable kosher ingredients and the mindful preparation that keeps these ingredients from mingling in unacceptable ways. *Halevay*, as they say in Yiddish: If only it didn't turn into a reflex. Still, mindfulness of this type—intromitting a Higher Power into every morsel consumed—is the real purpose of these blessings; our failure to attain it is precisely that—*our* failure, not the system's.

CHALA, THE HEART OF FRIDAY NIGHT

Probably the best-known Jewish bread of all, certainly the most prestigious within the culture itself, chala is based on non-Jewish German models and became part of Jewish life scarcely five hundred years ago. A braided wheat-flour bread made with sugar, eggs, and oil, the chala—often called an egg loaf or Jewish egg loaf in non-Jewish English—seems to have been adapted from German breads baked for special occasions, especially Sundays. The Jewish version was redirected to Friday night and Saturday, and thence to other religious holidays and celebrations.

Since Jewish law demands that we eat three meals over the twenty-five hours of the Sabbath, you can't have *shabbes* without bread. Halacha is also adamant about the presence of *lekhem mishne*, a double portion of bread, at each of these meals, in commemoration of the double portion of manna that the Israelites received on Fridays. Double portion is defined as two whole loaves, though the definition of loaf—any independent unit of bread at least the size of an olive and made of wheat, rye, oats, barley, or spelt not previously cut, torn, or bitten—leaves quite a bit of room for portion control.

Most non-Ashkenazi communities simply try to come up with unused loaves of the same bread that they eat during the week. Although many people claim that there is a tradition of baking on Fridays in order to be ready for the Sabbath, no such tradition really exists. There is, however, a statute supposed to have been instituted by Ezra in the fourth century BCE that appears in the same list of regulations that mandates the eating of garlic on Fridays. It states simply that "a housewife should rise early and bake, in order that there be bread for the poor" (*Bovo Komo* 82a), which Rashi explains as meaning that she rise early on whatever day that she bakes and do her baking in the morning.

This point is underlined in the Jerusalem Talmud, which states that Ezra "made an enactment that they bake bread on the eve of the Sabbath in order to provide for the poor" (*Yerushalmi Megilo*, 4:1). The baking is not done in honor of the Sabbath per se, but in order to help those who cannot afford bread of their own to observe it in the regulation manner. It's a prescription for community service, not ritual zeal. The only thing special about bread baked on a Friday morning is that neither the housewife nor her family are going to eat all of it.

Most Jewish communities were satisfied—were probably even happy—to be able to come up with enough bread of any kind to get through the three Sabbath meals. Ashkenazim were no exception until sometime in the fifteenth century, when Jews in Germany arrived at a new understanding of a well-known Mishnaic passage and, late though it was, finally established a tradition of baking something special for *shabbes*. The second chapter of tractate *Shabbos*, called *Ba-Meh Madlikin*, "What may we light [candles] with," has been recited as part of the Friday night liturgy since at least the ninth century, when Rov Amram Gaon included it in his siddur, the oldest Jewish prayer book known (Hasidim and other Ashkenazim influenced by Hasidic practice replaced this chapter with a different recitation in the late eighteenth century, long after the customs described had established deep roots in all Ashkenazi communities). The second-last paragraph in the chapter, recited just as the supplicant is beginning to slow down and pay attention again, has nothing directly to do with the materials from which Sabbath lights may be made. Instead, it informs us that:

> *There are three transgressions that cause women to die*
> *during childbirth: laxity with respect to the laws concerning*
> *menstruation, taking chala, and lighting candles on the Sabbath*
> *and holidays.* (Shabbos 2:6)

The mention of women and childbirth has long since led the observance of all these laws to be considered the particular province of women, and they are often referred to under the rubric "women's mitzvahs" or, in Yiddish and Hebrew, *Khanoh* (i.e., Hanna), after the acronym formed by the first letters of the Hebrew words for each category: **kh**ale (chala), **n**ide (menstrual laws), **h**adloke (lighting candles).

The connection between the latter two categories and the Sabbath is quite straightforward. Lighting candles is pretty much self-explanatory. The rules concerning menstruation determine the permitted times for marital intercourse. A man whose wife has just returned from the ritual bath after a couple of weeks of forced abstinence is supposed to have sex with her that very night, if only so that she will feel attractive. Otherwise, the *Shulkhan Arukh*, basing itself on the Mishna, lays down definite rules for frequency in marital intercourse:

> *Men of strong constitution who enjoy the pleasures of life, who have profitable pursuits at home and are tax exempt, should perform their duty nightly. Laborers employed in the city where they live should perform their marital duty twice weekly, once a week if they're employed in another city. Merchants who travel into villages on donkeys . . . and other such people should perform their marital duty once a week. Those who convey baggage on camels from distant places should have an appointed time every thirty days. [The Mishna adds: Sailors should have an appointed time once in every six months.] The time for scholars is from Sabbath to Sabbath . . . One should not deprive [his wife] of her rights unless by her consent, and only after he has fulfilled the duty of propagation.*

This passage adds a whole new dimension to the idea of tax reform—and we finally have the means of surveillance to make it stick. More traditionally, every married Jewish male is considered a scholar for these purposes and is expected to "give his wife her due," as the rabbinic euphemism has it, on all Sabbaths when the laws of *nide* allow him to touch her.

Taking chala is the only one of these mitzvahs with no direct connection to the Sabbath. The literal meaning of chala in this context is "portion of dough set aside for the priests," and the act of taking chala consists of removing a small amount of dough from every batch of baking and burning it in the oven to commemorate the offering made to the priests when the Temple was still standing. If this has not been done in advance of the actual baking, a piece of the finished product can be tossed away later, which is why packaged kosher baked goods often have cryptic statements on the boxes reading "Chala is taken." All it means is that you don't have to worry about what's inside; you can eat everything that you've paid for, secure in the knowledge that all the minutiae of the laws of ritual fitness—the laws of kashrus—have been observed.

Although everyone who bakes is obliged to take chala, Ezra's statute—along with the undeniable fact that women did most of the household cooking and baking—led the mitzvah to be associated with women as long ago as the time of the Mishna. Ten or twelve centuries after the Mishna was completed, someone noticed that while two of the women's mitzvahs mentioned in the Friday night prayers were intimately linked with *shabbes*, the third was admitted to the festivities only by chance. The general Jewish way of thinking, which hates a trinity but loves a hat trick, led them to go all the way and make it three for three; the custom of baking bread especially for *shabbes* originated less from a desire for sensory pleasure than out of a wish to honor the Sabbath by turning it into a literal source of life for the Jewish people. Having women perform all three of their admittedly sense-oriented mitzvahs in a timely and careful manner would help these women live to produce more Jews.

We don't know much about these early chalas. The first use of the word to mean "bread baked specially for the Sabbath" occurs in a book called *Leket Yosher*, whose author, Joseph ben Moses, died around 1490. The passage in question describes one of the customs of his teacher, Israel Isserlein (1390–1460), the leading halachic authority of the day and a major influence on Moses Isserles (with whom he is not to be confused):

> *I recall that every Friday they would make him three thin chalas, kneaded with eggs and oil and a little bit of water. He would put the mid-sized chala in the middle of his table that night . . . He put it on top of a large uncut loaf, even though it [the large uncut loaf] was of black bread, rather than on a small roll of white bread called a* zeml. *In the morning, he put the large chala and a large loaf on the table, as he had done the night before, and for the third meal he would use the small chala and a whole loaf.*

Whatever they looked like, the chalas were thin enough to rest comfortably on top of a loaf of bread. In two of the three meals, chala is opposed to the Hebrew word for loaf, *kikar*, suggesting that these chalas, which were not big enough to be called loaves, would have been made with the minimum amount of flour needed to fulfill the commandment, the same volume of 43.2 eggs that we saw in the matzoh bakery, roughly 2.7 pounds of wheaten flour. Each of the three chalas would thus have weighed about .9 of a pound before baking.

Joseph goes out of his way to point out that Isserlein avoided using a *zeml* as part of the ritual. The word *zeml* is regularly used in Yiddish for a small roll made of fine wheat flour kneaded with eggs; these days, it is more commonly known as a *bulke* or *bilke*. A hot one with butter was regarded as the breakfast of kings—it's what Bontche Shvayg asked for back in Chapter Four—and the *zeml* or *bilke* is still considered quite a treat. The difference between the *bilke* and what we have been calling chala for the last few hundred years seems to be entirely a matter of time, date, and size. A well-known Yiddish bon mot, usually attributed to the eighteenth century wit, Hershele Ostropolyer, claims, "It's called *bulke* all week, but on *shabbes* they call it chala." Indeed, later in the *Leket Yosher*, Joseph mentions that as Isserlein got older and started to lose his teeth, *zeml* (the plural is the same as the singular) were the only kind of bread he could eat.

Isserlein is acting, though, as if he were determined to invent the Yiddish proverb that warns, "If you have bread, don't go looking for *zeml*"—that is, learn to leave well enough alone. By avoiding *zeml* on *shabbes*, Isserlein seems to be saying that at least one of the two breads needed for each Sabbath meal has to have been baked for the sole purpose of taking chala as close to the Sabbath as possible. The other must be a full-sized loaf that, except for its size, will not overshadow or be confused with the bread that's been specially baked.

The chalas' pride of place depends on intent, not ingredients: They were baked as much for the sake of taking chala as for honoring the Sabbath, which means baked by a Jew, most likely a Jewish woman—neither of which was necessarily the case with the *zeml*, which would have been much more likely to be purchased from a baker. Yet had the *zeml* not been commonly used at the Sabbath table, Joseph would have had no need to mention his teacher's custom or stress the plainness of the loaves on which he rested his chalas.

The sense of chala as "bread baked for the sake of taking chala before *shabbes*" was already well established by the time the *Leket Yosher* was written. Joseph never bothers to explain the term and even talks in a later passage about "the thin chalas made for *shabbes* that are called *kuchen*." *Kuchen* is what they were *called*; what they were, in fact, was chala, baked specifically for the sake of the commandment. Three-quarters of a century after Isserlein, Moses Isserles mentions that "it is the custom to knead enough [dough] to take chala at home in order to bake breads for the Sabbath and festivals." Although Isserles nowhere refers to such bread as chala, it is clear that he is talking about the type of chala described by Joseph. Indeed, the term *kuchen* for certain types of *shabbes* chalas persisted in Polish Yiddish for centuries after both Joseph and Isserlein; the *kuchen* was a round, unbraided bread, pan baked with oil, that was usually eaten on Friday nights, while the braided egg chala came out with the *cholent* at Saturday lunch.

The original German *kuchen*-chalas were probably pan baked over a fire, too; this would explain their thinness and their name. Although *kuchen* now refers to a range of baked products that can all be described as cake, it seems originally to have been closer to what supersizing Yiddish-speakers would now call a *kichel*. In his definitive article on Yiddish baked goods, Mordecai Kosover describes this *kuchen*, which he characterizes as "one of the older dry baked products":

> *They were and still are [1958] baked for* shabbes *and also during the week. They are all flat. They are sometimes baked in bake pans with schmaltz or butter, mixed with cheese or baked with onions. They are not eaten on their own, but are always either a side dish during a meal or a dessert afterwards.*

The thinness, the greater crunch, must have distinguished Isserlein's chalas from the *zeml* that became the prototype for the chalas baked today. As a point of interest, Kosover mentions that a *fleyshik kuchen* baked with schmaltz (and nothing else) was commonly used for *hamoytse* on the Sabbath, and that Malke Berlant, a Vilna midwife and author of *Di Gliklikhe Muter* (*The Happy Mother*), published in 1836, described such *kuchens* as "harmful even for healthy people, especially those who suffer from bellyaches." This is possibly the first recorded instance of the shmaltzophobia that is killing Yiddish cooking even while saving Yiddish lives.

The earliest chala of which we have any description thus seems to have been more of a crisp- or flatbread than a roll and was hardly the cakey treat that we think of today. This unrisen form seems to have been a by-product of a desire to perform the chala ritual as close to the Sabbath as possible—baking, of course, being forbidden on the Sabbath itself—in order that there be no mistaking the reason for its performance.

Even though the *kuchen* type of chala enjoyed a long life in Europe, Isserlein's real contribution was to help establish or revive the link between the mishnaic passage and the Sabbath. Records of how this came to pass are spotty, to say the least, but the Jewish masses seem to have embraced the idea without any particular difficulty and then applied it to precisely the kind of bread that Isserlein avoided on *shabbes:* the *zeml.* Most writers on chala have mentioned the close resemblance between our braided loaves and those that non-Jewish women in southern Germany and Austria (where Isserlein lived) are said to have baked on Sundays. All that was necessary to get from the *zeml* that the Jews also borrowed from their German neighbors to the elaborate braided productions now associated with chala was to start a *zeml* train by making a whole bunch of *zeml* in the same tin and eliminating the space between them. Braiding would have been a way of preserving something of the *zeml's* original appearance while making it easy for the person who said the blessing to break pieces off for the rest of the diners.

Braided chalas were originally a little less cakelike in taste and texture than they are today. Although German Jews departed from Isserlein's recipe by leaving both eggs and oil out of their chalas, these ingredients, along with a nice egg wash to make the upper crust glow, were common in the chalas baked elsewhere. Sesame or poppy seeds were sometimes scattered over the top to allude to the manna which the chalas represent; fennel flowers were used in Lithuania.

Once the beet-sugar industry took off in Poland in the early nineteenth century, sugar began to be added to chalas—and just about everything else—by Jews who thought of themselves as *poylishe*, Polish-but-only-in-a-Jewish-way. Jews so dominated the sugar industry in Poland and Russia that it can be considered the Hollywood of the human mouth, and sugar rapidly became the defining feature of Polish-Jewish cooking. In addition to the sugar in the chala dough, granulated sugar was often sprinkled over the top of the loaf. A friend of mine replaces the granulated sugar with cake sprinkles on Rosh Hashana, thus proving that there really is nothing that sprinkles cannot improve. As with Polish *lokshn* kugels, raisins— the most beloved of Yiddish fruits—often find their way into a chala, especially on Rosh Hashana. Jewish food encyclopedist Gil Marks says that such raisin bread is another idea that we borrowed from the Germans.

The ability of a piece of bread to be both chala and *kuchen* simultaneously indicates why the name chala never caught on in all parts of the Yiddish-speaking world and is the default term only in countries where Jews from chala areas are strongly represented. Its most popular competitor for a Hebrew-based name was *berkhes*, sometimes pronounced *barkhes*. *Berkhes* has been the object of some rather fanciful stabs at etymology, ranging from the Latin *bracellus*, "arm," which ultimately gives us the word "pretzel," to the name of a pre-Christian Germanic goddess, Berchta. Though possibly introduced as a substitute for Berchta, in whose honor similar breads are said to have been baked, the real origin of *berkhes* seems to be exactly what the "folk" has always said it is: the Hebrew *birkas* (*birkat* in Israeli Hebrew), the first word of the biblical phrase *birkas hashem hi sa'ashir*, "The blessing of the Lord enriches" (Prv 10:22), which is often inscribed on the ornamental handles of knives used in the *hamoytse* ritual on *shabbes*. Some early sources even refer to *berkhes kuchen*, the *kuchen* over which the blessing is said. Confusion between *birkas*, which is singular, and *birkhes*, the construct or possessive form of the plural (as in, "blessings of," a frequent heading in prayer books and guides to the various blessings; it's pronounced *birkhot* in Israeli Hebrew), led to the latter being substituted for the former, possibly on the basis of the undeniable but grammatically irrelevant fact that multiple breads were being blessed at each of the Sabbath meals.

Berkhes/barkhes was widespread in Western and Central Europe; in Lithuania, braided chalas were called *kitkes*. The Polish *kitki* means "bunches, pigtails," as does *kitke* in Slovenian. Among Lithuanian Jews, the word was initially applied to the individual braids of bread—"Mendel baked a bread with six *kitkes*, but the baker can make one with twelve"—and then came to mean all the braids together. The term was as universal among Lithuanians as chala is among contemporary Americans; South African Jews, almost all of whom are descended from Lithuanian immigrants, still refer to their braided *shabbes* breads as *kitkes*. They use the term chala only for the dough that gets tossed.

Not every *kitke* was a plain old chala. In Poland, Belarus, and Ukraine, the large, round, braided chala without which no Purim or wedding feast was considered complete was known as a *koyletch*. The image of an older woman dancing with a *koyletch* during a wedding celebration is something of a cliché in Yiddish depictions of such events, but it helps to provide a link to the Slavs with whom the *koyletch*-eaters lived. *Koło* is Polish for a circle or wheel and a *kołacz* is a round cake that was originally served at weddings. The Ukrainian *kalach* is a round, sweet, braided bread, traditionally served on Christmas Eve. It also stands for good luck, fertility, and prosperity, an association that must have been absorbed by the people who danced with *koyletchn* at weddings or ate them on Purim, the one holiday on which the Jews were rescued before any harm befell them.

Despite their importance in Jewish life, neither regular bread nor chala figures very prominently as a source of Yiddish idioms. Most expressions that mention bread are easily paralleled in other cultures, though a couple seem typically Yiddish. "His bread always falls

butter side down" anticipates all those involved and utterly apocryphal attempts to define the difference between a shlemiel and a
shlimazl, while *Az men bakumt shoyn broyt, kumt der toyt*, "You finally get bread just before you drop dead," encapsulates the "Life's a
bitch, then you die," attitude common to so many Yiddish speakers.

Chala fares a little better, probably because of its association with
weekend sex. For many an Orthodox or formerly Orthodox adult
male, the smell of chala baking or the sight of a fresh chala, deco-
rously covered and waiting expectantly on the dinner table, evokes
the thought of hot crumpet for dessert. As such, chala figures in a
couple of fairly racy locutions. *Es nisht di khale far hamoytse*, "Don't
eat the chala before the blessing," is standard motherly advice,
especially to a daughter. It means no sex before marriage; the ritual
obligations, the sanctification of the act, must be performed before
the act itself. Similar, but slightly more vulgar, is *Iber an ongehoy-
bener khale iz nisht gut ken hamoytse tsu makhn*, "It's no good making
hamoytse over a chala that's already been sliced." In other words, no
man wants damaged goods.

The ritual of taking chala comes up in older German criminal
slang, where *Chale* meant a robbery in which care was taken to leave
enough behind to keep the robbery from being noticed too quickly.
The deliberately unstolen merchandise was like the dough put aside
for the priests. The people who did such things also used to refer to
jail food as *bilke*.

Finally, Gary Shteyngart paid tribute to the physical properties
of the doughy, nicely risen chala when he used it as the name of the
protagonist's girlfriend in *The Russian Debutante's Handbook*: "This
large pale woman . . . with the bulging cheeks." If she can be described as pale, the chala has already been sliced.

A NOTE ON THE MENU

Once the head of the household has made *hamoytse* and everyone at
the table has eaten a piece of bread, all that stands between you

and starting with dessert are tradition, decorum, and mother. The sequence of courses that follows represents the standard convention. While occasional substitutions are included to account for allergies, personal taste, and unavailability of ingredients, the big questions—Is gefilte fish really prior to soup? When should the side dishes discussed in Chapter Five come out?—are left to the discretion of the reader. The order here is the most common, but it isn't the only one.

STUFF IT: GEFILTE FISH

It's a good thing that Jews seem to like fish, because we've been stuck with it ever since the sages of the Talmud decided to make it meritorious, if not quite compulsory, to eat it on *shabbes*. "How do you make the Sabbath a delight?" they ask. "With a dish of beets and big fish and heads of garlic. Rov Hiya ben Ashi said in the name of Rov: Even if it's something small, as long as it's been done in honor of the Sabbath, it's a delight. And what did he mean by that? Rov Papo said: A fish-hash pie." (*Shabbos* 118b)

The beets seem to have been replaced by *tsimmes* and potato kugel, the garlic couldn't be chased out if you tried, and the fish abides as an essential component of every traditional Friday-night meal. Although some authorities go out of their way to stress the need to eat fish at all three Sabbath meals, *cholent* doesn't leave much room for fish at Saturday lunch and many observant people content themselves with gefilte fish on Friday night and herring at the third Sabbath meal, usually begun an hour or so before *shabbes* concludes. The Hebrew word for fish is *dag* (which rhymes with "rug") and the two letters that make up the word have a numerical value of seven; Saturday, of course, is the seventh day. Hence the Hebrew expression, *ha-oykhel dag be-dag nitsul mi-dag*: whoever eats fish on the seventh day is saved from being sentenced to hell (*din gehenom*, the initial letters of which also spell *dag*).

The Hebrew verb from which the noun *dag* derives means "to

increase, to be abundant," and fish have long served as a symbol of increase and prosperity in Jewish culture. When the dying Jacob blesses Joseph's sons, he says, "May they grow [*ve-yidgu*] into a multitude in the midst of the land" (Gn 48:16), a verse recited every night as part of the prayers before going to bed. Just as garlic is supposed to be eaten on the Sabbath for its aphrodisiac effects, so too fish; beets—by which the Talmud means the greens, not the bulbs—were also considered an aphrodisiac. Where Friday night chala, as we have seen, is there to give people ideas, and the kugel represents the masculine enabler of those ideas, the fish, gefilte or not, are supposed to provide some of the wherewithal to make those dreams come true.

It is therefore all the more surprising that a rather odd custom regarding the fish sprang up in certain Hasidic circles:

> *Eating fish in honor of* shabbes *was so incredibly important to rebbes and men of distinction that they used to eat it with their bare hands, without using any utensils. But they were careful to do so only with their first two fingers, rather than with all five, so as not to look like gluttons.*

The same people who considered touching the kugel a form of public indecency had no problem handling the lead that was supposed to fill the kugel's pencil. And if the fish that they were eating were gefilte, this might be the place to mention once again that *gefilte* in Yiddish means stuffed.

Now that the bagel has shed so much of its Jewish identity, gefilte fish is probably the Jewish dish most closely associated with Jews by people who aren't Jewish, even if they have never seen the food or met a Jew. No matter how little a given American might know about Jews or Judaism, she will still understand that a car bearing a stylized metal fish that says gefilte instead of Jesus or ΙΧΘΥΣ belongs to someone who has rejected Christ's offer of salvation.

Once ubiquitous by reason of its irreplaceable role in traditional Friday night dinners, gefilte fish—even more than chicken soup, which is eaten by plenty of people who might never have heard of Jews—became a sort of shorthand for the Jewish way of life, the charming but rather stodgy Tradition-with-a-capital-*T* that we're always leaving behind, but at the cost of a certain warmth and sense of belonging, that sense of psychic place that forms the national and familial bond that gefilte fish comes to represent. You might not have liked it; you might have sat and stared defiantly at the albino turd on the plate in front of you while the grown-ups kvelled all over it and told you how lucky you were to live in a time when you didn't have to come home from school to find a carp in the bathtub, that in the old country or the new country in the olden days of Harding and Coolidge and Hoover—*shoyn oopgeret*, forget already, about Roosevelt and Truman—kids looked *forward* to gefilte fish like it was a Saturday matinee, a double feature with newsreel, serial, and cartoon, and all strictly kosher because you paid your way in before *shabbes* with the Jew who owned the theater. Gefilte fish isn't Mom and apple pie; gefilte fish is Ma and Pa and DNA.

Which is not to say that the DNA of East European Jews tastes like shit, only that the standard commercial product, the stuff in jars and cans that can be bought in the supermarket—much of it made by people who also make matzoh, the rest by people firmly convinced that photos of grandmotherly women on their labels are a philosopher's stone that transforms the jellied dross in the jar into Neptune's kosher gold—is as close to proper gefilte fish as kohlrabi is to *Kol Nidre*. It sucks because people chose convenience over pisciculture, only to find that a spotless kitchen and a less hectic Friday left them no choice: for most producers of mass-market gefilte fish, good enough has always been more than enough.

Homemade gefilte fish was once a big production that began with a trip to the fishmonger sometime on Thursday or very early Friday morning for the best fish that a housewife's budget would allow. Once home, the fish was scaled, then sliced down the middle, gutted, opened up, and filleted. The bones were left attached to the skin. The flesh was chopped up, then mixed with bread crumbs (some recipes call for a whole *zeml*), egg, onion, salt, pepper, and—in Poland—sugar. The mixture was formed into slices or balls and stuffed back inside the skin, nestling between it and the bones. The skin was then sewn shut and the whole thing was put into boiling water with an onion and cut-up carrot and left to simmer for anywhere from ninety minutes to three hours. It was served cold, often straight out of the skin, along with the gel formed during the poaching.

As the time and effort that go into the dish might suggest, this was originally food for people who could afford kitchen help. The earliest surviving German cookbook, *Daz Buoch von Guoter Spise* or *The Good Food Book*, which is dated to about 1350, includes a recipe for stuffed pike. The merest glance at the manuscript confirms that it—the manuscript, as distinct from the fish—was a reasonably expensive production, with a good and very tidy hand; it wouldn't have come cheap. We can guess where German Jews got the idea for such a food. The thought of eating something associated with higher levels of society and even with the nobility—non-Jewish as such nobility might have been—appeals as much to traditional ideas of the Sabbath Queen, of *shabbes* as the one time when every Jew is a king and every Jewish woman a queen, as it does to the desire to ape one's betters that exists in every society. If gefilte fish wasn't quite the food of the gods, it was certainly the food of the lords.

Another compelling reason for its adoption is the complexity of the religious laws that deal with separating fish from bones on the Sabbath. While not absolutely forbidden, the proper manner of doing so, the conditions under which it can be done, and just about anything else connected with an act that falls under the rubric of "selecting," one of the thirty-nine types of activity prohibited on the

Sabbath, are so convoluted and contentious that it is easier to avoid the problem altogether by deboning the fish beforehand, thus giving your *frumer*-than-thou relatives one less thing to complain about. While this is not the sole rationale for eating gefilte fish on *shabbes*—plenty of nongefilte fish continues to be prepared and eaten in honor of the Sabbath—it certainly contributed to the alacrity with which gefilte fish seems to have made its way to the center of the Ashkenazi table. If nothing else, serving the fish cold also allowed the pot it was cooked in to be used for something else.

Like its German model, gefilte fish was originally made with pike. Once carp became established in Central and Eastern Europe, it began to figure prominently in the Jewish diet, in both gefilte and ungefilte form, much as it also did in France. The oldest recipe we have for gefilte fish made of carp is found not in a Jewish source, but in François Massialot's *Le Nouveau Cuisinier Royal et Bourgeois*, first published in 1691. Massialot was *officier de bouche*, head chef, to such luminaries as Louis XIV's brother, Philippe. His *carpes farcies* differ in only a couple of details from Jewish gefilte fish. After the carp has been scaled and the flesh drawn out of the skin (leaving the head and tail, as in the traditional Jewish recipe), one is to "make a forcemeat with the carp flesh, the flesh of an eel and soft carp roe, seasoned with herbs, salt, pepper, cloves, nutmeg, thyme, fresh butter and mushrooms, all of it ground very fine. Stuff your skins, and sew or tie them shut." Massialot then says to bake the carp in an oven, either on its own or in a casserole with a *beurre roux*, white wine, and fish bouillon.

The eel puts his recipe rather beyond the pale of any traditional Jewish cook; the butter isn't much help in preparing fish to be served at a meat meal, and the seasonings sound more like Versailles than Vitebsk. Still, the basic idea is no different. Although gefilte fish was usually poached, it was sometimes baked, though never with butter and white wine. But this is a local peculiarity. We're dealing with gefilte fish here, gefilte fish that might have been eaten by the Sun King himself and was certainly eaten by his courtiers—possibly even on Friday nights.

The spices and butter are there for a reason. Carp lends gefilte fish a darkish hue and a stronger taste than pike, and many women preferred to mix the carp with whitefish and pike. Even today, whitefish and pike in jelled broth is the Cadillac of packaged gefilte fish, possibly because whitefish and pike sounds like the name of a law firm, while mullet and carp combos are there for the budget-minded.

The slight taxidermic effect of presenting the sewn-up fish as if it were real, rather than an empty skin stuffed with forcemeat made from its own flesh, was highly prized in medieval and renaissance cooking and is yet another point of correspondence between the tastes of the Jewish masses and those of the feudal aristocracy.

The stuffed fish skin is rarely seen anymore and began to disappear decades ago. Making the stuffing takes enough time and trouble, and most women began to content themselves with preparing the fish balls and skipping this annoying and fundamentally unnecessary step. Bodiless versions of gefilte fish have become so prevalent that people who know that "gefilte" means stuffed are sometimes puzzled by the dish's name. They've been eating the stuffing without knowing that that's what it is.

Gefilte fish styles have nothing to do with the type of fish used; this was understood to be a matter of personal taste, finances, and availability. The big question, the real debate, is: Sugar or pepper? Sweet or savory? Polish or Litvish? If you were living in Eastern Europe, the answer was probably the easiest way of letting a stranger know who you were, where you came from, and what other features of your cultural orientation were also likely to provoke disgust or scorn. The nations of the world have their Maginot Line, their Siegfried Line; we have the Gefilte Fish Line, so named by linguist Marvin Herzog in 1965, on one side of which the gefilte fish is sweet, while the unfortunates on the other—or wrong—side, use pepper.

The fish changes from sweet to savory at almost exactly the same points as the main Yiddish dialects change from Central to North- or South-Eastern, a phenomenon responsible for even more intramural cavils than the food. To anyone able to read common Jewish cultural signifiers, the kind of gefilte fish you like is the key to your whole personality, or at least to those cultural leanings and prejudices that are going to determine much of its contents. As mentioned earlier, gefilte fish really is DNA.

DNA doesn't come with horseradish, though. *Khreyn*, as it is called in Yiddish, is one of the all-purpose Yiddish condiments and comes, like wine, in two main styles: white and red. Ground white horseradish is plain, while the red has been mixed with beets, a popular combination in much of Central and Eastern Europe. The red is usually preferred, especially when gefilte fish is involved; white produces too much of a monochrome effect. While horseradish is generally considered an integral part of the gefilte-fish experience, everyone knows that it's really just the icing on top of the fish cake and that gefilte fish will get you through times of no *khreyn* far better than *khreyn* will get you through times of no gefilte fish. Hence the ironic Yiddish idiom, "To give someone fish without *khreyn*"—to let someone off with a slap on the wrist, a laughably light punishment for whatever crime he has committed. They're going to fix his wagon all right—*Me vet im gebn fish on khreyn;* they'll make him eat his fish without horseradish, but he'll still get the fish.

Carp has long ranked among the more popular Jewish fish. Cold poached carp in jelly was once a common *shabbes* dish that, unlike gefilte fish, actually became popular among non-Jews. Though no longer part of the standard American Jewish menu, *karp po zydowsku*—carp *à la juive*—is still reasonably popular among non-Jews in Poland, where it can be found in restaurants that serve no other Jewish dishes.

As with most other fish that were not herring or sardines, the carp's head was considered a particular delicacy and tended to be punningly reserved for the head of the household, who would of-ten not think twice about eating the eyes. According to the Talmud (*Brokhos* 20a), the evil eye has no power over fish; eating the eye of a fish was considered a kind of homeopathic way of dispelling any evil eye that might have been cast your way. The fact that the head always went to the paterfamilias, whose position in traditional Jewish life is but little lower than God's, led the term *karpn-kep*, carp heads (as in "heads of carp," rather than "carp addicts") to be used as a slightly jocular or even pejorative designation for community lead-ers and other such big shots.

In a less conventional and completely non-Yiddish vein, the *Dön-meh*, descendants of those followers of seventeenth-century false messiah Shabbetai Tzvi who emulated his conversion to Islam but continued to think of themselves as Jews, sometimes called them-selves *sazanikos*, after the Turkish *sazan*, which means carp, "a fish that lives in both fresh and in seawater. Thus the converts conducted their double lives under Judaism and under Islam; and just as the carp seems to change color, so they changed external appearances in accordance with changing needs and circumstances." This is about as far from Friday night as you can get.

LETHAL CHEMISTRY

Like all other fish, gefilte fish is parve—neither meat nor dairy—and can be eaten together with anything else. At least that's the way it's supposed to be, but just try asking for real Worcestershire sauce, either for your food or your Bloody Mary, in a kosher steak house. You might get a knockoff, you might get a shrug, what you won't get is the real Lea & Perrins, even though it's been certified as kosher. The problem is that it's made with anchovies, and fish and meat cannot be eaten together. The *Shulkhan Arukh,* echoing the Talmud (*Pesokhim* 116b), tells us why: "Caution must be exercised not to eat meat and fish together, as doing so can lead to leprosy." Together is meant quite literally; they can be eaten at the same meal, just not at the same time. The text goes on to recommend washing the hands and eating something neutral between the two, but Isserles says that cleaning the mouth is sufficient.

Watch Orthodox Jews on Friday night; the gefilte fish is served on separate plates and eaten with separate knives and forks, often disguised as *haute goyishe* "fish knives" or "fish forks." See how many of the men have a shot of whiskey after eating it; watch the women take a sip of something; think deeply about why there is often a slice of lettuce underneath the fish. And that's the problem with a Bloody Mary; it's benign by mixology, malignant by meat-adjacent location—if you can find a kosher dairy restaurant with a liquor license, you'll be laughing. The medical reasoning might be a little weak, but you've got to admire the commitment to tradition: this extrabiblical prohibition is as carefully observed as the separation of meat and dairy.

I HATE FISH

"And if you don't like fish?" It's a question worthy of at least a couple of pages of Talmud, but if they're there, I have yet to find them. While there's a good deal of traditionally exerted pressure to eat fish on *shabbes*, that pressure has to bow before the positive commandment to make the Sabbath a delight. If you don't like gefilte fish, you're not obliged to eat it. If you like it but don't have time to make it and can't abide the stuff from the bottles and cans, you don't have to force yourself. What you *do* have to do, if only for the sake of culinary decorum, is provide something else between the bread and soup courses. Like so many others—my mother had a full-time job that left her no time to make gefilte fish and none of us liked the commercial stuff—my family filled that gap with chopped liver.

Often served today in delicatessens, chopped liver is among the oldest Jewish dishes still being eaten. Ancient Roman techniques of force-feeding geese seem to have been preserved only among Italian Jews, who passed the secret along to their Alsatian coreligionists. Foie gras as we know it is generally credited to Jewish methods of force-feeding, which were said to be "the exclusive possession of the Jews of Strasbourg and Metz." Rashi, who lived in Troyes in Champagne-Ardenne, which is not quite Alsace, in the eleventh century, alludes to goose fattening in his commentary on the Talmud (*Bovo Basro* 73b), and the Maharil, who lived in Mainz in the late fourteenth and early fifteenth centuries, discusses the practice with reference to chickens, rather than geese:

> *Chickens are not to be stuffed on the Sabbath, that is, to be fed against their will by shoving food into their throats in order to fatten them. This is not to be done on the Sabbath, as stated [in tractate* Shabbos *155b] "The camel is not to be stuffed."*

Goose and chicken liver, along with the livers of beef and calves, remained popular among Jews in Eastern Europe as well, so much so that Sholem Aleichem once described chopped chicken livers with schmaltz as the Jewish national dish. Cheap, nourishing, exempt, like all other offal, from the kosher-meat tax, and going well with even cheaper and more abundant onions and chopped eggs, liver from these animals was more than just a European Jewish superfood; free to flourish in America, it became a medium of artistic expression. Those who condemn the chopped-liver sculpture as tasteless should try eating a Giacometti; there is a direct line from stuffing an empty fish skin with balls of its own boiled flesh to those hepatic swans, chickens, bar mitzvah boys, and bridal couples. In five hundred years they, too, will be another link in the golden chain of tradition. Until such time, they—like so many of us who feel overlooked or underappreciated—are nothing but chopped liver: so commonplace, so everyday as to be unworthy of notice.

The sometimes insalubrious consequences of too much chopped

liver are graphically portrayed in a *King of the Hill* episode in which
Hank Hill's eleven-year-old son develops gout after becoming ad-
dicted to chopped chicken-liver sandwiches from the newly opened
Show Biz Deli. As far as unchopped liver goes, Jews born since 1971
will never know how lucky they are to have dodged any chance of
being confronted with the traditional but nonetheless frightening
lung and liver. By banning human consumption of lung, the USDA
delivered us from the worst of all kosher evils. Slathered in tomato
soup fresh from the can, lung and liver was enough to make a kid
beg for Brussels sprouts. And when it turned cold and the sauce
congealed in the face of repeated refusals to swallow so much as a
bite . . . there's a reason why someone like Calvin Coolidge, so
phlegmatic that you want to take his pulse, is called *a kalter lung-un-
leber*, "a cold lung and liver," in Yiddish. The blood doesn't seem to be
flowing and you don't want to know from the taste. Lung and liver
also gives us the fabulous *onhengen a lung-un-leber af der noz*, "to
hang a lung and liver from someone's nose"—that is, to trick them,
dupe them, leave them with something far worse than egg all over
their face.

Liver is also the now-lost operating principle behind one of the
best known insults or curses in Yiddish, *gey kakn afn yam*, "Go shit
on the sea." Not in, on. Originally, you'd have told someone to *gey
kakn afn leber-yam*, "Go shit on the liver sea," a world away from the
Big Rock Candy Mountain. *Leber*—liver—is closely related to the
Yiddish verb *glivern*, "to congeal," and *leber-yam* originally meant
"the congealed sea." The Yiddish version of the Hebrew *yam ha-
kerakh*, sea of ice, *leber-yam* is a direct translation of the Middle
High German *Lebermeer*, a congealed sea in which ships were unable to move. The German seems to have referred to a somewhat
mythologized version of the Arctic Ocean; *leber-yam* retained this
meaning and was also used for a time to denote the Dead Sea. In
either case, the liver sea where you were supposed to go was far away
and unpleasant. And you weren't coming back. As Sholem Aleichem

explains in his novella, *The Song of Songs*: "The water is as thick as liver and as salty as brine. No ships can pass through it, and anyone who somehow manages to get there can never come back." As the literal meaning and probable location of the *leber-yam* became ever more obscure and hard to fathom, speakers—all of whom knew what and roughly where a plain old sea was to be found—began to drop the *leber*, which no longer meant anything but "liver" outside of this phrase, and head straight for the sea itself.

INTO THE SOUP

Liver, fish, or even, God help us, a salad, the appetizer is traditionally followed by the most emblematic of all Jewish foods. While chicken soup figures in the cuisine of peoples who have had little or no contact with Jews, it has come to be thought of as so typically Jewish that a sitcom starring Jackie Mason, who has based his career on the idea of the typically Jewish, wasn't called *Matzoh Balls* or *Kugel*, but *Chicken Soup*. It isn't the soup's fault that the series didn't fly. More than just a dish, chicken soup has served as a specific for what ails the Jews for close to two millennia. The Talmud even discusses its progenitor, the so-called "chicken of Rabbi Abba," which was left to soak in hot water for days until the chicken was completely dissolved. "Rov Safro said, 'I happened to be at Rabbi Abba's once and he gave it to me to eat. Had he not [also] given me some three-year-old wine to drink, it would have made me vomit" (*Shabbos* 145b). Rashi tells us that the chicken was prepared this way for medicinal reasons.

The recipe had been refined by the time of Maimonides, who believed that such soup helped balance the humors and, among other things, was effective against leprosy, even if the latter had been induced by eating meat and fish together. Chicken soup was so important in the treatment of the sick and weak that Joseph Saul Nathansohn, the eminent mid-nineteenth-century proponent of machine-made matzoh, exempted chickens from a ban on the meat of a supplier whose kashrus he deemed suspect, on the grounds that, "Were chicken to be prohibited, what would the sick and women in childbed, not to mention people of frail constitution, do? There are certain people who simply cannot live without chicken soup. What will they do?"

That's why it's Jewish penicillin, a phrase that Rabbi Nathansohn, who died in 1875, could never have known. As medicine, it was fine as long as there was nothing better at hand. Once antibiotics made their appearance, chicken soup began to lose some of its cachet as a universal nostrum. It's great for colds and other minor ailments, and can't be beat as a source of comforting nourishment for those too ill to be able to eat as they please, but that's about as far as it goes. It's medicine for people who can't afford a prescription. As the Yiddish saying has it, "When a poor person eats a chicken, one of them must be sick."

JEWISH PENICILLIN

Jewish penicillin the phrase, rather than the soup—gives us a clue to at least one reason behind the decline of Yiddish cooking in the mainstream Jewish community. When used as an adjective in Yiddish, "Jewish" sometimes denotes something second-rate, jerry-built, not quite up to the noun that it's modifying. So you get such phrases as *yidish glik*, "Jewish luck," always the opposite of good luck; *yidish ashires*, "Jewish wealth," the source of which is described as the money you save by not eating; and *a yidishe yerushe*, a Jewish legacy: hemorrhoids. Even more mordantly, Jews in the Warsaw Ghetto referred to typhus as *yidishe* tuberculosis.

To Yiddish speakers, this sense of "Jewish" connotes what "separate but equal" does to African-Americans: the also-ran version, the version the others didn't want, the bullshit version. To call chicken soup "Jewish penicillin" is to point to its limitations, not its virtues. The real tragedy is the number of Jews whose cultural identity and pride in what they are has become a product of missing the point.

BACK TO SOUP

The recipe isn't terribly involved. Chicken, water, heat. Include the chicken's feet and giblets if they're available. Toss in some carrots and parsnips, dill and celery—don't forget the leaves—maybe even an onion, and simmer till ready. Dill, incidentally, has been associated with *shabbes* food since Talmudic times:

> *The emperor asked Rabbi Yehoshua ben Khananyo, "Why is your Sabbath cooking so fragrant?" He replied, "We have a certain spice called dill that we put into it and its aroma carries."*
> *"Give me some," said the emperor. He replied, "It only works for someone who observes the Sabbath. It doesn't work for anyone who doesn't." (Shabbos 119a)*

The Talmudic word for dill, *sheves*, looks exactly like the word for *shabbes*—שבת—a bit of playfulness that has led people many to translate Rabbi Yehoshua's first answer as "We have a certain spice called *shabbes*," if only to bring out the homily concealed in the pun.

Once the soup is ready, pay special attention to the floating fat slicks known as *rendelekh*, golden ducats. Toothsome and slurpy, their likeness to gold coins has made them an augur of good fortune, especially in *gildene yoykh*, golden broth—the clear chicken soup traditionally shared by the bride and groom at their wedding feast.

For the rest, chicken soup is as notable for what comes with it as for what it is. We've already had a look at matzoh balls and noodles (the original accompaniment), but they are far from the soup's only partners. *Mandlen* are one of the Yiddish kitchen's more bizarrely addictive productions. Their name means almonds (or tonsils) in Yiddish, but just as there are neither rocks at Rockaway nor eggs in egg creams, soup *mandlen*—sometimes called soup nuts in English—are made with neither almonds nor tonsils, just eggs, flour, schmaltz or oil, and a pinch of salt. The dough is rolled into tiny balls that can be baked or fried at the cook's discretion.

Mandlen are both an adornment to any chicken soup and a great straight-from-the-package TV snack. Purists who shy away from using them in tandem with matzoh balls don't know what they're missing; they taste very much like small unsweetened versions of the popover-like pastry known as nothings, which look like tiny, fissured kaiser rolls sprinkled with crystallized sugar. They are hollow in the middle, though. They're light—hence the name—and leave a pleasant taste behind. Although the ingredients do not differ significantly, if at all, from those of the packaged egg *kichelach* made by the large kosher food companies, nothings that come from a bakery lack the musty afterbite of the more widely distributed product.

KREPLACH

Until Behr Manischewitz turned matzoh meal from a seasonal necessity to a year-round treat, kreplach were the solid food most closely associated with chicken soup. Like wonton or ravioli, to which they are undoubtedly related, kreplach are stuffed pockets of dough, usually triangular and usually stuffed with liver, kasha, cheese, mushrooms, or potatoes; lung was popular in the old country. Kreplach are first boiled, then fried or baked. When not served in soup, they are spread with schmaltz, sour cream, or butter. There used to be special Purim kreplach filled with fresh fruit, preserves, raisins, or nuts, that had honey and spices—and sometimes even schmaltz—kneaded right into the dough.

Kreplach are mentioned as early as the thirteenth century. The name comes from the Middle High German *Krapfe*, which is also related to the French *crêpe*; the Modern German *Krapfen* is a hole-free doughnut and a *krap* in Yiddish—*krepl*, the singular of kreplach, is its diminutive—was a triangle-shaped dough-pocket, stuffed with apple and fried in honey. *Krapfe* had two meanings in the thirteenth century, one of which is already obvious; the other, as Matthias Lexer explains in his classic Middle High German dictionary, was *"obsc[ene] für testiculi."* These were the original soup nuts.

The testicular sense of kreplach persisted in Yiddish for quite a long time, although it does not seem to be attested in Yiddish literature. Yehuda Elzet, who died in 1962, writes: " 'Kreplach' was considered an impudent, disreputable expression. I know from personal experience that older women used to call kreplach 'unmentionables [*oser ledaberlekh*]'." The idea that generations of Jewish grandmothers thought of kreplach soup as soup with balls—balls that they themselves had made—might help to explain some of the more grandiose restorative powers sometimes ascribed to it.

Kreplach were always a treat; they are a pain to make and were reserved for holidays and special occasions. Yet they were never able to shake off that air of disreputability. One of the greatest food-based expressions in Yiddish translates literally as "You should eat kreplach." It isn't dietary advice. Sometimes it even comes out as "You should eat kreplach for talking like that." The person being addressed is being told that they're cruising for a bruising, that they've said something impertinent, indelicate, unmentionable, and had better not do so again. Indeed, you can even say *Kreplekh zolstu* nisht *esn far di reyd*, "You should *not* eat kreplach for talking like that," lest someone—God, His angels, the petty demons and supernatural troublemakers who never stop paying attention—overhear you telling someone to eat kreplach and decide to take you at your word and provide them with kreplach just to spite you.

As the Yiddish saying has it, *Az me' shlogt, est men kreplekh*, "When you hit, you eat kreplach." Although there are no hard and fast rules governing when kreplach are to be eaten, it has been traditional for centuries to eat them at least three times a year: on Purim, the eve of Yom Kippur, and Hoshana Rabba, the seventh day of the holiday of Sukkos or Tabernacles, when worshippers recite a large number of supplicatory prayers called *Hoshanas* (from which we get the English word Hosanna). Something is hit or beaten, at least idiomatically, on all three of these days. The Yiddish verb *shlogn*, "to hit, beat, strike," has a wider range of meanings than any of its standard English translations, and things that you *shlog* in Yiddish are not always hit in English.

On Purim, Haman is metaphorically beaten when the children let loose with their noisemakers (often called *homen-klappers*, Haman hitters) whenever his name is mentioned during the reading of the Book of Esther. The ritual of swinging a chicken around your head on the eve of Yom Kippur is known in Yiddish as *shlogn kapores*, beating *kapores*, even though a beating is about the only thing that the poor chicken doesn't get. On Hoshana Rabba, willow twigs called *heshaynes* are beaten on the floor of the synagogue. Kreplach and beatings thus became as closely associated as turkey and football; telling someone to eat kreplach is a subtle way of offering them a strictly kosher knuckle sandwich.

The same idea of eating kreplach when there's a beating going on comes up in a once-widespread rhyming proverb, *Yidishe keplekh— klogn un veynen un esn vayter kreplekh*, "Little Jewish heads—they wail and cry and eat some more kreplach." They're crying because they're being hit, and when something gets hit, you get kreplach— which makes it all worthwhile. This is the Yiddish version of national codependency.

Kreplach also come up in a delightfully contemptuous expression of disbelief. If someone's claim to have seen or heard or done something strikes you as patently untrue, you can say, *"Zol er zen kreplekh*, He should see kreplach, the way he saw Mick Jagger at McDonald's"—and once he sees them, I can hit him. *Krepl-fleysh*, kreplach meat, was the cat's meat of the Yiddish-speaking world; you were never quite sure what it was. According to Alter Druyanow, a Hebrew writer and folklorist from Russia whose three-volume collection of Jewish jokes continues to be plundered by academics and performers alike, "When an innkeeper had meat that he couldn't decide whether or not to throw out, he made kreplach with it."

SEVEN

It's All Meat
Sabbath Main Dishes
and Some of Their Accomplices

Forget about Jesus. On a day to day basis, meat was the wall that separated Jews from the people around them. Jewish meat differed from non-Jewish not so much in being kosher as in being. Peasants living in the Moscow region at the beginning of the twentieth century—admittedly well outside the Pale of Settlement in which Jews were allowed to live—apparently consumed an average of 200 kilos of barley and rye, 150 kilos of potatoes, and 80 kilos of sauerkraut per annum. Meat was a rare treat, usually reserved for religious festivals.

Shabbes, a religious festival that takes place once a week, was responsible for much higher levels of meat consumption among Jews; even the poorest would do their best to come up with at least a token piece of chicken. Although many people who would hardly have been considered destitute saw meat only on *shabbes* and other holidays, they still ate it once a week.

It wasn't as if they didn't miss it the rest of the time, even if they'd never really had it. Yiddish ideas of fine dining took shape a long time ago and have remained fundamentally unchanged since the sixteenth century. While cooking styles and modes of preparation have been influenced by improvements in technology and the culinary styles and fads of the countries in which Yiddish speakers lived, the basic idea that a really good meal should center around meat or poultry has not changed significantly. At the height of

East European Jewish immigration to the United States, from the 1880s to the 1920s, Jews became notorious, not least among public-health workers, for eating meat as often as they could afford to, sometimes more than once a day. While not all Jewish immigrants had the money or the inclination to do so, and while virtually none had done so in Europe, the idea—or ideal—of all meat most of the time, was a preference that grew out of strong historical conditioning.

We saw a long time ago that Jewish food started off with a plague, so it shouldn't be too surprising that the Black Death continues to be the single greatest influence on Ashkenazi ideas of food. The death of somewhere between one third and one half of the European population had a drastic impact on the need for arable land and the number of people available to work it. The dead, who weren't eating any meat themselves, left plenty of room for cattle.

The effects of the Little Ice Age, a major drop in temperature that lasted until the nineteenth century and had far-reaching effects on European life and culture, were also beginning to be felt, especially in a growing season that lost as many as two full months in certain areas. Much farmland was thus turned to pasture, leading to a considerable increase in the numbers of sheep and cattle available for eating, and a concomitant drop in the price of meat. Although lamb and mutton were never hugely popular among Jews (except on Passover, when veal or lamb were a matter of tradition), beef, in every form permitted by halacha, most certainly was, and by the time the meat surplus ended around the middle of the sixteenth century, the idea of having meat at every meal of any consequence had become entrenched in the Ashkenazi psyche. The Talmud says that there is no celebration without meat (*Pesokhim* 109a), and many Jews still choose to ignore the first clause of that sentence—"When the Temple was standing"—so that they can change the tense from past to present and allow themselves to celebrate another day of living. Just as Yiddish notions of European geography reflect a reality that ended in 1569, so the Yiddish menu—or the Yiddish fantasy menu, at any rate—has never acknowledged the end of the post-Black Death meat surplus in Europe.

Some typical dishes have not come down to us. The signature Jewish dish until poultry conquered all was a meat pie called a *pashtet*, with the accent on the last syllable, or *pashtida*. If you failed to go home for Friday night dinner in the fifteenth century, your mother would have made a big *tsimmes* about the nice *pashtet* that she'd spent all day making and that you—Mr. or Mrs. Big Shot—were too busy being important to come by and eat. Although there were fish *pashtetn*, meat in pastry dough, along with onions, garlic, and spices, was by far the more popular combination. Given the low status that meat pies, especially frozen ones, tend to enjoy among contemporary Jews—it's the goyishness of the pastry that does it—it is sobering to recall that such pies were the centerpiece of Ashkenazi cookery for a very long time, and that no noses were ever turned up at the thought of eating one. *Pashtidas* made with eggs and cheese have become popular in Israel over the past few decades, but the meat pies which so delighted Rashi and most of the other early sages mentioned in this book are nowhere to be seen.

Udder, already noted as kosher in Chapter Three, was popular in West European *pashtetn* long before the Black Death; Rashi mentions it in the eleventh century. The standard wisdom is that if the udder is to be roasted, you have to cut an X into it and press it against a wall to squeeze out any remaining milk. If it's to be boiled, the cutting and pressing can be skipped, but udder in a *pashtet* is supposed to be treated as if it were being roasted. Non-Jews, incidentally, usually soak the udder for a couple of hours to get rid of the milk; a standard German recipe—insofar as any recipe involving udder can be called standard—has it breaded and then fried, much like a schnitzel. Samuel Pepys mentions roasted udder, and cold udder cooked in milk was not uncommon in British sandwiches until surprisingly recently. Although a recipe for stewed udder and vegetables can be found in Regina Frishwasser's 1946 *Jewish American*

Cookbook (and Frishwasser, it should be noted, was the food columnist for the *Jewish Daily Forward*, the most popular of the Yiddish
papers), udder disappeared from the standard Jewish menu a long
time ago.

SHIT ARAYN

Take out the potatoes, and virtually all of today's more common
Yiddish dishes would have been recognizable to our grandparents'
grandparents' grandparents. And probably to their grandparents,
too. They all come from the same five cuts and have been prepared
for generations by the *shit arayn* method of cooking. The *shit* has
nothing to do with quality or taste; it's Yiddish for a pinch or a bit
of something that is tossed in, i.e., *arayn*. Although the Yiddish
cookbooks that we have were designed to improve the culinary skills
of the average housewife, which often fell short of the exalted levels
reached in folklore and memory, their main aim was to expand the
range of food that that housewife might prepare. The bulk of
the recipes are for new and "foreign," that is, *goyishe* dishes, rather
than the traditional ones, which most *balebustes* were assumed to
have learned from their own mothers, who would have been describing ingredients in pinches and handfuls rather than ounces or
grams. Indeed, the only real variations in recipes for traditional
dishes are regional; otherwise, a *krepl* is a *krepl* and matzoh fried
with eggs in butter, oil, or schmaltz is matzoh *brei*. Adding cinnamon or onions or anything else is a matter of family tradition or
individual imagination; it's the cook's talent that makes the real
difference.

The Yiddish cookbooks were trying to broaden their readers'
cultural horizons. *Dos Familiyen Kokh-Bukh* or *The Family Cookbook*, possibly the most ill-tempered guide to kitchen wizardry ever
written, was published in New York in 1914 and is full of unsolicited advice about hygiene and proper deportment. The author's
general attitude can be summed up as, "Eat poorly, eat well, you're

still going to die. Don't blame me if you do so with a stomachache."
His introduction to the chapter on meat deserves to be quoted at
length, as much for its cultural prejudices as its attitude to meat:

> *Until such time as science discovers what can take the place of*
> *meat, people will have to eat meat. Human beings have been*
> *eating meat since they became human beings, and might have*
> *been doing so even earlier. Not only does the whole human body*
> *need meat, but the stomach simply has to have it in order to*
> *function properly. . . . The meat-eating nations are the most*
> *capable and progressive. The Chinese, the Russians, the people*
> *of the Baltic islands eat little meat; the servile Hindus do not*
> *eat meat at all. The English, the Americans, are the biggest*
> *meat-fressers; the French and Germans come next. But we are*
> *not here to philosophize. . . .*
>
> *A butcher will realize right away if the woman who is buying*
> *meat from him knows what she is doing and if she would know*
> *what to do with a good piece of meat if he were to give her one.*
> *If he sees that she doesn't know, he will give her the worst meat.*
> *But if he knows that she is a maven and also knows how to*
> *cook—then he's going to be careful.*

It's like Rudyard Kipling meets Molly Goldberg. Later in the
book, he provides instructions for cooking an egg—twenty minutes
till hard-boiled—and how best to digest it.

Although the English-language Jewish cookbooks also included a
great many recipes for foods that could never be described as Jewish,
their rationale is the opposite of that of the Yiddish cookbooks.
They are there to supply the instruction, to pass down the traditions
that a girl or young woman would once have received directly from
her mother. People who were already Americans were being taught
how to act like Jews. Leah W. Leonard's *Jewish Cookery*, published
four years after the end of World War II and still in print thirty years

later, opens with a "Calendar of Jewish Holiday and Food Associations" that has nothing to do with sodalities or consumer groups. The lunar calendar is explained, the names of the Hebrew months are listed. There follows a four-column table of holidays and the foods associated with them, information that any Jewish six-year-old in Eastern Europe would have mastered by the age of four. "Kosher Kitchen Questions and Answers," a sort of catechism of kashrus arranged in question-and-answer format, follows a few pages later.

A subgenre of the Leonard-type of cookbook was the folksy, *yidishe mama* cookbook, written (except for the recipes) in Yinglish and making no bones about its real function: to help newlyweds learn to cook the dishes that their husbands' mothers used to make. But if today's girls had any natural feel for these dishes, they wouldn't need the cookbooks: they would have been raised properly. The opening chapter of *Love and Knishes* sums up the dilemma:

> *The true art of Jewish cooking is based on inexactness. . . .*
> *[but] this modern generation has gone to college so how can you*
> *teach them how to cook? You've got to put it into their heads by*
> *the level teaspoon yet. If you tell them, "Put in a little flour,"*
> *so they ask you, "How much?" and when you say, "Put in till it*
> *looks right," so do they know what you are talking about? Can*
> *an artist measure out a masterpiece? . . . When you go to college*
> *you can cook only from a book.*

We are dealing with food that was cooked by instinct—not always well, but not ever wrong—and the prime target of that instinct, when applied to anything that once walked on hooves, was the braised chuck or brisket known as *gedempte fleysh* or pot roast. Since Ashkenazim in the diaspora rarely go to the trouble and expense of preparing the hind parts of a kosher animal in kosher fashion (see the discussion in Chapter Three), all that is left them are the tougher and less tasty forequarters, cuts that benefit from long, slow cooking in liquid. A little water, or better, stock; some onions and garlic, carrots, potatoes, any other vegetables that take your fancy (celery was standard for many years), and the indispensable schmaltz; the usual spices—don't forget the bay leaves. Cover the pan tightly—some older recipes recommend sealing it—and place over fire or into oven. And whatever you do, *cut crosswise, against the grain*, once you've taken it out.

When Howard Wolowitz's mother starts screaming about her brisket on *The Big Bang Theory*, this is probably what she means. Known as *brust* or *brist* in Yiddish, brisket—the standard anatomical term for the breast of any four-legged animal (a discovery I made while helping my daughter assemble her Visible Dog)—is a technical term once confined to ranchers, butchers, and veterinarians that became part of day-to-day Jewish English only because there is no other generally accepted name for it. "Breast of beef" does not—you'll pardon the expression—cut it. Brisket is big; brisket is—or used to be—cheap, because nobody but Jews wanted it. A pariah cut dear only to those who had no other choice, brisket from any knife but a *shoykhet's* tended to end up as hamburger. Only with the advent of Texas barbeque did it gain any real popularity among non-Jews; the Lone Star made common cause with the Star of David, and the brisket, hitherto the meat of exile, finally found a land of its own and a price more suited to its newfound popularity.

FROM BRINE TO BORSCHT

At about six untrimmed kilos per cow, a single brisket, properly portioned out and preserved, could keep a family going for a very long time, or provide a butcher with enough meat to give four or five or six different families a reasonably festive *shabbes*. It is a lean, dry cut, though, and needs time and liquid to come into its own, which is why it is at its best in such dishes as pot roast and *cholent*. While pot roast can be made with stock instead of water, the brisket doesn't really sing until it has been braised in either vinegar or *rosl*. The vinegar version—*esik-fleysh* in Yiddish—doesn't differ essentially from sauerbraten, but the *rosl*—well, *rosl* opens the gates to a whole new kingdom of Yiddish food.

Rosl, which means broth, brine, or pickle (the liquid, rather than the thing preserved in it), can mean wildly different things to wildly different people, depending on where they or their forebears come from. It can be a sort of soup that looks and tastes like the liquid in which the brisket has been resting, a sort of brisket version of chicken soup, complete with all the other ingredients that have been tossed in to accompany the meat.

More commonly, though, *rosl* refers to a brine made from fermented beets. Peeled beets are sliced into quarters or thirds and put into a vessel—a barrel in the classical versions—along with some water. The vessel is covered and left to stand for three or four weeks, until it has fermented into a scarlet vinegar with plenty of bite, which is then strained through a tablecloth. Although this can be done whenever you have enough beets to make it worthwhile, it was almost always done in time to have the *rosl* ready for Passover, when it was used in the borscht that is traditional, though not exclusive to, that holiday. The meat borscht involves brisket, *rosl,* and eggs, along with sugar, salt, an onion, and spices. Potatoes are sometimes added. Meatless, it is made from *rosl* and the beets from which it grew, usually thickened with egg yolks or sour cream and often adorned with a boiled potato. It can be served either hot or cold and is the origin of the bottled borscht sold in supermarkets.

The *rosl* that goes into the borscht is what most people think of when they hear the word *rosl*, though to many others it also denotes any kind of pickle brine: The stuff in a jar of herring or pickles is as much *rosl* as the fermented beet liquid. Pronounced *rusl* by most Yiddish-speakers, the brine was still well known enough in the '40s and '50s that both Rosalind and Jane Russell were often called Rosalind and Jane *Rusl* by people familiar with kosher food. (When

I attempted the same joke about Bertrand in a college philosophy seminar, the professor, a Jewish refugee from Vienna, told me to stop parading my ethnicity. I was wearing a yarmulke at the time.)

Lign in rosl, "to be lying in *rosl,*" means to be in a pickle, a bad situation. When Alonso asks Trinculo at the end of Shakespeare's *Tempest,* "How cam'st thou in this pickle?" he would have said, "*Vi azoy ligstu in aza rosl?*" in Yiddish. *Rosl* also figures in what is arguably the single greatest expression in all Yiddish: *dreyen zikh vi a forts in rosl,* "to blunder around like a fart in the brine." The person doing so has no idea where he is, why he's there, or where he's supposed to be going. He is bubbling frantically, but the bubbles that he's making have nothing to do with fermentation.

With brisket or without, borscht is one of those iconic foods that signify Jewish in America, even though beet and cabbage borscht (substitute cabbage for beets; keep the brisket if you want it *fleyshik*) are eaten throughout Eastern Europe, where they are considered no more Jewish than the grilled-cheese sandwich is in the USA. But when Abel Green coined the term borscht belt, it wasn't because Sullivan County was full of hotels catering to ethnic Lithuanians.

Borscht meets love in a modern Yiddish song by Meir Charatz and Efim Chorny. "I have never eaten such a borscht," say the lyrics, "nor known such a taste. I can't forget you, darling, because I love you." An English-language song about a desire to eat your beloved would have an entirely different subtext; the Yiddish makes you yearn for soup.

Borscht turns up in a number of Yiddish idioms and expressions, the most common of which are *bilik vi borsht,* cheap like borscht, and its intensive form, *biliker vi borsht,* cheaper than borscht, meaning that it can't get any cheaper. The magnificent and woefully under-used *tsu borsht darf men nisht hobn ken tseyn,* "For borscht, you don't need any teeth," is the Yiddish counterpart of "It isn't rocket science." Next time a fellow movie-goer asks you how you figured out that the cop with two weeks left to retirement was going to die in the next ten minutes, tell them that you don't need teeth to eat borscht—a person with a working brain doesn't have to think to figure it out. It's subtler, nastier, a little more insulting, than the rocket science expression.

Just as popular as *rosl* and better balanced nutritionally, sauerkraut has also remained a Yiddish staple. In the old country, it would be prepared at home, usually in the fall. Cabbage leaves were cut into strips, sprinkled with salt and caraway seeds, then layered into a saltwater-filled barrel and pounded down with a pile driver until the cabbage gave up its juice. There would be a layer of apples, carrots, beets, and cranberries between each layer of cabbage. Men would press all the layers together as snugly as they could, then leave the barrels to ferment for five or six days, prodding the contents periodically with sticks to release the foul-smelling gas and guard against explosions. Once the cabbage was fermented, the barrels would be rolled to a basement, pantry, or outhouse, depending on the resources at the householder's disposal. A barrel or two would last the whole winter, staving off hunger and scurvy alike.

Making sauerkraut was child's play in comparison with what Jews in rural Lithuania had to do to pickle cucumbers. These were salted in big barrels, oak leaves and dill were added, and the barrels were hermetically sealed and rolled into a local lake, where they remained ("not too far from shore") for the whole winter. When the barrels were fished out of the water before Passover, the cucumbers were sour but firm. They were eaten in place of fruit.

Today's kosher dills are among the best known Jewish contributions to American cuisine and were once considered a sign of the moral and nutritional rot that our ancestors brought to this country from Europe. Nutritionists and social workers despaired of the Jewish love for such food, especially its effects on children, who were in a fair way of using this easily affordable stimulant as a gateway to smoking, drinking, and who knows what else. "The Jewish children," said a well-meaning Boston nutritionist, "suffer from too many pickles, too few vegetables, and too little milk."

Pickles could be purchased every few feet in the Jewish areas of larger cities; mothers could make them at home and sell them as a way of earning a few extra pennies. *Dos Familiyen Kokh-bukh* devotes a fifteen-page chapter to pickles and pickling and provides recipes for various vinegars, including mint, cayenne, and mustard, along with instructions on how to pickle beets, red cabbage, cauliflower, cucumbers, onions, peppers, green tomatoes, cherries, currants, grapes, peaches, and watermelon rinds.

The father of one of the main characters in *The Old Bunch*, Meyer Levin's 1937 novel that was a kind of a *Big Chill* for the children of Jews who came to America in the first decade of the twentieth century, dies of a heart attack induced in part by overindulgence in sour pickled tomatoes.

Pickles were probably never strangers to brisket, but the two cemented their association in kosher or kosher-style delicatessens, some of which still bring a plate of pickles to any newly occupied table as a suitable vegetable prologue to meat that has been treated in essentially similar fashion.

THE YIDDISH EAGLE

Judaism and poultry have been inextricably linked in the Yiddish mind ever since the Talmud informed us that a town called Tur Malka was destroyed because of a rooster and a hen. The people there were accustomed to have a cock and hen lead the bride and groom to their wedding, "as if to say be fruitful and multiply like chickens." When some passing Roman soldiers steal the birds from one such wedding, the Jews fall upon them and beat them, leading the soldiers to tell the emperor that the Jews are revolting. He responds with troops and the Jews decide to revolt for real, but their leader is killed in a privy when a snake appears and pulls his intestines out through his anus. God has mercy and delivers the Jews. Instead of offering prayers of thanksgiving, though, they hold a party to congratulate themselves on having frightened the emperor. Offended, the emperor sends his troops back in: three hundred thousand swordsmen slaughter for seventy-two straight hours, even as the partying continues on the other side of town (*Gitin* 57a).

And all on account of chickens. Although chickens pop up frequently in ancient and medieval Jewish literature, the goose was the Ashkenazi bird of choice for a very long time. The only area in which chickens have never had to compete with geese is a pre-Yom Kippur ritual called *kapores*, literally "atonements," which is only obliquely related to dining. On the eve of Yom Kippur, a Jew who is about to be judged by the only Judge who matters will wave a live chicken around his or her head three times while reciting the following formula: "This is my stand-in, this is my substitute, this is my atonement. May this hen/rooster go to its death while I go off and continue on a good, long, and peaceful life." Men use a rooster, women a hen; using a goose would probably prove fatal.

The *kapores* ritual has given birth to a considerable number of Yiddish idioms that have nothing to do with food but have helped keep chickens at the forefront of the Yiddish-speaking mind. Ranging in meaning from "to revile a person" to "to fall hopelessly in love with them," idioms featuring *kapores* have accustomed Yiddish-speakers to the idea that there is no human activity that cannot be mediated through poultry.

Jews sometimes took the chickens' side. In one of his best-known and most deeply cynical stories, Sholem Aleichem writes about a chicken strike: They're sick of being used as *kapores* and walk off the job. The local Jews enter into negotiations with them, but the chickens have no interest in improved *kapores* conditions. They eventually mount a physical attack on the humans, from which they emerge victorious: "And ever since . . . they are slaughtered exactly as before. They are plucked, cut up; they are boiled, roasted and fried, brought to the table with all kinds of sauces and other dishes, exactly as before. But they are no longer used as *kapores*." Like Bontche Shvayg, who couldn't conceive of anything better than a hot roll with butter, the chickens missed the real point. The Jews in this story represent the Russian government, the chickens the Russian and Polish Jews. It is one of the great portrayals of futility in all world literature.

The *kapores* ritual spun off some unusual subrituals of its own. A book published in 1734 in Moravia, then under Habsburg rule, recommends a sort of backwards *kapores* ceremony for gravely ill infants: "If a newborn child appears to be dead, take a hen and place her beak in the child's rectum. If God so wills it, the child will live and the chicken die."

The chicken came into its own as the standard *shabbes* fare in Eastern Europe around the end of the meat surplus in the mid-sixteenth century, when it became the buffalo of the Jewish people: Not a piece, not a part, went to waste. While there were solid economic reasons for this ascent to glory—the rising cost of meat, the chicken's relative cheapness and ubiquity, the bonus that came with hens in the form of eggs—there also seems to be something about the taste that appeals to the Yiddish palate. And we're not talking secret blends of herbs and spices. Samuel Chotzinoff, who came to the United States in 1906 at the age of seventeen (he was two years younger than Chagall, who came from the same town), describes the traditional bird: "I had known chicken exclusively in its austere boiled state, garnished with whole, waterlogged onions or accompanied by masses of noodles, the whole swimming in an overgenerous supply of broth."

This is classic *bubbie*-style chicken, the path-of-least-effort tasteless mass that explains why such *bubbies* found *Father Knows Best* entertaining rather than bland and why chicken soup has always had a greater mystique than the bird itself: It's where most of the taste, and apparently all of the virtue, ended up. Gizzards (*pipkes* in Yiddish), feet, any neck that wasn't being stuffed, all ended up in the soup pot.

It's hard to blame those *bubbies*, though; a chicken demanded a real commitment of time and effort. A woman would go to the market and check a few chickens, picking each one up by the legs and blowing on the feathers near its rear end. As her breath separated the feathers, she'd be able to see the skin and form an opinion as to the age and schmaltz content of the bird. She'd pick one out and have it slaughtered. If she was in America and the chickens had already been killed, she'd try a few by pressing her index finger against the chicken's breastbone; the springier the flesh, the younger the bird. Once she got the chosen one home, she would scald it quickly, let it cool until the wing feathers could be pulled out easily, and then get down to the plucking. The bigger feathers were pulled out by hand, the pinfeathers with the help of a tool, and the remaining hairs were singed away. Gas burners, alcohol lamps, even candles would all do the trick, and I have vague memories of overhearing heated discussions of the pros and cons of the different methods when I was very young.

The chicken must now be cleaned and *kashered*, according to the steps laid out in Chapter Three. The hours of soaking and salting attendant on the *kashering* process give the woman time to feed the kids, clean the house, and begin to prepare the rest of the food needed for the Sabbath. *This* could well be the reason why so many of those old ladies were content to throw a chicken into a pot and then walk away. Boiling a chicken in Europe also freed up oven space—if there *was* any oven space at home—for the other dishes that had to be made.

Chicken plucking as an activity commanded little respect— the Anglo-Yiddish "chicken flicker" is a term of opprobrium for a nobody who's not even very good at being a nobody—the very sort of person that you are not: "What do you think I am, some kind of chicken flicker? First pay me, then I'll finish the job." Low as plucking ranked on the Yiddish scale of activities, though, no one could deny its necessity. Not only could feathered chickens not be eaten, but goose feathers were essential household items. Every year around

Chanukah time, right after the big goose slaughter, women would organize plucking bees. These tend not to get much attention in Yiddish literature, but Hirsh Abramovitch, a Yiddish writer and scholar who was born in 1881, provides a description that also sheds a fair bit of light on social relations in late nineteenth- or early twentieth-century Lithuania:

> At the feather plucking people told wonderful tales that had been handed down as traditional, or new ones that they had heard somewhere or other or even got from a storybook. Non-Jewish women from the neighborhood would also be invited, and everybody sang songs—Yiddish, Lithuanian, Polish, Belorussian and Russian. . . . Plucking feathers was a well-established tradition in every Jewish family. Sacks or pillowcases would be filled with feathers plucked from geese, and sometimes from ducks. Poor families would often get their feathers from roosters and hens. Every daughter had to be supplied with bedding, that is, pillows and featherbeds. The girl whose wedding was closest would do her utmost to pluck as many feathers as possible, so that she would be able to show off her bedding.

Little as we might think we have in common with people whose matrimonial prospects could be materially affected by a bad goose harvest, the effort to understand a world in which outfitting yourself for that marriage was also a means of preparing food and maintaining friendly relations with neighboring members of other communities is worth a little effort. This is what organic is really supposed to mean, and a single bad goose year could change people's lives. The lack of goose schmaltz could affect more than the taste of latkes during the upcoming Chanukah, and possibly even bring about a reversion to latkes made of cheese. The menu for the entire year could be affected: A shortage of goose fat could lead to a run on chickens, which could drive up their price—making chickens and their schmaltz harder to acquire—and produce significant changes in the usual *shabbes* and holiday menus, not to mention the quality of the local bedding, especially among newlyweds. Cancellation of the feather-plucking bees could have an adverse effect on intercommunity relations. Blizzards of feathers wafting through the air and onto the ground are among the most iconic images of pogroms: Attackers would rip open comforters and pillows, shake their contents out the windows and scatter them through the houses, as if to deny the possibilities of harmonious coexistence held out by the bees and deprive marriageable girls of their trousseaus, leading at least temporarily to a decline in the Jewish birthrate. A non-Jewish participant in feather-plucking parties could well prevail on her husband to leave that nice Mrs. Abramovitch and her friends alone. It's no wonder, then, that poultry figures so prominently in the Ashkenazi worldview. Every chicken, every goose, was a walking, clucking, honking sign of a whole communal and religious ecology.

TREATS AND DESSERT

In accordance with the rabbinic dictum that anything edible can qualify as a Saturday delight as long as it's been purchased or prepared with *shabbes* in mind, *shabbes* treats, both desserts and casual snacks, have been part of the Sabbath experience for centuries. Long before the advent of packaged snack foods, kids would look forward to *shabbes oyps*—*shabbes* fruit—as a more child-friendly Sabbath delight than calf's-foot jelly. Often fresh, sometimes dried, the fruit was occasionally accompanied by nuts. Aside from the fruit compote, which can seem rather redundant to someone who's just eaten a *tsimmes* that includes many of the same ingredients, the more prominent *shabbes* confections tended to be baked. Effort and expense aside, there was no compelling reason to confine such treats to the Sabbath, but their function as food for fun in a world where dessert was a very sometime thing meant that they tended to be associated with special occasions and uncommon conviviality. Virtually none of the dainties that we're about to look at is really thought of as *shabbes* food, but any of them was likely to appear toward the close of a Sabbath meal.

One of the oldest such treats, still popular today in somewhat altered form, came to the medieval Jewish snack menu from a most unlikely source. The *oblata*, the most Catholic-sounding of all Jewish dishes, takes its name from the past participle of a Latin verb meaning "to offer" and originally referred to an unconsecrated host wafer. The Roman host is made of unleavened wheat flour baked into a wafer in an iron mold (Orthodox and Eastern Catholic Churches add yeast to symbolize the resurrection); it lent its name to similar-looking, highly un-Jewish pastries—cookies, if you will—that were baked with eggs and sometimes sweetened with honey. Such *oblatn* are still widely available in Germany and there is even an American company, based, appropriately, in New Germany, Minnesota, that specializes in their production. Sales to Jews are probably nugatory, but Jews in medieval France and Germany bought *oblatn* from non-Jews and also baked them themselves. According to Rashi, *oblatn* were like tiny wafer sandwiches filled with spices, almonds, and nuts. Though popular in France and Germany, *oblatn* do not appear to have made much headway with Jews in Eastern Europe, despite the popularity of the *oplatek*, the Polish version of the *oblata*, on Christmas Eve; they don't seem to have recognized the word when they encountered it in Hebrew texts from the West. While not all authorities allowed *oblatn* to be bought from gentiles—because of the rules about gentile cooking, rather than their all-too-obvious connection with the Mass—no one had any problems with *oblatn* baked by Jews. Guides to blessings even specify which are to be made over thin *oblatn* and which over thick.

Along with their genealogical link to ice cream wafers (which, as *vafelim*, are quite popular in Israel), these strictly kosher communion wafers prefigure equally kosher chocolate Easter bunnies, Easter Eggs, Santa Clauses, and plain old crosses by nearly a millennium and would have turned Yalso, who wanted to eat milk with meat in Chapter Three, green with envy. They also give us a pretty clear picture of the degree to which Jews can allow themselves to be influenced by their neighbors. As long as non-Jewish religious references could be removed, forgotten, or ignored, there was no barrier to adopting the basic recipe (much as the Church had done in transforming matzoh into hosts). Eating real communion wafers, though, even if they were unconsecrated, would have been another matter entirely, especially in light of the accusations of host desecration that became so popular in the thirteenth and fourteenth centuries, and that might have had something to do with the disappearance of *oblatn* from the Jewish menu. You know that there has been a radical break with the European past when Lang's Chocolates of Williamsport, Pennsylvania can offer "1 oz. Easter Crosses, Certified Kosher-Dairy & Certified Halal," in addition to kosher (and halal) Easter bunnies, Easter eggs, and full-sized Easter rabbits. Just the thing to give your seder an ecumenical bang. I'm waiting for a kosher-for-Passover version of the traditional Christmas fruitcake made with matzoh-meal honey cake and plenty of finely chopped prunes. I already know which blessing to make.

As venerable as the *oblata*, if not indeed older, *flodn* is basically a protocheesecake: layers of dough with sweetened cheese between them. When mentioned at all these days, it's usually called *fludn*, in accordance with the Yiddish spoken by the Jews of Hungarian origin who still eat it on a regular basis. But throughout the Middle Ages, *flodn* can be said to have ruled. We have references to it as far back as the tenth century, and by no less a personage than Rabbi Gershom, The Light of the Exile, one of the most influential rabbinic figures since the destruction of the Second Temple and the spiritual father of Ashkenazi Judaism. The near nonexistent waiting periods between meat and dairy discussed earlier made *flodns* a popular dessert on *shabbes* and holidays. Since desserts tended to come only with festive meals that also involved meat, cheese *flodns* receded in popularity after the near-universal adoption of the six-hour waiting period. Parve fruit *flodns* made with apples, plums, raisins, and other fruit have been holding their own for eleven hundred years, though. Elzet mentions a *khosn-flodn*, a bridegroom *flodn*, from Bessarabia, filled with farfel fried in honey and eaten not at weddings, but on the Sabbath immediately preceding Passover, when the Lord betrothed the Children of Israel to Himself. Jews from Hungary still make *flodns*, usually with apples, nuts, and poppy seeds, but the cheese *flodn* has all but disappeared from the standard menu.

Its place has been taken by cheesecake, basically a *flodn* of firmer cheese with all but the bottom layer of pastry removed. Where the cottage-type cheese in a European *flodn* needed a sturdy crust to keep it in place, the American—more properly, New York—cheesecake is firm enough to be self-supporting, thanks to an almost entirely nontraditional list of ingredients. Only sour cream could have been found in Europe, and it is the least important of the three; the cream cheese and the graham crackers used for the crust are purely American creations. These impeccably goyish ingredients—think of sour cream as the one Jewish family on a street where everyone else is either Lutheran or Methodist—were put together by Jewish restaurateurs whose original clientele was largely, though not exclusively, Jewish, and provide a perfect, if unwitting, illustration of one way that a new dish, one with no associations at all, can still be born Jewish: ingredients that are common in a given country or geographical area are combined in a novel way by Jews, who pass the results along.

Arnold Reuben, who also gave himself credit for the Reuben sandwich, claimed to have invented New York cheesecake by substituting cream cheese for cottage in a recipe that he took home from a dinner party. When he started serving this new creation in his Jewish-oriented delicatessen at about the same time as Leo Lindemann began to offer a similar cheesecake at Lindy's—using either his own recipe or one borrowed from Reuben, depending on whom you believe—the cheesecake absorbed the Jewish associations of its native environment. A cake you've never seen served in a place that serves blintzes and gefilte fish is going to look somehow Jewish: Jews assume that anything they eat with gefilte fish is Jewish and develop proprietary feelings toward the dish; non-Jews from New York assume that anything they eat at a place that also serves gefilte fish is Jewish, and see the dish as yet another ethnic specialty that they can even eat with the bacon and soft-shell crabs that were also on the menu at Lindy's; tourists from the hinterland think that anything that they eat in a restaurant immortalized by Damon Runyon and mentioned by people like Walter Winchell must be typical New York fare. And so, as Kurt Vonnegut used to say, it goes. A dish with no claim to tradition introduced in restaurants with strong Jewish associations became a prime symbol of America at its most urbane for everybody except Jews and their immediate neighbors, for whom it acquired an instant Jewish heritage. Apart from the identification with New York or America, this is roughly what happened with such European pastries as strudel, babka, and even Danish, which only Jews think of as Jewish, the difference being that none of the latter is of Jewish origin. In areas with no German, Austrian, or specifically East European bakeries, the Jewish ones were the only places to buy such things, which then assumed an ethnicity that they would never have dared claim in Europe.

Thanks in no small part to the success of Sara Lee, cheesecake has been so completely assimilated into the mainstream American diet that Penny on *The Big Bang Theory* can work in The Cheesecake Factory and never have to explain what cheesecake is. The restaurant's name says something, but with locations in Kuwait, Dubai, and Abu Dhabi, it definitely doesn't say "Jewish."

O*blatn* and cheese *flodns* have had their day. For centuries now, first place, top of the charts, the little black dress of the Yiddish treat has been sponge or honey cake, known in Yiddish as *lekach*. The name and the cake both come from the German *Lebkuchen*, yet another Christmas-oriented progenitor of typically Jewish food. But where today's *Lebkuchen* are usually quite heavy on ginger, traditional Yiddish honey *lekach* rarely gets fancier than chopped nuts or the occasional raisin, while the sponge variety is just that: a simple sponge cake.

The honey cake came first. All early references to *lekach* that make any mention of ingredients include honey, but the original does not seem to have borne much resemblance to the honey *lekach* that we eat today, as this thirteenth-century recipe, taken from a guide to religious customs, indicates: "The cake is prepared from three measures of fine flour . . . one mixes into it honey, oil, and milk." This is a far cry from modern recipes, which often feature brandy or even rum, which was completely unknown in medieval Europe; coffee, which was likewise unknown; sugar and various spices, all of which were rare and very expensive. Nor could it be baked without the help of such chemical leavening agents as baking powder or baking soda, which help lend the cake its springiness. Eggs, which are also there to help the dough rise and which certainly existed in the middle ages, are also absent. It's no wonder that most early authorities considered *lekach* subject to the *hamoytse* blessing for bread, as long as it contained no spices.

Mordecai Kosover lists five different kinds of *lekach*: plain, extra honey, *lekach* made from rye flour, bread *lekach* from dark rye flour, and sugar *lekach*. A recipe for an apparently typical early-modern honey cake appears in Pauline Wengeroff's *Memoirs of a Grandmother*, an invaluable portrait of Jewish life in nineteenth-century Russia. Wengeroff (1833–1916) describes how her husband's grandmother added white honey and ginger to rye flour. She would then take bits of dough from the mixture and knead nuts into them, rubbing and pulling at each piece until it slipped easily through her fingers. Once the whole mixture had been kneaded with nuts, she poured it into a bake pan and put it in the oven.

Arguments over what constitutes *lekach* were as popular among a certain set of Yiddish speakers as fights about whether windows in the synagogue should be open or closed. In many areas of Eastern Europe, *lekach* on its own—for the last 150 or 200 years, at any rate—meant sponge cake; if you wanted honey cake, you had to specify by calling it *honig-lekach*. People from other regions understood *lekach* only as honey cake, although those whom I've had occasion to ask did not seem to know of a separate word for plain old sponge cake. It would seem that as tastes began to change and honey became less prominent in the general diet, sponge cake came to the fore in some areas—especially those in which sugar now played a major role in general cookery—and simply took over the name reserved for what Claudia Roden has called "the all-purpose Jewish cake."

With honey or without, *lekach* has been ubiquitous in Yiddish social life for the better part of a millennium. By the early thirteenth century, it had been promoted from a casual snack to an essential element of certain rites of passage. Eleazar of Worms, known as Ha-Rokeach (no relation to the soap company) after the title of his magnum opus, describes how little boys were taken to school for the first time on Shavuos and set down on the teacher's lap. The teacher would take out a tablet with the Hebrew alphabet written on it in regular and reverse order, along with three scriptural verses appropriate to the occasion. He would go through the alphabet twice, once forwards and once backwards, reading out the names of the letters and having the child repeat them, pointing to each letter as he did so. Finally, they would go through the biblical verses word by word. Then the teacher . . .

> . . . *puts a bit of honey onto the table and the boy licks up the honey that is on the letters with his tongue. Then they bring out a honey cake, on which is written, "The Lord God gave me a skilled tongue, to know how to speak timely words to the weary.*

*Morning by morning, He rouses, He rouses my ear to give heed
like disciples. The Lord God opened my ears, and I did not
disobey, I did not run away." [Is 50:4–5, JPS] The teacher reads
each word of these biblical verses and the boy repeats them. Then
they bring out a peeled egg on which is written, "He said to me,
'Mortal, eat what is offered you; eat this scroll, and go speak to
the House of Israel.' So I opened my mouth, and He gave me this
scroll to eat, as He said to me, 'Mortal, feed your stomach and fill
your belly with this scroll that I give you.' I ate it, and it tasted
as sweet as honey to me." [Ez 3:1–3, JPS] The teacher reads each
word and the boy repeats it. Then they give the boy the cake and
the egg, for it [the egg] is good for opening the heart.*

Forget about the size of the cake; the real question is how they
got all that writing onto a single egg. Those biblical verses are no
shorter in Hebrew than they are in English, but there were giants
on the earth in those days, and nothing is too difficult for a heart
that is open. A couple of other roughly contemporary accounts of
this ritual have survived; the basic features of honey cake and egg
remain the same, but the biblical verses change. According to the
Talmud (*Horayos* 13b), eating a roasted egg is good for the memory, and later mystical practices noted by historian Ivan Marcus involve inscribing magical formulae on both eggs and cakes, though
not on honey cakes.

Lekach was still commonly used in first-day-of-school rituals well
into the nineteenth century, long after it had come to stand for conviviality and good times. *Makhn a lekakh mit bronfn,* "making a
lekach-and-liquor," can still sometimes be heard as a synonym for
putting on a *simkhe*—a bar mitzvah luncheon, for instance—or at
least a congregational kiddush. *Lekach* and whiskey were the scotch
and soda of the Yiddish-speaking world; the *lekach* was often dipped
into the whiskey before being eaten, a mixture that works much better with sponge than honey cake. I can still recall old men in the

shuls I went to as a kid who would always take two shot glasses of whiskey after the morning service: one for drinking and one for dunking. Or, as they tended to put it, "One for me and one for the *lekach*." It isn't called sponge cake for nothing.

Lekach was the visible sign of festivity and was served "at every celebration, large or small, weddings, engagement parties, circumcisions, redemptions of the first born, the completion of a Torah scroll or of studying a tractate of Talmud." If Paddy Chayefsky had written *Marty* in Yiddish, the question that haunts the title character would have been, "When you gonna give *lekach*, Marty?"

Since *lekach* requires no yeast, it is quite easy to adapt for Passover. Matzoh or potato flour are substituted for the wheat, and egg whites are used to get the air into it. I had never given it much thought until Fred Levy, an accountant in Toronto, told me of a kid with whom he went to public school in Hamilton, Ontario, who would bring lunch to school on Pesach. Instead of the usual depressing out-of-the-house Passover lunch of a hard-boiled egg sans inscription and two pieces of matzoh with something or other smeared between to make sure they're nice and soggy by lunchtime, this kid turned up with a sandwich: egg salad on Passover sponge cake. I'll never pack a matzoh lunch again.

Often served with *lekach* these days, *mandelbroyt* (or *komish-*, or *kamish-*, or *kamis-broyt*), is often compared with biscotti. Although both are baked twice, the Jewish cookies are not quite as heavy as the Italian. The difference, if any, between *mandel-* and *komishbroyt* is another highly contentious question of nomenclature: In some areas, twice-baked loaves of almond cookies were known as *mandelbroyt,* in others the same thing was called *komishbroyt*. *Mandelbroyt* is still widely known as *komishbroyt* in Winnipeg, even among people who otherwise know no Yiddish at all.

As traditional as *mandelbroyt*, the *rugelah* is another highly popular cookie with no significant folkloric attachments, even though it is traditional to eat it on Chanukah. *Rugelach* are crescent or horn-shaped cookies of such seemingly universal appeal that they could well become the most successful Jewish crossover since the bagel. It might have something to do with the cream-cheese dough that's become so popular over here and that gives the *rugelah* the feel, and sometimes even the taste, of a cinnamon bun. Maybe it's the wide range of possible fillings: walnuts, pecans, cinnamon, and poppy seeds are only some of the more common. Many bakers use lekvar or more American jams. Chocolate joined the club fairly recently, and Nutella followed soon in its wake. Although more traditional *rugelach* are often made with butter or sour-cream dough, those that I was unfortunate enough to grow up with were made with parve pastry dough indifferently stuffed with farfelized nuts and whatever the bakery had too much of. I didn't like them. I wouldn't eat them. I, who crushed a prune hamantasch into my kid sister's hair, once resisted a suggestion to put a *rugelah* on her pillow. It would have been going too far.

And the rest of the world loves them. Myself, I preferred the same bakery's blueberry buns. Like *mandel-* and *komishbroyt*, buns filled with fruit were a popular treat that changed names from locality to locality while retaining the same basic concept, in this case a fruit filling wrapped in chala or pastry dough. The Toronto blueberry bun provides an excellent example of the vagaries of nomenclature, not to mention the permutations of traditional pastry in North America.

Wildly popular as blueberries have become in contemporary Poland, they are indigenous to North America and seem not to have been cultivated on a large scale in Europe until 1923, when they began to be grown in Holland and Germany. Although I have seen claims that blueberries have been grown "on a commercial scale" in Poland since the 1870s, it is difficult to determine whether these were the North American variety or the smaller bilberries, which are not uncommon in Europe and grow wild all over Poland. Fine points of species aside, one or the other—or perhaps even both—of these berries was popular in Poland between the two world wars. Mayer Kirshenblatt, who left Poland for Canada in 1934, talks about one of the local bakers' "*shtritslekh*, blueberry buns, [which] were extraordinary: lots of blueberries, thin dough, full of juice."

Whether these were blueberries or bilberries, the buns sound very much like *jagodzianki*, the bilberry buns that are "all over Poland" today and were popular enough in the late teens and twenties of the last century for Annie Kaplansky, the Polish-born founder of Toronto's Health Bread Bakery, to start baking and selling them in 1928, thereby putting Toronto onto the world Jewish food map: These buns don't seem to be sold anywhere else, and most non-Torontonians have never heard of them. Kaplansky's son says, "I think my mother used to make blueberry buns in Poland."

Although we have no Polish recipes for the *shtritslekh* described by Mayer Kirshenblatt—which were also called *shtritslekh* by other Jewish immigrants in Toronto—the recipe popularized by Matthew Goodman a few years ago does not differ significantly from a recipe for Polish *jagodzianki* that I was able to find online; both consist of a sweetened yeast dough stuffed with berries, brushed with an egg wash, and sprinkled with sugar.

From a food history point of view, the most interesting thing about the Toronto blueberry bun—aside from the fact that it seems never to have been made commercially anywhere else in Canada or the USA—is its name. A *shtritsl*—*shtritslekh* is the plural—was a Polish-Yiddish designation for an unbraided chala loaf, "wide in the middle and narrow at the ends"—an accurate description of the Toronto blueberry product: a *yagde shtritsl* would be a small unbraided loaf with berries. The buns in Kirshenblatt's hometown must have looked enough like an unbraided chala to be graced with its name. Over here, where almost no one called a loaf-shaped chala a *shtritsl*, the term lost its association with *shabbes* just as certainly as the *oblata* once lost its connection to the Catholic host.

EIGHT

Pancakes, Crepes, and Sexy Baking
Other Holiday Foods

CHANUKAH AND SHAVUOS

It might look like an incongruous coupling: Chanukah, the post-biblical semiholiday that takes place around the winter solstice and commemorates the miracle of a single cruse of oil that lasted for eight days, wouldn't seem to have much in common with Shavuos, or Pentecost as it's sometimes called in English, the Torah-mandated festival of first fruits on which the Jews received the Torah (and when tongues of fire rested upon the Apostles in the New Testament Book of Acts). As one of the three pilgrim festivals, Shavuos is attended by the same restrictions as the Sabbath, except for the latter's ban on cooking and carrying. You can cook on Shavuos, as long as the oven is already on and you don't adjust the temperature. You can't drive, ride a horse, turn electricity on or off, touch money, write, or go skeet shooting. On Chanukah, you can do whatever a Jew is allowed to do, except on that part of the eight-day holiday that falls on Saturday.

The one thing, possibly the only thing, they have in common is that both have been closely linked with dairy. As Moses Isserles puts it, "There are those who say that cheese should be eaten on Chanukah because the miracle [of deliverance] was effected through the milk that Judith gave the enemy to eat." The apocryphal story of Judith and Holofernes has long been associated with the Maccabeean struggle against the Greeks. Judith, the Jewish heroine whose actions are based on those of Jael in the Book of Judges, deliberately stuffs the randy Holofernes with milk and cheese in order to make him drowsy; once he has fallen asleep, she decapitates him and makes off with his head.

Until the second half of the nineteenth century, when potatoes became ubiquitous in Eastern Europe, most Chanukah latkes were made from the same curd cheese that still finds its way into blintzes on Shavuos. A 1956 recipe for cheese latkes calls for a half pound of dry cottage cheese, six eggs, four tablespoons of flour, and a pinch of salt. Eight days is a long time to eat nothing but cheese, though; buckwheat latkes were also popular and, when the fixings could be found, latkes made of distinctly nondairy brains, as if the Maccabees had also defeated the zombies. Made with matzoh meal instead of flour, these crêpes *cérébrales* were even more popular on Passover as a fancier version of the matzoh-meal latkes called *chremslach*. Brains, in fritters and latkes, fried by themselves or along with scrambled eggs, were a common Yiddish dish until relatively recently; you just had to be sure to remove the membrane before cooking.

Those who wanted dairy potato latkes would fry them in almond oil, but potato latkes were more commonly *fleyshik*, often eaten with *gribenes* and fried in schmaltz. Chanukah was when geese were slaughtered for winter, and the schmaltz would flow like wine. The yearly release of the schmaltz nouveau seems to underlie the now widespread idea that we're supposed to eat greasy food on Chanukah to commemorate the miracle of the unexhausted oil. But the Maccabees didn't drink the oil. The miracle of the oil explains why we light candles, which for many people are not wax tapers but small glass or metal containers that hold wicks floating in olive oil. Although Isserles, as we have seen, mentions eating dairy on Chanukah, the *Shulkhan Arukh* is silent about any obligation to induce acid reflux. The chocolate latkes introduced by Bartons in 1951 are no more or less halachically valid than the slightly more nourishing potato variety; those made by Gayle's Chocolates of Royal Oak, Michigan actually look pretty good. "Oy, they're so good!" reads the ad. "Sixteen mouth-watering chocolate latkes. . . . Premium dark chocolate poured over crunchy potato chips and formed to look just like the latkes grandma made. (No offense, but they probably taste better.)." They've got the potatoes, but lack any sign of rabbinic approval. The same company also makes dark chocolate yarmulkes and chocolate-covered Oreos topped with crosses—everything but chocolate e-meters.

Although there is a large and not terribly convincing apocrypha devoted to explaining why we eat dairy on Shavuos, Gil Marks's explanation in his *Encyclopedia of Jewish Food* probably comes closer to the truth. This late spring festival "corresponds," he says, "to the time of the year when young animals are able to graze and dairy products are in abundance." Cheese *flodns* were once as common on Shavuos as cheesecake is today, but the Shavuos dish par excellence is, of course, the blintz, which has only increased in popularity since Jews borrowed it from their Slavic neighbors sometime around the fifteenth century. Described in *The Joseph Jacobs Handbook of Familiar Jewish Words and Expressions* as "Crepe Suzette with a Yiddish accent," the blintz—*blintse* in Yiddish—consists of a *bletl*, literally a leaf, of wheat or, less frequently (much less frequently these days), buckwheat flour mixed with eggs and sugar and fried in butter, if dairy, or schmaltz, if not. The *bletl* is fried on one side, filled, and rolled up—not too tightly, according to Jerry Seinfeld.

Because of their close association with sour cream and Shavuos, many of us tend to think of blintzes as strictly *milkhik*, but as Marks also points out, "Traditional blintz fillings include curd cheese, mashed potatoes, kasha, chopped cooked beef, chopped liver, and fruit, or a combination of cheese and fruit." Cheese is still the filling most commonly associated with blintzes, though, and there are many blintz fans who have never heard of, let alone eaten, a meat or mashed-potato blintz.

The term *blintzkrieg*—blintz war, a play on the Nazi blitzkrieg—
has become a little stale over the past seventy years, but it was fresh
and funny when first used by The Three Stooges in 1940's *You
Nazty Spy!* Moe, as Hitler, says, "We'll start a *blintzkrieg*," to which
Curly, playing Hermann Goering, replies, "I just love blintzes,
especially with sour *krieg*." The same play on blitz and blintz comes
up with reference to football in a 2013 episode of *The Big Bang Theory* where Howard, the Jewish character, actually says, "I love a good
blitz, especially with sour cream," thus proving that a good Jewish
joke never dies.

Blintzes, as already mentioned, were once commonly made with
buckwheat flour rather than wheat. Buckwheat latkes were sometimes eaten on Chanukah to relieve the monotony induced by eight
days of cheese and/or potatoes, and buckwheat with noodles was
frequently seen at both Chanukah and Purim meals, though it was
also the sort of thing that could pop up at any *shabbes* or holiday
meal, or even during the week. Buckwheat, the quinoa of Jewish
cuisine, is technically a fruit rather than a grain and plays a major
part in East European Jewish cooking. It was made into flour, or
toasted and used in groat form; *retshinikes*, buckwheat cakes, were
once fairly popular (*retshene* is Yiddish for buckwheat). The groats
are still used to stuff kishka and knishes, and are indispensable to
the popular noodle dish, kasha *varnishkes*. Although the term kasha technically refers to any type of porridge, when it is used without any qualifying adjective in Yiddish, it is assumed to refer to the
buckwheat kasha still widely available in supermarkets and health-
food stores.

Buckwheat kasha was probably the second most widely consumed staple of the East European Jewish diet, and was even put
out for birds in winter; only bread was more common. The simplest
way of preparing it is to boil it in water, as if it were oatmeal. The
most common recipe, though, involves schmaltz and onions, lead-

ing most Yiddish-speakers to think of kasha as a *fleyshike* dish. To say that someone eats *kashe mit maslinke*—kasha with buttermilk—implies that there's something a little off about them, that while there is nothing that you can quite put your finger on, their general conduct or demeanor gives you reason to suspect that they are not on the doctrinal up and up. It's the kind of phrase that Fox News, were it ever to broadcast in Yiddish, would be hurling at Democrats every day.

In a slightly different vein, ill-paying work is said to yield *vaser af kashe*, "water for kasha," but not enough for the kasha itself. *Farkokhn a kashe*, to "cook up a porridge," is to land yourself or someone else in yet another fine mess. And people who take no crap from anyone are said not to let anyone spit in their kasha. According to another saying, *Ver es git nisht tsushtayer, tor nisht in der kashe araynshpayen*, "If you haven't contributed, you're not allowed to spit in the kasha"—you can't criticize an enterprise in which you refused to take part. In Czarist times there was also *kashe gelt*, kasha money, which Jewish communities were forced to raise in order to provide locally garrisoned soldiers with the kasha that constituted their basic ration.

After kugel, kasha with *varnishkes*—often called kasha with bows, or bow ties with kasha in English—is probably the most popular of all Yiddish noodle dishes. *Varnishkes* come from the Ukrainian *vareniki*, which are small stuffed dumplings—kreplach, in other words. Jews were too busy stuffing poultry necks, kishkas, blintzes, kreplach, hamantaschen, and knishes to want to stuff *vareniki*, too, so they cooked the ingredients side by side. As we have seen, a similar impatience with the act of stuffing played a role in the history of gefilte fish. The bow tie shape of today's *varnishkes* is an American innovation introduced by A. Goodman & Sons, whose pioneering role in the kosher egg-noodle industry made the company more than just another matzoh bakery.

Kashe mit varnishkes is a fairly simple dish; aside from the principals, it needs schmaltz, onion, and chicken stock. It pops up surprisingly often on *Seinfeld*. In the episode about the doorman, George complains to Kramer that his father, who is living with him, cooks kasha that stinks up the whole house. In another episode, Jerry complains about the smell in George's parents' home: "Dandruff, kasha, mothballs, cheap carpeting"—and George isn't even supposed to be Jewish. The *varnishkes* finally come in when Rabbi Glickman offers Elaine, who is upset over George's engagement, some kasha *varnishkes*.

Our final Chanukah treat is the still-popular pastry known in Yiddish as a *pompeshke*. Ukrainian *pampushky*, like Polish *pączki*, are deep-fried and holeless, much like jelly doughnuts, and filled with poppy seeds or fruit jam. (There is a second type of Ukrainian *pampushok* that is baked, but it is more in the nature of a garlic roll and is served, unstuffed, with borscht.) While the Roman Catholic Poles eat *pączki* on Fat Thursday, the Thursday before Lent, Ukrainians, most of whom are members of the Orthodox Church, traditionally serve *pampushky* on Christmas Eve. They must have looked good enough to give their Jewish neighbors ideas; Christmas and Chanukah usually fall in fairly close proximity, and the Jews began to make their own *pompeshkes* on Chanukah, changing the recipe only to keep from frying the doughnuts in lard. They are known today by their Hebrew name, *sufganiyot*, and, dusted with granulated sugar, are generally thought of as an Israeli or Israeli-style treat. They were, however, very popular among Jews in Poland and Ukraine, whose descendants would probably turn several different colors if anyone were to present them with a flaming plum pudding in honor of the miracle that kept the menorah burning for eight whole days.

The link between doughnuts and Chanukah was reinforced at the other end of the Ashkenazi world, where Jews in German-speaking countries had long since embraced the deep-fried *Berliner*

Pfannkuchen (the thing that John F. Kennedy claimed to be when he declared, *"Ich bin ein Berliner"*; today I am a Chanukah treat) that non-Jewish Germans were accustomed to eat on New Year's Eve.

PURIM

The hamantasch is an open-faced triangular pocket of yeast or cookie dough filled with fruit, nuts, or preserves that is traditionally eaten on Purim, when Queen Esther and her uncle outwitted the evil Haman, who was planning a legally sanctioned massacre that would have left the Persian Empire *Judenrein*. The most common fillings are prune, poppy seed, and chopped walnut, though more up-to-date fillings have been available for many years. I have seen and tasted hamantaschen into which Marshmallow Fluff has been lovingly spooned after baking, though without the peanut butter necessary for a Fluffy Hamanutter.

Hamantaschen—pronounced *homon-tashn* in Yiddish—were originally *mon-tashn*, poppy-seed pockets. The similarity between *mon*—poppy seeds—and *Homon* led to the name change, and with it a raft of after-the-fact attempts to explain what the pastry had to do with the villain of the Purim story. Variously said to represent Haman's ears and nose, his hat, and even his pockets, hamantaschen are more convincingly explained by a pun on the various biblical verses in which the Children of Israel are said to have eaten *ha-mon*, the manna, which would also help to explain the popularity of the poppy seed filling: Haman and *ha-mon* are spelled alike in Hebrew.

German and Dutch Jews took the pun one step further and began to make gingerbread Hamans—instead of *ha-mon*, they ate Homon himself, as if in fulfillment of these biblical verses and also as a reminder of what the Lord Who had us eat the gods of Egypt finally does to our adversaries.

Yiddish slang associates the hamantasch with two other well-known, though not especially festal, Yiddish dishes that also involve a filling wrapped in dough. Closely related to kreplach, pierogis—which most people tend to think of as Polish or Ukrainian, rather than Jewish—were once eaten quite widely by people who never dreamed of not keeping kosher. These crescent-moon-shaped pockets of dough were filled with meat or fish, kasha, potatoes, or other vegetables and served with fried onions and sour cream. *Milkhike* pierogis, not surprisingly known as *pirogn* in Yiddish, were once a staple in Catskill hotels and Jewish dairy restaurants, but seem to have fallen off the menu of most contemporary Jewish eating places.

Another stuffed, grain-based food, the knish was originally fried, but has been baked like pastry for the past century and a half or so, anticipating the "baked not fried" selling point of so many of today's other healthy low-cal snacks. There's nothing low-cal about a knish, though; its major health benefit lies in being too heavy for anyone of normal constitution to be able to eat more than two at a time—and two is already a superset. This Jewish Cornish pasty—cheap, filling, and designed for dirty hands—was once a real street food, sold from carts like hot dogs. Yonah Schimmel's knishery has been a fixture on lower Manhattan's Houston Street since 1910, unaffected by the fact that Schimmel (or *shiml*) means mold in Yiddish, and many New Yorkers of a certain age retain vivid memories of the knish men who used to set up outside their schools in time for the final bell.

The thick shell of dough is stuffed with the familiar ingredients: beef, liver, kasha, potatoes, or cheese. No one seems to dislike the result; there is a Yiddish saying, "To kill someone with a knish," which means to end up benefitting a person you were trying to harm. "He killed me with a knish"—I got the better of him without having to do anything but let him attack. If it isn't quite the Yiddish version of "hoist with his own petard," it is proof that for Yiddish, revenge is best served *fleyshik*.

Members of the rapidly dwindling cohort of people who grew up speaking Yiddish in Eastern Europe can sometimes be seen smiling or shaking their heads when someone asks, "Would you like a hamantasch?" or "How about a little knish?" Much as they probably appreciate the attention, that's not why they're grinning. The general appearance of the hamantasch and its cousins in geometry, the knish and pierogi, has given all three a special place in colloquial Yiddish as slightly coy vulgarisms for the human vulva, roughly equivalent to "pussy" or "beaver," neither of which is even vaguely kosher. *Pireg*–pierogi–is the most vulgar, hamantasch the cutest. Its triangular shape and varicolored stuffings make it a natural. Knish occupies the sort of middle ground that allows it to be used informally between consenting adults of either sex. People who wonder about the possibilities for erotic literature in contemporary Yiddish need only consider that Anaïs Nin's *Delta of Venus* would come out as *Love Hamantasch*, a great title for a B-52s song, but not the sort of thing to set pulses racing.

On the other side of the anatomical coin, there used to be a number of very different dishes known as *shkotsim*, young gentile boys, or *shkotsim mit mon*, young gentile boys with poppy seeds. Harkavy's dictionary defines them as "a kind of cakes with poppy seeds and honey." A slightly different recipe describes *kneydlekh* made of wheat-and-potato flour: "Round *kneydlekh* that we called *halkes*, or oblong ones that we called *shkotsim*, or flat *kneydlekh* like cookies that we called *shikses*." The ones with which I was familiar were a cross between the two: oblong strips of honey-glazed dough rolled up like cigars around a poppy-seed filling—and it is probably no accident that I had a grandmother who came from Lomza, the same part of Poland as the woman who described the *kneydlekh*. The name, as everyone recognized and no one ever mentioned, came from the finished product's resemblance to a gentile boy's uncircumcised member. There was nothing off-color or indelicate about it, and no one ever tried to avoid calling *shkotsim* by their name. The not-so-veiled allusion to centuries of ritual murder libels in which Jews were accused of killing Christian children to use their blood in baking makes the name a prime example of characteristically Yiddish irony. As to the flattened-out *shikse*, I have to admit that I've never had one.

NINE

———

Is That All There Is?
Weekday Food

THE BREAD OF GETTING BY

Fresh bread made of wheat tended to be a once-a-week treat; the rest of the time it was rye or, less frequently, barley. There were types of rye bread, degrees of light and dark, but virtually any nonchala loaf not qualified by the word barley can be assumed to have been made of rye, and far too many an East European *shabbes* began, faute de mieux, with a pair of meagre rye rolls. This preeminence was hardly a matter of choice. Rye is the main cereal crop in those areas of Eastern Europe that were most densely populated by Jews and was correspondingly inexpensive, especially in comparison with wheat. An 1894 guide to blessings published in Slovakia—slightly removed from the main centers of Jewish population—explains over which bread *hamoytse* is to be said when there's more than one loaf to choose from: Wheat takes precedence over barley or rye bread, barley comes before rye, and rye before oats. Most people, Jews and non-Jews alike, were subsisting on their third choice in a field of four.

The most common type of rye bread, the one with the highest proportion of rye flour, was called *razeve broyt*, literally "rye bread," but a rather different rye bread from anything found in a contemporary Jewish bakery, where rye bread actually contains more wheat flour than rye. *Razeve broyt* was usually baked—or at least prepared—at home and consisted of as much rye flour as rye bread can bear. The Yiddish writer and scholar Hirsh Abramovitch, our source for the feather-plucking bees, provides a detailed description of making such bread from single-grind rye flour:

> *The whole kernel was used—the bran, the starch, the germ, and*
> *everything else. Some flour and warm water were mixed together*
> *in a kneading trough and left to stand overnight, covered with*
> *a tablecloth which was covered in turn with a fur coat or a pillow.*
> *The warmth made the mixture start to ferment. Sometime before*
> *dawn, the sourdough was kneaded by hand for about three-*
> *quarters of an hour, while more flour and water were added.*
> *Once everything was thoroughly mixed, the trough was covered*
> *up again and left to stand somewhere warm for four or five hours*
> *until the mixture had risen, when it would be formed into loaves*
> *of between fifteen and twenty-five pounds . . . The loaves would*
> *sit in the oven for four to six hours, depending on their size.*
> *Women who didn't want the tops of their loaves to be*
> *black would sift rye flour in a thick sieve, mix the sifted flour*
> *with water, and smear it on the tops of the loaves before putting*
> *them into the oven . . . They called this mixture* kharmushke;
> *it gave the bread a "Jewish look," in contrast to gentile bread,*
> *which was "as black as coal."*

This is as far removed from the wheaty light rye served in most delicatessens today as the PGA is from miniputt. Our ancestors had guts of iron rather than abs of steel. Although twenty-five pounds sounds like a lot of rye bread, if the old saw that East European Jews ate an average of two pounds of rye bread a day is true, it would have lasted a family of four only half a week.

A nice, heavy, low-gluten bread like this has a relatively long shelf life and goes well with the sharpness of the sour and tangy foods favored by many Jews from Eastern Europe: sour cream, herring, sauerkraut, borscht, schmaltz-dipped onions and radishes, and pickled anything. Black bread dipped in sour cream was so closely identified with Jews from Lithuania, Belarus, and the formerly Lithuanian areas of Poland and Ukraine, that my father once accused my maternal grandparents of trying to make a Litvak of me when I came home from visiting them and asked to have some. No such combination had ever been seen in our home.

Pumpernickel or dark rye has been doing duty for *razeve broyt* in American Jewish bakeries for more than a century now. Made of rye meal or dark rye flour in a forty-sixty ratio with wheat flour, pumpernickel gets its characteristic dark hue by adding caramel color or molasses to the mix. It is subtler than *razeve broyt* and a good deal springier, but with more bran than the lighter deli ryes.

Razeve broyt was the food of poverty; people without the money to be poor would stretch their rye flour by grating potatoes into it. If even that was a stretch, what they finally ate was called *pisne*: dry bread, bread with nothing on it, the unwilling European counterpart to Elwood's order of dry white toast in *The Blues Brothers*.

The Jewish rye, so-called, that caught on in America, the stuff that comes with pastrami, began as a bread in which 30 to 40 percent of the flour was either medium or white rye, the most finely milled rye flour, with the rest coming from wheat. The mixture lets the rye shine through without taking over; the whiter the rye, the milder the taste. Caraway seeds are baked right into the dough and scattered on top of the loaf, lending the bread a fleeting savor of licorice or anise. When buying rye bread from a baker, rather than in a package, you would specify the kind you wanted, seedless or plain, otherwise it came with *kimmel*, as caraway seeds are called in Yiddish. If the usual amount of *kimmel* wasn't enough, you asked for double or—if you had a good enough baker—even triple *kimmel*. The 20-percent rye bread common in today's delis is lighter and less crusty than the 40-percent version and rarely seems to come with *kimmel.* It's a little pallid compared with its cousin, a sort of Pat Boone version of the other rye bread: whiter and nowhere near as Jewish.

Jewish-style ryes have been readily available in supermarkets for quite a while, but rye bread's real contribution to mainstream American culture comes not so much from the bread itself as from a series of advertisements for Levy's Real Jewish Rye, né Levy's Real Rye, that turned "You don't have to be Jewish" into a catchphrase that is still in use and made Levy's bread the first product to attract a non-Jewish public by emphasizing, or even overstating, its Jewishness. The campaign was helmed by Phyllis K. Robinson and Bill Bernbach, but the slogan itself was the work of copywriting legend Judy Protas. Photographed by Howard Zieff, who became a well-known Hollywood director, the campaign featured photos of obviously non-Jewish people—Irish, Italian, Native American, Chinese, African-American, and, most memorably, Buster Keaton (as if silent movie comedians were a race to themselves)—enjoying sandwiches made with Levy's rye, under the caption "You don't have to be Jewish." The rest of the message ("To love Levy's Real Jewish Rye") ran beneath the pictures.

The campaign not only resuscitated a dying brand, but the slogan lost no time entering the language. Suddenly, there were all kinds of things that you didn't have to be Jewish to do—generally, enjoy something that only Jews might have been thought able to appreciate, though I still treasure the memory of a protest button I bought in 1967 that said, "You don't have to be Jewish to oppose the war in Vietnam." The locus classicus for post-Levy use of the phrase is the 1965 gold record, *You Don't Have To Be Jewish*, written and produced by Bob Booker and George Foster. The album was a considerable mainstream hit and spawned a number of sequels, the first of which, *When You're In Love, The Whole World Is Jewish*, not only scored a Top 40 hit with Frank Gallup's "The Ballad of Irving"—which begins, "He was short and fat and rode out of the west," and was written by Frank Peppiatt and John Aylesworth, who later created *Hee Haw*—but also marks Valerie Harper's first appearance in a Jewish role; like Peppiatt, Aylesworth and Bob Booker, the producer and author of many of the sketches, Harper really *didn't* have to be Jewish. It's interesting, and not a little frightening, to think that if not for a series of ads for a rather undistinguished rye bread, *Hee Haw* might never have happened.

THE BAGEL: BEGINNINGS

If rugelach and chala have become moderately well known outside of the Jewish community, the bagel has managed the near unimaginable feat of actually becoming American, despite the fact that unless it's come hot from the oven, this "unsweetened doughnut with rigor mortis," as it has too often been called, has half the shelf life of a fruit fly, a best-before-date of fifteen minutes prior to purchase. More than any other food discussed in this book, the bagel has been the focus of a great deal of talk about authenticity: Can bagels be frozen without losing their character? Are blueberry or cinnamon-raisin swirl acceptable bagel flavors? Are flavors acceptable at all, and if so, why stop with onion and garlic? Are sesame seeds better than poppy seeds, or should a proper bagel be seedless?

Frivolous as they might seem, these questions have a lot to do with such larger issues as the differences between regional and national; ethnic and American; Jewish and non-Jewish; and the boundaries between all of these. Is a plain, frozen bagel purchased in a supermarket in Casper, Wyoming any more or less Jewish, any more or less authentic, than a fresh-baked whole-wheat pesto bagel at a Jewish bakery in Brooklyn?

To try to come up with an answer, the first thing we need to do is figure out just what a bagel really is. While most of us tend to associate bagels with rolls, buns, or even loaves of bread, the bagel's closest living relative is the pretzel, especially the kind of soft pretzel that has been popular in southern Germany for over a thousand years. Jews living in that area seem to have been as partial to pretzels as their gentile neighbors, perhaps because the basic ingredients—aside from the yeast, of course—could just as easily turn into matzoh. But the pretzel's real secret lies elsewhere: Once the dough has been kneaded and shaped, the pretzel-to-be is dipped into a solution of water and lye, the stuff that puts the lute into lutefisk, then dropped into boiling water for about half a minute before being baked. The lye makes the outside brown and crispy, but keeps the inside soft and moist, so that a pretzel can stay fresh for about as long as a bagel.

Pretzels are mentioned in a guide to circumcision written in the early thirteenth century by Gershom ben Yaakov, known as *Ha-Gozer*, The Clipper. He says, "The boy's father increases joy and feasting and festivity by sending gifts to all and sundry: rolls known as pretzels, and eggs." The father of a boy who has just been circumcised is supposed to throw a celebratory meal after the completion of the ceremony; the gifts here are clearly intended to provide that meal to those who were either unable to attend or—given the size of the average medieval house—unable to fit into the home in which the circumcision had taken place. The eggs, clearly hard-boiled if they're being sent all over town, represent the baby's entry into the world—Jews still use hard-boiled eggs to symbolize the circle of life—but it's the pretzels that make it a meal. Soft pretzels (as distinct from hard pretzel sticks, which fall into a different halachic category) are subject to the blessing of *hamoytse* and count as bread; you have to wash before eating them and say the long Grace after Meals once you've finished. By sending these fun little breads along with an egg, the father has sent meals all over town centuries before the first kosher pizza delivery, thereby giving all and sundry a share in the festivities that accompany circumcision.

The Slovakian guide to blessings groups bagels and pretzels together as foods that are boiled before being baked, but the parallels might extend even further. The earliest extant reference to bagels complements the idea of pretzels at a bris, albeit at a distance of nearly four hundred years. The 1610 bylaws of the Cracow Jewish community list bagels among the gifts that can be sent to a new mother and her helpers. Something about boiling before baking must have suggested a connection with birth, infant health, or the power to frighten or vanquish evil spirits bent on harming mother or child. No one seems to know quite how boiling and baking are connected with childbirth, but the similarity of the gifts is too striking for simple coincidence, especially since the circular nature of the bagel comes to the fore at the other end of the life cycle: Like hard-boiled eggs, bagels are traditionally served at the first meal after a funeral. Assuming that the father of the boy being circumcised could never have afforded to send a whole loaf of bread to everyone in town, we would still have expected some kind of *zeml*, a miniature version of whatever type of bread was associated with the Sabbath or festivals, rather than the considerably less-dignified pretzel. Likewise, the circumstances surrounding the birth of a child make it likely that the bagels mentioned in the Cracovian bylaws would have been made with eggs, heretical as this might sound to bagel purists, for the simple reason that egg bagels are not subject to *hamoytse* and thus require neither washing nor a lengthy after-blessing, both of which would probably have come as a relief to a group of exhausted women living well before the invention of running water.

The pretzel is not the only other boiled-before-it's-baked delicacy to which the bagel is related. In light of the fact that bagels are first mentioned in Cracow, it's probably no coincidence that they bear a suspiciously close resemblance to the popular Cracovian snack specialty known as an *obwarzanek*. *Obwarzanki*, which can be bought from vendors on any major Cracow street, differ from bagels chiefly in being made with two pieces of dough rather than one; their name comes from a Polish verb that means—what else?—to parboil. *Obwarzanki* are made pretty much the same way as bagels, and even come sprinkled with sesame seeds, salt, or poppy seeds. But while the *obwarzanek* has remained primarily a Cracow specialty, the bagel spread all over the Yiddish-speaking world.

A handmade bagel contains high-gluten flour, yeast, salt, and far less water than a similar volume of bread. Some bakers add sugar. Malt syrup is a popular optional extra which is compulsory in Montreal. Once everything has been kneaded together, the dough is shaped into the familiar ring, traditionally by being wound around the winder's four fingers in a move that bears a marked resemblance to the way in which the end of a man's tefillin strap is wound around the width of his hand. The dough is then left to stand in a cool place—a refrigerator, in recent times—for somewhere between twelve and twenty hours before the baking begins. This retardation, as bakers call it, pays tribute to matzoh by inhibiting the fermentation process while promoting the growth of the lactic-acid bacteria that lend the bagel its characteristically tangy bite. The lengthy waiting period is also responsible for the bagel's crust, without which it would be nothing more than characterless dough.

Once the dough has been sufficiently retarded, it is plunged into boiling water. The timing here is crucial—boiling the rings before they go into the oven lets them retain their shape while baking. There is a whole oral law about the duration of the boiling time, but two minutes is considered by all as the extreme outside limit. The boiled dough then goes into the oven, preferably wood fired, where it bakes for no more than half an hour at high heat. The bagels that come out stay fresh for about five hours.

People will tell you all kinds of tales about what qualifies as "authentic" and what does not. Bagels are supposed to be made from a single coil of dough, but no one bothered to tell the bagel baker in Opatòw in the 1920s, whose bagels are described as . . .

> . . . just like the obwarzanki *still sold on the streets of Krakòw today. . . . made of two thin coils, which he twisted, bringing the ends together to form a ring. He would put the bagels on a stick,*

several at a time, and drop them into boiling water. When they
floated, he would lift them out with the stick, let them drain,
and place them on a peel. Before setting them directly on the floor
of the oven, he would sprinkle them with poppy seeds and salt.

The real issue is the boil. For the rest, it was a matter of local preference and tradition, the baker's skill, and the nature of the water. The hoo-ha over flavoring bagels is a red herring. Flavors come and flavors go; we have nineteenth-century evidence for almond bagels, egg bagels like the ones from the seventeenth century, and dairy bagels kneaded with milk instead of water. The flavor problem—if it is a problem—is merely a matter of taste. The thing that defines a real bagel and separates it from simple bread dough baked in the shape of a ring are those few precious seconds in boiling water. Think of that water as a *mikve*, a purifying ritual bath; a ring of dough that has not been inside it suffers from an ineradicable defect and can never be considered a proper—that is, a truly kosher— bagel. A never-boiled ring of baked dough is no more a bagel than a man who wears a skullcap but lives in the Vatican is a rabbi.

Despite its lengthy history, the bagel didn't really come into its own as an everyday snack until the mid-nineteenth century, when it developed its first real connection to the USA. The large scale importation of American wheat that began in Europe in the 1850s had so stimulating an effect on European wheat production, especially in Ukraine, that the consumption of wheat in the Pale of Settlement began to skyrocket. By 1900, it had risen to an annual total of fifty-seven kilograms per person (as compared with over four hundred kilos of potatoes) and the bagel had turned from an occasional treat into a ubiquitous street food. Yehuda Elzet, who was born in Plock in central Poland in 1887, says that a bagel cost a groschen—the same as a penny—and that three of them made up a *shiur seudah*, enough to be considered a meal. Elzet is making a bit of a joke on the Yiddish saying that claims that it's the third bagel that fills you up. *Shiur seudah* is a rabbinic way of letting us know that the average bagel would have weighed between 2.2 and 2.3 ounces—only slightly smaller than the roughly 2.5-ounce contemporary handmade bagel, as compared with the 4 ouncers sold by the chains.

The idea that a bagel would never cost more than a groschen was so deeply ingrained that the phrase, "like a bagel for a groschen," was used to mean something with a fixed or invariable price.

The standard handmade New York bagel, sometimes called a water bagel, is made with nothing but flour, water, yeast, salt, and malt syrup. Its only real competition, so far as connoisseurs are concerned, is the Montreal bagel, which dispenses with salt and adds sugar, oil, honey, and egg to the mix. These bagels are unusual in having a retardation time of only twenty minutes or so; the sugar is there to help the yeast do its thing, the oil keeps the insides nice and chewy, and the salt isn't there at all—it would get in the way of the yeast. Unlike New York bagels, the Montreal variety is baked *only* in wood ovens. The finished product is sweeter than the puffier, much more chewy New York version.

The origins of the Montreal bagel are somewhat obscure. Although no one denies that Isadore Shlafman, who opened Fairmount Bagel in 1919, was the first to sell them from a store, there are those who claim that a man named Chaim Seligman had been selling the same kind of bagels on the street before Shlafman arrived in Montreal. No one seems to have recorded precisely where either man came from and whether or not the recipe had come over from the old country or been developed in Canada. Shlafman's legacy lives on in Fairmount Bagel, which is still in operation, and its main rival, St-Viateur Bagel Shop (usually pronounced *à l'anglais* as Saint Vee-ate-er), established by a former Fairmount employee in 1957. Feelings between partisans of the two bakeries can run high; it isn't unusual for fans of one to refuse to eat bagels from the other, and many native Montrealers claim to be able to tell their bagels apart in blind taste tests—a fact that doesn't do much for the city's image as a citadel of swinging nightlife.

ALL-AMERICAN TOPPINGS

Purists for whom the Lender family, whose innovations will be discussed shortly, is the snake in Bagel Eden, might be disappointed to find out that corruption really set in the day some unnamed New World yahoo decided to split a bagel down the middle, coat the insides with cream cheese, and top that cream cheese off with lox.

The old-country bagel was usually eaten on its own, with minimal toppings or condiments. It was never cut into equal, toaster-sized halves, never saw itself covered with anything more than a very occasional *shmir* of butter. A lullaby published in a 1901 collection of Yiddish folk songs gives us a spicier-than-usual look at the place of the buttered bagel in the Yiddish folk mind:

In mark darf men loyfn,	We've got to run to the market,
Beyglekh darf men koyfn;	We've got to buy bagels;
Mit puter darf men shmirn,	We've got to spread them with butter,
Der tate un di mame	So that mom and dad
Zoln zikh tsu der khupe firn.	Will go off and get married.

Like the children in the folk song, the buttered bagel was a little unusual and not entirely legitimate.

The average Jew not engaged in circumcision, kosher butchery, or leatherwork tended not to wander the streets with anything sharp enough to cut through a bagel more than a few hours old. Cream cheese is a purely American product, invented in upstate New York in 1872, but close enough to the soft curd cheeses to which East European Jewish immigrants were accustomed to enter the Jewish diet without fanfare or difficulty. The Standard Yiddish term for it, *shmirkez*, "cheese for spreading," appears to have been coined in the

United States (possibly by Uriel Weinreich, in whose *Modern English-Yiddish Yiddish-English Dictionary* the word is found) and to have been based on the way in which a bagel with cream cheese would be ordered in Yiddish: "*Gets mir a beygl mit a shmir kez*, Give me a bagel spread with cheese," where "cheese" means the only cheese that would have been considered in such circumstances. Put the *shmir* and the *kez* together and you've got a perfectly serviceable new noun to represent something utterly unknown in Yiddish-speaking Europe. I've never heard anyone other than earnest students and highly committed Yiddishists use the noun, though; the Yiddish-speakers whom I knew as a kid tended to call it "cream cheese," much as they didn't call peanut butter *stashke-piter* or *stashke-shmir*, or refer to Maurice Chevalier as Moyshe.

If cream cheese fit naturally with East European Jewish food preferences, lox, which was scarcely better known to the bagel eaters of Europe, didn't require much more of a leap. Salmon was not a particularly Jewish fish in the old country; of the thirty-three fish recipes in the 1896 Yiddish cookbook, only two are for salmon, one fresh and the other marinated. Smoked salmon came onto the Jewish menu in England and North America where, along with cisco, Winnipeg goldeye, and the sable that Larry David didn't want his name attached to, it was being prepared in smokehouses run by immigrants from Germany and Scandinavia, two other cultures in which salmon is also called lox (or *lachs* or *lax*). The Jews soon developed their own take on it, "soaking it in light brine or occasionally dry curing it with salt and sometimes brown sugar, then cold-smoking it." This is the process that gives us what is now called Nova. Lox, properly considered, is not smoked at all; it is cured in brine and emerges with a stronger, much saltier taste. All belly lox is by definition brined, not smoked. If the lox, so called, that you're eating today seems weaker than the stuff you used to have as a kid, it is probably because belly lox has been replaced—in most common uses, at any rate—by the milder and much more expensive Nova.

Cream cheese and lox seem to have met the bagel sometime in the 1930s, making this beloved traditional dish slightly younger than Tony Bennett. Many writers on the subject have adopted anthropologist Stanley Regelson's suggestion that the combination posed an implicit challenge to the dietary laws because of the ham-like quality of the salmon—a quality for which I've yearned in vain for over half a century—while others, like Gil Marks, prefer to see a bagel with cream cheese and lox as a kosher response to eggs Benedict, with each ingredient replacing its goyishe counterpart. Regrettably, there is nothing inherently unkosher about either English muffins or Hollandaise sauce, though the butter in the sauce would be a bit of a problem even if the bacon were kosher. The real question is how all those lower-middle and working-class Jews in the depression would have known from eggs Benedict to begin with. Eggs Benjamin, a more direct Jewish response to eggs Benedict, have long since proven that Hollandaise can go just fine with the smoked salmon that replaces the ham, if you like that sort of thing, while the Jewish breakfast classic *vursht* (salami) and eggs proves that when we want to go head-to-head with breakfast *treyf*, we tend not to pull any punches.

Still, the eggs Benedict comparison has an elegance of its own, once we stop to consider the degree to which Sunday replaced *shabbes* for earlier generations of American Jews, most of whom worked, however unwillingly, on Saturday. The real advantage to cream cheese and lox on a bagel lies in the fact that you don't have to do much more than open packages, slice bagels, and spread. No one has to cook. You could have your parents or religious relatives over without having to answer any embarrassing questions about where you bought the meat. And best of all, there was nobody, absolutely nobody, who could tell you that it was done better in the old country.

Cream cheese and lox on a bagel is a good thing. The ingredients taste better together than they do individually (especially if they can tempt an onion along), but slicing that first bagel into two thinner rings and then treating it as the launch platform for what is essentially a sandwich initiated a subtle change in our way of looking at the bagel. From something sufficient unto itself, the bagel came to be regarded as somehow lacking, as needing something to complete it and make it perfect. When something similar happened with the Hebrew Bible, Passover turned into Easter.

Remaking the bagel into something that was always accompanied, no longer just a bagel but "a bagel and," "a bagel with," or a bagel that was the object of the preposition "on," was a lengthy process that was helped along by the legions of Jewish entertainers who took to mentioning both bagels and lox in public. There are hundreds, if not thousands, of jokes and throwaway lines, the most memorable of which is probably Phil Silvers's quip in the 1954 film version of his Broadway hit, *Top Banana*. Playing a thinly disguised version of Milton Berle, Silvers sends out for lunch near the start of the film. "I got an idea for a new sandwich," he says. "Jerry Biffle's Interracial Special: ham on a bagel."

RISE OF THE MACHINES

All the jokes and comedians in the world were of no avail against the one stubborn fact that militated against mass adoption of the bagel: If you didn't live near a bakery that made them, there was no way you would ever be able to try one. Since most bagel bakeries were located in Jewish neighborhoods, few of the bakers gave much thought to trying to expand beyond the Jewish community. It took a second-generation bagel family in New Haven, slightly off the beaten Jewish track, to start thinking about how to get bagels to people who would have to learn to want them.

Murray Lender, one of four brothers who worked in their father's bagel bakery, got the idea from cheesecake, Sara Lee frozen cheesecake, which made the New York cheesecake a staple of American recreational eating. If non-Jews outside of major Jewish centers had even heard of cheesecake before Charles Lubin began to freeze it and ship it cross-country in 1954, it was probably through the short stories of Damon Runyon—who arguably did more than any other individual, Jewish or non-, to raise awareness of Jewish food in the vast non-Jewish hinterland—or, even more likely, through stage or movie versions of his work, especially *Guys and Dolls*, in which cheesecake figures quite prominently.

Harry Lender, the paterfamilias and founder of what was still a fairly modest operation, had started to freeze bagels in the '50s in order to get them to the stores he supplied before they had a chance to go stale; freezing was a convenience for the manufacturer, not a selling point for the consumer. The Lenders had long sought to expand their operation, but could neither produce enough handmade bagels to compete in a larger market nor get the bagels to those markets before they started to get hard. New Haven was too small for them to be able to go on thinking locally.

A few years after Harry's death, his sons, impressed with Lubin's success, began to think that if Lubin could freeze a cheesecake and have it thaw into something close enough to the original that people would buy it again, he and his brothers could do the same with bagels and break into the lucrative New York market. The stores would receive bagels that would stay frozen until their customers decided to take them out of their freezers when they felt the urge for a "fresh" bagel.

In order to make this work, though, they had to be able to make the bagels more quickly than they could by hand. Desperate, they tried to adapt a machine for making Italian bread sticks to the needs of the bagel business:

Sam Lender mixed the bagel dough and one man cut it into small slabs and fed it into an Italian breadstick machine.

The Italian breadstick machine made bagel dough strips that were then distributed to workstations where six to eight men rolled them by hand into bagels. With this system they averaged 50 dozen bagels per hour per man.

By 1961, Daniel Thompson had succeeded in inventing a dedicated bagel maker that could replace those eight trained men with three unskilled workers. Thompson's invention was the culmination of a two generation effort; his father, a bagel baker himself, had started work on a bagel machine sometime around 1918 and finally passed the task along to him. The story should have been written by Robert McCloskey; instead, we have the Web site of the Thompson Bagel Machine Mfg. Corp. The Lenders were the first people to express a serious interest in Thompson's machine—which is now used by virtually all national bagel concerns of any consequence, including Lender's and Einstein Bros.—and Murray Lender was the first person to lease one, in 1963. As Thompson describes it:

With the advent of the Thompson Bagel Machine any entrepreneur that wanted to enter into the bagel business or expand their business was now provided with the ability to produce unlimited quantities of bagels without expensive skilled help. This brought the price of bagels down and made them more readily available. Bagels started to shed their ethnic roots and more people started eating them. *Ultimately tens of millions of people enjoy eating bagels and tens of thousands of jobs were created by the advent of the Thompson Bagel Machine.*

The bagels were adjusted to the needs of the machine, and with each adjustment shed a little more of their ethnic roots. The dough had to be softer; at 52 or 53 percent water, traditional bagel dough was too recalcitrant for the machines, which could only work with a thinner batter. Oil also had to be added to keep the dough from sticking to the hoppers. The Lenders had already been tinkering with the recipe, adding eggs and shortening to make the finished product noticeably less dense. In a move designed to save time and money, the national bagel makers dropped the crucial retardation process and substituted dough conditioners for the twelve- to twenty-hour waiting period, thus allowing them to move the dough straight from the shaper into the oven and reduce the bagel's characteristic acidity to virtually nothing. Such conditioning is the bagelian counterpart of wine or beer that has not been aged, and such bagels are, bagelistically speaking, little more than baked bum wine, Thunderbird with a crust, but without any kick. But at least they won't turn your tongue black.

The kicker, though, the real nail in the coffin of the traditional bagel—and traditional Jewish coffins don't have nails—is the complete elimination of boiling. These so-called steam bagels are baked in ovens equipped with steam-injectors that fire a blast of steam onto the bagels manqués for about thirty seconds. This would not be a problem if the oven were turned off and each bagel was Marilyn Monroe; as it is, all that comes out of those ovens are the simulacra of bagels, Potemkin bagels made of authentic looking facades and meaningless prop material.

A ring-shaped, high-gluten, cinnamon-cucumber-sun-dried-tomato concoction left to stand for the right amount of time and then boiled before being put into the oven is a bagel. It might not be a bagel that *you* want to eat, but the flavor that repels you is what philosophers refer to as accident: a property with no necessary or organic connection to the essence of the thing itself. The substance, the essential qualities that make something a bagel and not a sports car—high-gluten dough left to retard, then dipped into boiling water before being put into the oven—is still there. The problem with chain and frozen bagels lies not so much in their attempts to provide flavors for Americans to love, as in the fact that they aren't really bagels.

The shedding of the bagel's ethnic roots that Daniel Thompson mentions would never have been so complete without the visionary marketing ideas of Murray Lender, who seems to have learned a great deal from the Levy's rye bread campaign that got underway around the time that the Lenders began to look seriously at the Thompson Bagel Machine. Where Levy's slogan played up its Jewish origins to imply that Jewish rye was the *only* rye and that Levy's was the only *real* Jewish rye, the photos on the posters made it clear that, Jewish as their bread was, it was precisely that Jewish element that made it so attractive to those who were not members of the tribe (and it's no accident that one of the most popular posters featured a Native American, just in case anyone might miss the pun). The bread was good *because* it was Jewish.

Lender took the opposite tack. Where price and convenience might have helped the brand in New York—Lender's frozen bagels were even precut so that you didn't have to fight to get them into a toaster—they were not much of a selling point in the vast regions of America where no one but Jews had ever eaten a bagel. The Jewish origins of the bagel were alluded to only very subtly, and only in the television commercials featuring Murray, Sam, and Marvin Lender, all of whom had or assumed typically "Jewish" voices and vocal inflections. Murray would often invert his English syntax in characteristically Yiddish fashion: "On bagels, I'm an expert; people, I'll never understand."

Otherwise, though, the emphasis was on taste and wholesomeness: "After all those years of eating toast for breakfast, now there's something better," because it was "crispy outside, soft and chewy inside." Similarly, the Bruegger's Bagels Web site informs us that their "New York style" bagels (which, according to Bruegger's, are still boiled) are "crisp on the outside, chewy and flavorful on the inside." Four decades of bagel jokes in the popular media might have helped produce a willingness to give bagels a try, but it was taste and texture that led people to buy them again and again, until they became so popular that even fast-food chains like McDonald's and Dunkin' Donuts added bagels to their menus.

While only certain Lender's bagels are labeled "New York Style," all of their products feature a logo that shows the Statue of Liberty, the Empire State Building, and a bevy of other skyscrapers. Melvin and Elmo, the two guys in the Einstein Bros. logo, have a distinctly old-world cast to their features, slightly reminiscent of Otto Soglow's Little King; and Einstein, like Seinfeld, is a name that suggests but does not insist upon Jewishness. With the New York water bagel as the touchstone for virtually all bagels baked in the USA, bagels retain their Jewish identity only among Jews themselves, or non-Jews living in heavily Jewish areas; elsewhere, they behave more like *Seinfeld*, where George and Elaine, who are both supposed to be gentiles, act no less Jewish than the explicitly Jewish Jerry. Many viewers think of them all as Jews, even Kramer (who was supposed to have worked long enough at H&H Bagels in Manhattan to be on virtually permanent strike), but these viewers tend to be Jewish themselves. For the rest of the world, they are New Yorkers—zany, lovable, post-Woody Allen neurotics whose *meshugas* has more to do with where they live than what they are.

To return, then, to the question about the Casper and Brooklyn bagels, the real question is: Was either of them boiled? Otherwise, there is no difference between the imported frozen bagel and the fresh-baked but eccentrically flavored local product: They both say New York, they say affluence and urbanity, hipness and sophistication—there's nothing square about a bagel. The same bagels in Seoul or Manila have all the same qualities attributed to them, but as a component of their Americanism. From Jewish to New York to American—the adjectives tell the bagel's whole story. The pejorative use of bagel as a term for a Jew, either on its own or accompanied by "baby" or "bender," seems to have died out a long time ago. "Tell that bagel-bender to shut his trap," isn't the sort of thing you expect to hear from today's anti-Semites.

Often as the bagel turns up in movies, on TV, in novels and plays, it usually plays itself—the preferred informal food of sophisticated urbanites who are sometimes Jewish. Once in a while, it serves as a talisman, a symbol of older, better times, although the bagel's current ubiquity means that such nostalgic capering tends to be confined to articles about the decline of the bagel itself. There is, of course, Abbott and Costello's version of the vaudeville set piece, *Floogle Street*, in which Floogle is changed to Bagel, home of the Susquehanna Hat Company; I don't think it is meant as a comment on anything, except that A and C must have thought that Bagel would get a bigger laugh than Floogle. A similar motive might well underlie the choice of the name Bagel for the nerdish, nebbishy character played by Michael Tucker in *Diner* and *Tin Men*.

We have already noted that mourners eat bagels after the funeral, and bagels meet death in a couple of widely used Yiddish idioms that have nothing to do with being crispy on the outside and soft within. A relatively nasty way of saying that someone is dead—croaked would be more accurate here—is *men est shoyn zayne beygl*, "We're eating his bagels already." The idiom paints a picture of the world as a fully automated prison, so indifferent to the fate of its inmates that the bagels on which each one is sustained continue to be disbursed even after the prisoner has died. The system will never notice; whoever grabs those suddenly ownerless bagels gets more to eat—it's in no one's interest for this guy's death to be noted officially, forget about mourned. We're eating his bagels; he's not greatly missed.

No discussion of bagels would be complete without at least a brief mention of the bagel's greatest symbolic contribution to Yiddish culture, the equally death-oriented *lign in dr'erd un bakn beygl*, "to lie in the ground, baking bagels." Writing about the dead who haunt burnt-out stores and archways now that the local synagogue has been shut, Isaac Mayer Dik, a nineteenth-century Yiddish writer whose novellas are a storehouse of otherwise forgotten folk customs and beliefs, says, "In the summer they lie in rows in the cemetery, baking bagels." Just dying is never enough. As I have written elsewhere:

> *You've got to spend all of eternity in hellishly hot bakery conditions, baking bagels that, being dead, you have no need to eat; that, being dead, you've got no one to whom you can sell them; that, being dead, you don't even know anybody except other dead people, who also don't need to eat and who also don't have any money and who are all busy baking their own lousy bagels that they can't get rid of either.*
>
> *This is the Yiddish myth of Sisyphus, but Sisyphus—Sisyphus is a mythological Greek. He pushes the rock, the rock rolls back. He pushes the rock, the rock rolls back—Sisyphus at least comes out with muscles.*

The Jew has only one tiny source of consolation: at least they aren't pizza bagels.

BIALYS

The bagel might be the best known Jewish bun or roll, but it is hardly the only one. If the bins in the local Jewish bakeries are any indication, *bulkes* and *zeml* are as popular as ever, at least among the baby boomers and their surviving parents who seem to make up most of the clientele, but I have never heard anyone argue about them. No one slaps a firm but aging hand onto a tabletop to lay down the law of *bulkes*; no one tells you that the *zeml* on sale across the street are no more *zeml* than Santa Claus is a *shoykhet*. No family or friendship has ever dissolved over *bulkes* or *zeml*, and any Yiddish food that does not serve as a *casus*, as well as an ache in, *belli* is in grave danger of losing its place on the Jewish menu. Food historians, cookbook authors, food writers of every stripe attribute variations in Yiddish cuisine to geographic and economic factors, to the agricultural policies of the countries in which Yiddish-speaking Jews were living—all the things that help to explain the food of every other national or ethnic group on earth—without ever stopping to consider that such differences could just as easily have developed as a result of sheer orneriness and the will to do anything but what *they*—whoever they are—might be doing: "I wouldn't give them the satisfaction of seeing me eat a salt-and-pepper kugel; if that's how those Litvaks are going to eat it, I'm going to put sugar in mine, they should all choke, the bastards." And vice-versa.

While rolls unquestionably vary from town to town and bakery to bakery, these differences don't seem to arouse the passion of true engagement the way the bagel does. Its chief competitor in what could also be called the Yiddish food-snob sweepstakes, baked goods division, is the bialy, which is, if anything, even more closely identified with New York than the bagel.

Not quite a category unto itself, the bialy is really a Bialystok variant of the onion *pletzl*. A *pletzl* is a flatbread quite similar to the Italian focaccia, thin enough to look from a distance as if it might also be crunchy in the middle, but not so thin as to be confused with a crispbread. Although it can, and apparently has, been topped with almost anything, it is most commonly baked with onions, to which poppy seeds are sometimes added. A wheat product, it didn't enter the Yiddish world in any significant way until the nineteenth-century wheat boom mentioned in connection with the bagel. Unlike the American bagel, the *pletzl* is never split; anything that goes with it goes on top.

The *pletzl's* German-language cognate, *Plätzchen*, means a cookie, with a more specialized meaning of "cookie baked during Advent in honor of the season." *Placki* (pronounced platski) is the Polish term for what Jews call a latke: *placki ziemniaczane* are potato latkes, while *krowie placki*—bovine latkes—is the Polish version of cow pie. All three come ultimately from the Latin *placenta*,

which means a cake, particularly a flat cake. The anatomical meaning of *placenta* comes from the Greek from which it is derived, which
means "flat" and is also a distant ancestor of the Yiddish word for flat,
platshik. The edible *pletsl* shouldn't be confused with the diminutive
of another Yiddish word, *plats*—place or square—which looks and
sounds the same and lent its name to the old Jewish area in Paris's
fourth *arrondissement*.

The bialy is the Bialystok take on the *pletsl*. Bialystok is a city in
eastern Poland that once had a considerable Jewish population, and
technically the bialy is a *bialystoker pletsl*, a Bialystok *pletzl*, or a *bialystoker kuchen*. Balls of dough (usually high gluten) that have
been left to rise are flattened into circles, which the baker's thumb
then flattens even further in the center. This depression, which can
range from the merest dent to a deep indentation, provides a home
for the onions and gives the fully formed bialy the "rubber wading
pool" look described by Leo Rosten in *The Joys of Yiddish*. Dull col-
ored and somewhat sallow in comparison with a bagel or *bulke*, the
bialy's pasty appearance is proof of its open-faced guilelessness; unlike the other rolls, it presents itself without cosmetic adornment,
free of the egg wash glaze that lets the others shine so bright.

Now that it is no longer to be found in Bialystok, the bialy's real
home is New York City, where it is well known and readily available. Elsewhere, where available at all, it appeals to more of a niche
market of ex-New Yorkers and non-New Yorkers who know what it
is. Unlike the bagel, it does not lend itself to either machine production or freezing; if it isn't baked locally, it cannot be eaten at all.
The bialy—or its name, at least—was given a bit of a boost in the
late '60s, when Mel Brooks used it as the diminutive by which little
old ladies addressed Max Bialystock in *The Producers*; the image of
a crash-helmeted Zero Mostel driving a motor scooter with an oc-
togenarian woman in the passenger seat screaming, "Go, Bialy
baby," is not easily forgotten. More elegiacally, Mimi Sheraton, the
former *New York Times* food critic, has devoted an entire book to

the bialy, its history, and its place in the culture. Most importantly, though, bialys go much better with herring, the national fish of Yiddishland, than bagels do.

HERRING

In an unpublished essay called "Jews as Fish-Consumers," a writer named Adam Gostony described the kinds of fish that Jews in New York were eating in 1942: "Gefilte fish, bismarck herring, roll mops, matjes herring, salted herring, homemade schmaltz herring, homemade pickled herring, homemade fried herring, smoked herring, chopped herring, herring salad ('a gray looking material'), whitefish and salmon."

Egg and Spam; egg, bacon, and Spam; egg, bacon, sausage, and Spam: I have looked in vain for Gostony's name in the credits for the Monty Python Spam sketch and am content to believe that he was no more than a patron saint, a mute, inglorious Mendel, rather than its source. Nearly thirty years before the Spam shtick was written and first performed, Gostony had already divined that those who live on Yiddish food are living a Monty Python kind of life. Only bad luck and Gostony's lack of publisher prevented unsolicited bulk e-mail messages from being called herring: "On Sunday, one had pickled herring; on Monday, soused herring; on Tuesday, smoked herring; on Wednesday, baked herring; on Thursday, herring fried in oatmeal (delicious!); and on Friday, one had herrings in sour cream."

Have a Spamwich in Adam's memory.

Aside from the carobs traditionally eaten on the fifteenth day of the Hebrew month of Shvat, herring was as close to an exotic food as most East European Jews were likely to come upon on a regular basis. In *Eat and Be Satisfied*, John Cooper makes the often-overlooked point that "between the two World Wars three-quarters of the fish consumed in Poland, chiefly salted herring, was still imported"—and Poland, like Russia and Ukraine, can hardly be said to lack for lakes and rivers full of freshwater varieties. The herring that the Jews were eating was caught, treated, and shipped by people who would have caught and treated it in the same fashion even without the Jews. It is a food that became Jewish strictly by virtue of the fact that Jews liked it, were able to afford it, and ate it in vast quantities; it was a major source of protein and vitamin D, not to mention sodium. The fishermen might not have been Jewish, but Jews were more than prominent as herring brokers, importers, and commission agents. North Sea catches from England and Scotland, Baltic herrings from Holland, Germany, and Scandinavia were bought by Jewish importers who shipped them to Russia and Poland, where they moved down the chain of distribution, much of it also run by Jews.

Herring is salted for the sake of preservation, and needs to be soaked in water before it can be eaten. Pickling makes it less intensely fishy. The fish, usually accompanied by slices of onion, is marinated in vinegar and sugar, sometimes with a few peppercorns added to give it a bit of zest. Rollmops are fillets of pickled herring wrapped around something like a gherkin or olive and held closed with a toothpick. Bismarck herring are pickled fillets with the skin removed.

The boss herring, at least for Yiddish speakers and their descendants, is the schmaltz herring, possibly because of its name. There is no schmaltz in schmaltz herring, just plenty of fish fat. A schmaltz herring is a decapitated, fatty, full-grown herring that was about to spawn; a matjes herring is a virgin that, thanks to you, will never spawn. It's milder and more expensive than the others. All that's left is *milch* herring, basically a schmaltz herring with cojones. The *milch*, or milt as it is called in English, is the sperm and seminal fluid that the male fish sprays onto the roe. It's the main ingredient in what I always think of as a characteristically Polish-Jewish dish called *kratsborsht*, or scratch-borsht. In our house, at least, the herrings were scraped on a grater, milts and all, and then served with finely chopped pieces of pickled herring mixed with vinegar, sugar, and onions. By us it was an appetizer; in Poland it was often the main course of a two-course meal, the other course being a piece of bread or a potato.

Similar two-course meals were made with other types of herring. Popular as it has remained, herring was always regarded as the kind of food with which you made do—okay for an appetizer, a snack, a light lunch, but an admission of defeat when served as the main meal of the day. As a folk song popularized by Theodore Bikel has it, rich people get a fresh, wiggling carp and we paupers get a piece of meagre herring. The carp, hardly the top of the fish chain itself, at least fills everyone up.

It should come as no surprise that The Three Stooges did their best to bring herring into the public eye. One of their films features a spy and femme fatale called Mati (after matjes) Herring, while in the fantastically titled *I'll Never Heil Again*, Curly, playing Hermann Goering to Moe's Hitler, is called Field Marshal Herring. Charlie Chaplin used the same joke a few months later in *The Great Dictator*, where Billy Gilbert plays Herring, the minister of war.

There is an old tradition behind this kind of nomenclature, although it is unlikely that Chaplin or the Stooges were aware of it. Pickle-Herring had been a stock name for clowns and tricksters on the German stage since the beginning of the seventeenth century, and was the name used for the comic-relief character in an early eighteenth-century Yiddish play from Germany about Joseph and his brothers.

Herring, pike, and carp might have been the main Yiddish fish in the old country, but they were far from the only ones. Roach and tench occupied a middle ground of affordability between carp and herring, but never seem to have developed much of a folklore. The giant pike-perch was popular when available and affordable; in Yiddish, it's called *sendak*. Yehuda Elzet says that Jews avoided eating the head because it had, or was believed to have, a bone there in the shape of a cross, a piece of folklore that would probably have delighted the late children's author.

There was also a dish called false fish—it sounds almost exactly the same in Yiddish, though mock fish is probably a better English translation. Made of chopped or ground chicken breast rolled into gefilte-fishlike balls and then poached, *falshe fish* provided a clever disguise for any leftover *shabbes* chicken. It wasn't the only false dish; *falshe zup*, mock soup, consisted of boiling water with onion or garlic. If Manischewitz still did Yiddish packaging, the recipe for mock kishka on boxes of their Tam Tams would be labeled *falshe kishka*.

Unrelated to meat of any kind is the equally well-known *puste fish*—empty fish, mock fish: potatoes, onions, pepper, and butter or schmaltz. In Lithuania, and possibly elsewhere, it occupied the place that pizza now has when people get their friends to help them move: an inexpensive communal snack as a reward for help with a tiresome but necessary task. Under Czarist rule, many Lithuanians might have relied more on herring and such fish substitutes as *puste fish* than residents of other parts of the Russian empire. Speaking of how "the more prosperous [Lithuanian] farmer bought a small wooden barrel of herring from the Jewish city merchant," Peter Paul Jonitis goes on to explain that "since the Russian authorities did not allow fishing in the rivers in Lithuania, fresh fish did not frequently appear on the peasant table." Jews living inland would, of course, have been subject to the same restrictions and were probably no less willing than their neighbors to take matters into their own hands. According to Jonitis, the usual punishment meted out to Lithuanians caught fishing illegally was to have their clothes confiscated "so that the Lithuanians had to furtively sneak back to their homes." Similar punishment meted out to a Jew would have been a small price to pay for the sake of fish for *shabbes*.

Epilogue
How Is It Jewish?

No one misses *cholent*. Most American Jews have never seen it; many might not have heard of it, either. Jews with direct experience either eat it or avoid it. De rigeur in the ultra-Orthodox world and popular, though not inevitable, among the Modern Orthodox, this definitive Ashkenazi dish has almost no currency among people who don't keep *shabbes*. Formerly ultra-Orthodox Jews who retain a taste for *cholent* might still eat it, but if they do so on the Sabbath, it's only because they're visiting family or friends who have not strayed from the path of righteousness. Otherwise, they tend to eat *cholent* almost anytime *but* the Sabbath, either in restaurants that serve it at least once a week, or at gatherings like the one mentioned in Chapter Five, where a melting pot of emigres from the old country of Orthodoxy tries to re-create the communal experience associated with eating it.

The *cholent* pot is both pretext and symbol, a means of recapturing the ancillary pleasures of a way of life that the participants might have rejected but have not entirely escaped. As the rabbinic proverb has it, "*Girso de-yankuso lo mishtakkho*, you never get over what you learned as a kid": the real point is to spend time with a large number of people with whom you can feel like family even if you've never met before—even if you might not like them—because you've all emerged from the same damned place. It's that bond, that sense of belonging that draws them to the *cholent*, which isn't really a food to be eaten alone. Refugees from Orthodoxy who don't want to be reminded of the past or their travails in escaping it don't go to the gatherings and don't eat *cholent* at all.

Such gatherings of former yeshiva students and their sisters (who were being raised to *make* the *cholent*) are like a Talmudically charged, single-dish reenactment of the history of Ashkenazi cuisine in North America. These people aren't eating *cholent* because you're not allowed to cook on the Sabbath. They're eating *cholent*, the one dish as redolent of *shabbes* as their *shabbes* once was of it, for strictly sociological reasons. There is a subtle but very real difference between serving pepperoni pizza or BLTs at a gathering of formerly Orthodox Jews and serving *cholent*. As a food now eaten almost exclusively by Sabbath-observant Orthodox Jews, *cholent* has come to be identified with the most conservative wing of Jewish society, the one most likely to be characterized as narrow by Jews who approach the religion differently. When former members of that community make a bit of a show out of eating a BLT, they're showing themselves and anyone who happens to be looking that they're emancipated enough to give their background the finger. In other words, they're acting like kids. When they make a similar show with a *cholent*, though, they're saying that there's more than one way of being Jewish; that even though they no longer keep *shabbes* or observe the dietary laws, they are just as Jewish as people who do. They're Jewish in a different way, but have no less right to the title. The *cholent* becomes an affirmation of identity whose connection to the religious constraints and occasions that it was developed to satisfy has become purely historical. It has become a sign of not *having* to eat *cholent*.

As the Jewish dish par excellence, *cholent* lends itself particularly well to such declarations of identity, especially since kugel and gefilte fish, the other contenders for the designation "par excellence," were deconsecrated, as it were, a long time ago. Since the Jews went into exile, their food has been different, even if only subtly so, from that of the peoples around them. Somewhat detached from the national diet of the lands in which Jews were living, Jewish food has always been a cuisine of coexistence, a diet that runs parallel to that of neighboring non-Jews and serves to mark the people who eat it as Jewish. Closely as an individual Ashkenazi dish might resemble its non-Jewish counterpart, each is part of a meal at which the other will never appear. What goes into the Ashkenazi mouth isn't much different from what comes out of it: Yiddish food in Europe related to the food cultures around it in much the same way as Yiddish itself did to German and the Slavic languages. The main difference was that a Yiddish speaker might abandon Yiddish for German or Polish when speaking to a German or a Pole; he would never voluntarily eat unkosher German or Polish food with them. For centuries, Ashkenazi food existed within a framework defined by Jewish law and Christian anti-Semitism. Ethnicity—the idea that a Jew stays Jewish even after converting to another religion—became part of that context in the mid-nineteenth century.

The nature of that context changed significantly in America (and, to a somewhat lesser degree, in Western Europe), where religious customs and imperatives tended to wither away in the face of a much more porous society than Jews had been used to. Once the restrictions associated with *shabbes* and kashrus began to fade, food that had been a matter of religious dictate and social duty became a cuisine of choice. As the mass of Jews grew less observant, but not necessarily less Jewish, dishes associated with religious occasions tended more and more to *become* the occasions: the Friday-night family dinner at which dinner itself is the only ritual; the Rosh Hashana feast that neither follows tonight's prayers nor precedes tomorrow's; the seder at which only the matzoh is kosher—for Passover or any other time. Dishes once fraught with religious significance became badges of ethnicity, affirmations of an innate condition that doesn't need to follow any stinkin' rules.

Rapid as the process was, it was also gradual; there was a time when most restaurants serving traditional fare were either strictly dairy or strictly kosher, but once the clients stopped caring, the owners stopped trying. Kosher eateries were eventually outnumbered by those that served their food "kosher style"—especially delicatessens, which also initiated the shift. Kosher style, which really shouldn't mean anything at all, is generally understood as traditional Ashkenazi food made from ingredients that aren't necessarily kosher, that have been prepared with utensils used indifferently for *milkhiks* and *fleyshiks* by workers who might be cooking the food on Yom Kippur: Plenty of kosher-style delicatessens have been serving bacon for a very long time, even if they keep it away from the chicken soup.

The standard delicatessen menu, kosher or not, is a fusion of such *shabbes* and holiday standards as chopped liver, chicken soup, matzoh balls, kugel, and kishka; Middle and East European dishes eaten by Jews and gentiles alike, such as cabbage rolls; street foods such as knishes; and pickles for customers who want to eat their vegetables. But the deli's defining dishes, the ones around which all the others revolve, came to prominence only in the New World.

FROM KOSHER TO JEWISH: DELICATESSEN

In an early chapter of his novel, *Blondzhende Shtern* (*Wandering Stars*), Sholem Aleichem mentions pastrami (which he calls *postrame*) and pauses for a second to explain it: "A Bessarabian dish with pepper and garlic," he writes, "that is eaten with *plentshites*, that is, cornmeal-and-cabbage blintzes." Though he was writing about Bessarabia (formerly Romania, now mostly in Moldova), the explanation makes it clear that Sholem Aleichem himself, who is to Yiddish literature what Shakespeare and Charles Dickens are to English, was a little vague as to what went into pastrami and how it was made, as well he should have been. When this chapter was first serialized in 1909 or 1910, pastrami was still a regional specialty. A Yiddish-speaking immigrant landing in New York a hundred years ago wouldn't have known what pastrami was unless he had been to Romania. Delicatessen as we know it, the food that kills those who love it best, is an American variation on a few themes with roots in Europe.

The pastrami in Sholem Aleichem's book was probably made of goose, the most common Jewish substitute for the pork, lamb, and mutton pastrami popular with Romanian gentiles; although Jews also ate beef and mutton pastramis in Europe, it is said that the lower price of beef in America prompted a definitive switch from goose. Today's pastrami is usually made from the navel, also known as the beef plate, or in kosher butcher shops, the *dekl* (deckle), a tough, fatty cut that lies behind the brisket. While the navel was originally rubbed with a dry mixture of spices and cured for a couple of weeks, most nonartisanal pastrami is now injected with *rosl* and left to marinate for a couple of days. Only then is it dry rubbed. Both types then go to the smokehouse.

Corned beef, pastrami's main rival, is pickled brisket that has been cooked in boiling water. Introduced to the US by immigrants from Germany, it was as unfamiliar to the mass of East European immigrants as the Romanian pastrami that was often sold alongside it. Montreal-style smoked meat, for which the world owes Canada an unpayable debt, has been described by deli expert David Sax as a combination of pastrami and corned beef, "A brisket cured and smoked like a pastrami, with slightly different spicing."

If not quite the origin of today's fast food, deli certainly played a role in its rise, not to mention its effect on the nitrate levels of American Jews. Folklorically, Bessarabia long enjoyed a reputation as the Playboy Mansion of Yiddish-speaking Europe: Romania or Bessarabia—the names were used interchangeably in colloquial speech—was regarded as the homeland of good food, flowing wine, and pretty girls—and it is definitely no accident that professional Yiddish theater was born in a Jewish wine garden in Iași.

Perhaps as a result of this heritage, Romanian-Jewish immigrants
to the United States tended to enter the restaurant business in dis-
proportionately large numbers. Figures from 1902 estimated that
"Romanians owned 150 restaurants, 200 wine cellars which all had
lunch rooms, as well as 30 coffee shops" in New York. The cramped
nature of the Lower East Side, not to mention the far greater numbers of Jewish immigrants from Poland, Russia, Ukraine, and so on,
indicates that they were not selling Romanian-style food solely to
other Romanians. Nine years later, a more exact but less nation-
ally specific study identified "one hundred restaurants and lunchrooms . . . within the area bounded by Grand, Chrystie, East
Houston and Suffolk Streets . . . less than one third of a square
mile." Such restaurants and lunchrooms, most of them still kosher,
helped introduce non-Romanian Jewish immigrants to such foods
as pastrami and non-German Jewish immigrants to corned beef and
the other cured meats and sausages so popular among Jewish and
non-Jewish Germans alike. As with other immigrant communities,
many Jewish males were either bachelors or married men trying to
save enough money to bring their families over from Europe. Those
who did not board with families who provided meals relied on these
restaurants and lunchrooms, along with pushcarts selling hot dogs
and knishes, for the bulk of their nourishment. The pastrami and
corned beef, the exotic salamis sold in Romanian-run delis—
whether sit down or strictly takeout—provided these men and their
unmarried female counterparts with inexpensive food that filled
them up and tasted good.

The deli owners, meanwhile, had adapted the selling of such
meats to American conditions. Not even in Romania had there been
any such thing as a pastrami sandwich. In New York and elsewhere
in the US, deli owners (or perhaps a single genius among them)
stumbled upon what might be called the Knish Principle: you can
only fit so much filling into a single knish. Enclosing the meat in

dough makes it easily portable, but neither pastrami nor corned beef is really at its best in a knishlike setting. Using the meat to stuff a sandwich lets the deli owner turn a higher profit; the customer is now paying by unit, not by weight, and—until places like the Carnegie Deli in New York began to sell sixteen-ounce sandwiches—the average generous deli sandwich contained about five ounces of meat. Slapped between two slices of relatively inexpensive rye bread and rounded out with an even cheaper pickle, the customer received a full serving at an affordable price, while the restaurant was able to sell those five ounces for considerably more than they would have cost as part of a take-home pound of meat.

Whatever the marketing strategies, the food was so enthusiastically received that people began to forget that they had not been eating it all their lives. Within a surprisingly short time, delicatessen of this type changed from Romanian to Jewish, from novelty to tradition. And it's as a tradition, something that's always been there—as long as you remember that there is really here—that such food has entered both Jewish and more general American culture.

The most significant thing about this tradition is its novelty. While "foreign" dishes that can be made to fulfill the demands of kashrus can become part of the Ashkenazi culinary repertoire, it generally takes quite a long time for them to become naturalized and have their outside origins forgotten. Foreign as their passports might have been, pastrami, corned beef, and other thinly sliced exotica could be immediately embraced as Jewish. They were kosher products sold and served by Jewish butchers, shop owners, and restaurateurs to customers who were also Jewish. The real deli difference for all those Jewish immigrants who discovered this cuisine only after getting off the boat was that it was as unmoored (and as free to re-create itself) as they were. Eating deli was a purely sensory experience. It was Jewish food that called forth no memories, reminded no one of difficulties overcome or loved ones left behind. It provoked neither nostalgia nor relief, reminded no one of home, had no religious associations to trigger pangs of guilt. Unlike chicken soup, kugel, or gefilte fish, corned beef and pastrami sandwiches were served on a blank slate.

Deli is the only kind of Jewish food that was only "culturally" Jewish from day one and it's no accident that virtually all so-called Jewish foods that are *treyf* by definition first appeared on delicatessen menus. The Reuben sandwich, the best-known and possibly oldest example, consists of corned beef, Swiss cheese, and sauerkraut, doused in Russian dressing and grilled on rye bread. The Reuben's origins are obscure and highly contentious, but no one seems to have seen one until either the late 1920s or early 1930s, by which time most of the more prosperous delis had long since abandoned kashrus in favor of an edible image of their customers: Jewish by nationality, unconcerned with (and sometimes even unconscious of) the day-to-day demands of the religion. But not even Reuben-serving delis dared put cream into their chicken soup or cheese on their brisket plates. Only deli, the food that seemed to have no history, could be treated that way; only deli could undergo such ritual defilement and still end up as the most "Jewish" food of all, the one most redolent of Jewish pride and Jewish identity.

From San Diego up to Maine, New York Deli equals Taste of Jew: sardonic, urbane, vaguely connected to show-biz, and neurotic in a way that makes *you* want to go into therapy, too. From Diane Keaton confirming her character's status as New York outsider and Eternal Shiksa by ordering pastrami on white with mayo in *Annie Hall*—there are limits to the amount of abuse even deli can endure—to the comics swapping stories in the Carnegie in *Broadway Danny Rose*, to Meg Ryan faking an orgasm while eating good, honest food in Katz's in *When Harry Met Sally . . .* , the deli is a place in which pretensions are no more welcome than butter, a suitable venue for revealing secrets and advancing the plot.

I have never met a Jew—Orthodox, Conservative, Reform, or otherwise—who doesn't consider himself an expert on deli and isn't ready to argue its fine points, along with the fine points of most other topics that come along, at a moment's notice. Debates as to the Judaism of a Reuben can be lengthy, heated, and surprisingly wide ranging, and are often conducted in a deli over corned beef and pastrami sandwiches, or even the offending article itself. Since recreational drinking wasn't looked upon as a terribly Jewish activity, the delicatessen became the Jewish bar, the place where dreams were hatched, boasts were bragged, and sorrows were buried under mounds of steaming meat. If Eugene O'Neill had been Jewish, *The Iceman Cometh* would have taken place in Harry Hope's delicatessen.

The literary high point of the deli as a secular *bes medresh*, a study hall in which mankind replaces Talmud as the text to be studied—but with no less disagreement, self-deception, and straight-ahead bullshit—is found in the works of Mordecai Richler, especially *The Apprenticeship of Duddy Kravitz* and *St. Urbain's Horseman*. Duddy hears many of the legends that shape his life in a candy store-cum-lunch counter that figures in both novels and is quite openly based on a real place. Wilensky's Light Lunch (*Casse-croûte Wilensky* in French) is still in business in Montreal, still serving its Specials: two kinds salami, one piece bologna on a kaiser with mustard. Grilled. It is never cut, and a sign behind the counter lets you know that the mustard is compulsory. You can get it with Swiss or cheddar. Wilensky's also serves chopped-egg sandwiches and hot dogs. And no other main courses at all.

The delicatessen might no longer be the social hub that it was for earlier generations, but the food that it serves is still recognized as Jewish, even when the ingredients are combined in ways that can't help but pain an observant Jew. And that, oddly enough, is delicatessen's real value, its real point, its real function in Jewish culture. A Jew's native expertise, the ability to designate at least one delicatessen as a place into which foot is never to be set, is all the reminding that he or she needs, all the proof that the outside world demands, that the person in question is truly a Jew: The less faith a Jew has in the Bible, the more Jewish meaning pastrami acquires.

Endnotes

ONE

B. Tsivyen: quoted, M. Weinreich, vol. 3, p. 180

Herodotus: Book II:46; de Sélincourt, p. 148

If the Egyptians wouldn't: *Sifre, Beha'aloskho* 29

Pyramid of Cheops: ibid., II: 125; de Sélincourt, p. 179

A handbreadth thick: *Shulkhan Arukh, Orekh Khayim* 460:5

Matzohs are to be made: ibid., 460:4

Matzoh is forbidden: *Levush, Orekh Khayim* 471:2

Never milled at all: *Sifre, Beha'aloskho* 89

The nations of the world: *Tankhuma, Beshalakh* 22

Rabbinic tradition: ibid.

They said: *Sifre, Beha'aloskho* 88

The *Jewish Encyclopedia*: s.v., Morbidity, www.jewishencyclopedia
.com/articles/10982-morbidity

Human beings cannot: Braun, pp. 262, 270, 263, 268

It is a custom in Israel: Lipiec, p. 82

Birds or animals on the matzoh: *Shulkhan Arukh, Orekh Khayim*
460:5, 460:4

J.D. Eisenstein: Eisenstein, p. 248

Arbo'oh Ha-Turim: *Tur, Orekh Khayim* 493

The Passover matzohs of our pious forebears: *Sefer Maharil,
Hilkhos Afiyas Matsos*, 1

Ezekiel Landau: *Noda Bi-Yehuda, Tnino,* p. 79

Gil Marks: Marks, p. 393

A point made by Baila Grunwald: www.chabad.org/library/article
   _cdo/aid/853153/jewish/Not-As-Simple-as-It-Looks.htm

TWO

Ikey, Mikey: Roth, p. 56

There are those: *Shulkhan Arukh, Yoreh Deah* 89:1

David C. Kraemer: Kraemer, pp. 94–7

So the Tosefta: *Tosefta Trumos* 8:16

Two separate tractates: *Zevokhim* 96B, *Khulin* 111B

Antonius Margaritha: quoted Kraemer, p. 109

Isserles comments: *Shulkhan Arukh, Yoreh Deah* 93:1

Marshall Brickman: Brickman, p. 68.

David L. Gold: Gold, p. 135

THREE

A fifth-century midrash: *Bereyshis Rabbo, Toldos* 65

The successors of Moses: Strabo in Stern, vol 1., p. 300

Even if the Jew: Petronius, Frag. 37; in Stern, vol. 1, p. 444

Quaestiones Convivales, or *Table Talk*: Plutarch in Stern, vol. 1, p. 555

Sinister and revolting: Tacitus, 5:5; Wellesley, p. 273

Avoid eating pork in memory: Tacitus, 5:4; Wellesley, p. 273

The Jews apparently abominate: Plutarch in Stern, vol. 1, p. 556

The Grifters: Thompson, p. 46

Henry Adams: Samuels, p. 469

Thomas Mann: Mann, pp. 432–3

Joseph Opatoshu: Opatoshu, p. 227

Milk that has been: *Shulkhan Arukh, Yoreh Deah* 115:1

The main thrust: ibid., 112:2

As Karo also: ibid., 112:1

Most places permit: Isserles, *Toras Khatas* 75:1

Mordechai Yoffe: *Levush, Yoreh Deah* 112:3

Maimonides: *Mishne Torah, Ma'akholos Asuros* 17:15

History of Grossinger's: quoted Gabaccia, p. 83

Kept a pegboard: Fox

Chazarello: Cooper, p. 84

Beef fry: Joselit 1994, p. 193

Joel Finkelstein: Fromson

And gentiles are never: *Eykho Rabba* 1:28

FOUR

The stuffed goose: Braun, pp. 152, 150

Calvin Trillin: Trillin, p. 64.

The holy Rebbe: Meisels, vol. 3, p. 246

It should not be mixed: ibid., p. 247

Cut fatty skin: Leonard, pp. 42–3

The Maharil: *Minhagey HaMaharil, Hilkhos Shabbos*, 16

They feed continually: Cooper, p. 154

Adult-flavored milk: see Rashi to Numbers 11:6; *Sifri,
    Be-Ha'aloskho* 29

So allium-friendly a land as Spain: Trachtenberg 1943, p. 50

Fifteenth century Judensau: Shachar, p. 34

Martin Luther: Jacob Marcus, p. 166

Procter & Gamble: Schisgall, p. 66

A food product: quoted Schisgall, p. 71

Crisco is Kosher: Neil, p. 19

Advertise in Yiddish newspapers: Heinze, pp. 158–9, 176–7

Borden's ad: ibid., p. 177

Put a fair amount: Braun, p. 116

Each croquette: ibid., p. 121

102 Barbara Kirshenblatt-Gimblett: Kirshenblatt-Gimblett, in
    Joselit and Braunstein, p. 94

Ever since it: quoted, ibid., p. 94, my italics

According to Joan Nathan: Nathan in Greenspoon, Simkins,
    Shapiro, p. 4

A bacon bandage: Kramer, p. 513

Central European bourgeois cuisine: Kirshenblatt-Gimblett, in Joselit and Braunstein, p. 81

How to set the table: Kramer, p. 475

In some families: ibid., p. 476

A 1912 invoice: http://www.flickr.com/photos/jhsum-commons /4419542548/in/photostream Retrieved Dec. 1, 2012

In these countries: *Shulkhan Arukh, Orekh Khayim* 462:4

The main Passover dish: Elzet, p. 44

Thoroughly soak: Blaustein, p. 196–7

Beat four eggs: ibid., p. 197

1910 business directory: see Williams

The basic ingredient: All quotations of case from: Parev Products Co. v. Rokeach & Sons, 36 F. Supp. 686 - Dist. Court, ED New York 1941, retrieved from http://scholar.google.com /scholar_case?case=11449435996579932240&hl=en&as_sdt =2,5&as_vis=1 Retrieved March 10, 2015

FIVE

Here is a shopping list: Mordkhe Spektor quoted Elzet, p. 38

David Abudarham: *Sefer Abudarham, Shakhris shel Shabbos*

Moses Isserles: *Shulkhan Arukh, Orekh Khayim* 257:8

In his third "Satire": Juvenal, 3:13–4

With her basket and hay: Juvenal, 6:541–4

According to John Cooper: Cooper, p. 186

Or Zarua: *Or Zarua*, ii, *Hilkhos Erev Shabbos* 8

Latin *calentem*: Weinreich, pp. 400–2

Daniel M. Pinkwater: Pinkwater, p.74

Well-stewed [barley]: Abramowitz, n.d., vol. 18, p.8

A recipe from *Kokhbukh far Yudishe Froyen*: Blaustein, p. 193

Take flour, chopped bits: ibid., p. 193

As one handbook: Meisels, vol. 3, pp. 231–2

Mayer Kirshenblatt: Kirshenblatt, pp. 208, 211

It is deeply to be regretted: Heine in Ausubel, p. 364

In order to fully enjoy: Saphir in Ausubel, p. 361–2

Then you put a cover: ibid., pp. 360–1

Tempting Kosher Dishes: *Tempting Kosher Dishes, forrede*

Take well-soaked rolls: Blaustein, p. 194

Many Jews go through: Saphir in Ausubel, p. 362

Creatio e nihilo: Elzet, p. 36

Since at least the eleventh century: Kosover, p. 62;
   Or Zarua ii: 256

Take a piece: Levy, p. 28

Added to the *cholent*: *Sefer Ha-Rokeach,* quoted Kosover, p. 64

Again in the following century: J. Weil, quoted Kosover, p. 65

Rabbi Kalonymus and the elders: *Or Zarua* 2:21

The Maharil mentions: Kosover, p. 66

Cholent, which is called *frimslekh*: *Shulkhan Arukh, Orekh
   Khayim* 168:13

Sift about one pint: Kramer, p. 224

Yiddish cookbook published in Warsaw: Shafran,
   quoted Kosover, p. 36

The ABC of Jewish: Kosover, p. 144

The farfel was made: Abramovitch, col. 426

When all the water: Kramer, p. 224–5

Kugl heyste: Rabinovitch 1925, vol. 14, p. 227

In 1728: Goldberg, p. 254

Mayerl Premishlaner: Meisels, vol. 3, p. 261

I once asked him: Shtam, p. 20. I would like to thank Alan
   Nadler for making me aware of this quotation

Joan Nathan: Nathan, p. 285

Lokshn kugel is the principal: quoted Nadler in Greenspoon,
   Simkins, Shapiro, p. 207

A coarse, doughy mess: Saphir in Ausubel, p. 362–3

If you didn't eat kugel: Tendlau, p. 225, #712

A hometown marriage: Elzet, p. 36

Martha Rose Shulman: Parker-Pope
Love and Knishes: Kasdan, p. 63
A real calf's foot: Elzet, pp. 34–5
A not entirely serious Hasidic tradition: Meisels, vol. 3, p. 250
The recipe begins with: Kramer, pp. 97–8
Le Ménagier de Paris: Ménagier, "Other Odds and Ends"
Recipe for turnip *tsimmes*: Blaustein, pp. 79–80
It was introduced into Russia: see Molokhovets, pp. 57, 350
Norman Salsitz: Salsitz, p. 83
Leah W. Leonard: Leonard, pp. 33–6
Gil Marks: Marks, p. 599

SIX

Men of strong constitution: *Shulkhan Arukh, Orekh Khayim* 240:1
I recall that: *Leket Yosher*, p.49
It's called *bulke*: Elzet, p. 26
The thin chalas made for: *Leket Yosher*, II, p.5
It is the custom to knead enough: *Shulkhan Arukh, Orekh Khayim* 242
Mordecai Kosover describes this *kuchen*: Kosover, p. 120
They were and still are: Kosover, p. 120
Harmful even for healthy people: quoted Kosover, p. 122
Jewish food encyclopedist Gil Marks: Marks, p. 497
This large pale woman: Shteyngart, p. 4
Eating fish in honor: Meisels, vol. 3, p.169
Daz Buoch fun Guoter Spise: Recipe 17
After the carp has been scaled: Massialot, p. 144
Sazanikos: Maciejko, pp. 13–4
Caution must be exercised: *Shulkhan Arukh, Yoreh Deah* 116:2
The exclusive possession: Kirshenblatt-Gimblett 1986–7, p. 85, n. 21
Chickens are not to be stuffed: *Minhagey HaMaharil*, 206:10

As Sholem Aleichem explains: Rabinowitz 1925, vol. 2, p. 18.
Were chicken to be prohibited: *Shoel u-Meyshiv*, vol. 3, part 3,
    resp. 84
Kreplach was considered: ibid., p. 47
Alter Druyanow: quoted ibid., p. 43, n. 5

SEVEN
Peasants living in: Cooper, p. 152
Udder in a *pashtet*: Kosover, p. 95
Until such time: Braun, p. 84
The true art: Kasdan, pp. 12–3
Prepared at home: Abramovitch, col. 418–9
These were salted: ibid., col. 426
The Jewish children: quoted Joselit 1994, p. 181
And ever since: Rabinovitch 1925, vol. 8, p. 126
If a newborn child: Ashkenazi, 34B
I had known chicken: Chotzinoff, p. 154
At the feather plucking: Abramovitch, col. 422
According to Rashi: Kosover, p. 131
Chocolate Easter bunnies: http://www.savingforsomeday.com/wp
    -content/uploads/2011/04/KosherEasterCandy.png Retrieved
    Nov. 18, 2012
Fruit *flodns*: Kosover, p. 99
Elzet mentions: Elzet, p. 46
The cake is prepared: quoted Ivan Marcus, p. 30
Mordecai Kosover lists: Kosover, p. 104
Wengeroff (1833–1916) describes how: quoted Kosover, p. 106
Claudia Roden: Roden, p. 187
The teacher would take out a tablet: *Sefer Ha-Rokeach, Hilkhos
    Shavuos*, p. 296
Noted by Ivan Marcus: Ivan Marcus, pp. 59–67
At every celebration: Kolp, p. 58

Mayer Kirshenblatt, who left Poland: Kirshenblatt, p. 42
All over Poland: Barbara Kirshenblatt-Gimblett, private
    communication
Kaplansky's son: Gould
Popularized by Matthew Goodman: http://www.food.com/recipe
    /toronto-blueberry-buns-120460 Retrieved Sept. 10, 2015
A recipe for Polish *jagodzianki*: http://forthebodyandsoul.blogspot
    .ca/2008/09/jagodzianki-wild-blueberry-buns.html Retrieved
    Sept. 10, 2015
Wide in the middle: Elzet, p. 27

EIGHT

There are those who say that cheese: *Shulkhan Arukh, Orekh
    Khayim* 670:2
A 1956 recipe: Kasdan, p. 113
Dairy potato latkes: Abramovitch, col. 421
The Bartons company in 1951: Joselit 1994, p. 239
Oy, they're so good: http://www.gayleschocolates.com/spotlight
    .php?id=18-015 Retrieved Nov. 16, 2012
Gil Marks's explanation: Marks, p. 550
Crepe Suzette: Joseph Jacobs, p. 7
As Marks also points out: Marks, p. 57
Only bread was more common: Elzet, p. 91
Round *kneydlekh* that we called: Erlich, p. 63

NINE

An 1894 guide: *Mekor Ha-Brokhe*, quoted Kosover, p. 33
The whole kernel was used: Abramovitch, cols. 424–5
If the old saw: quoted Ginsberg and Berg, p. 56
Stretch their rye flour: Abramovitch, col. 421
The 20-percent rye: see Ginsberg and Berg, pp. 72–4
An unsweetened donut: Beatrice and Ira Freeman, *NY Times*,
    May 22, 1960

The boy's father increases: quoted Kosover, p. 117
The Slovakian guide: quoted Kosover, p. 118
Two pieces of dough: Dembinska, p. 116
A handmade bagel contains: Balinska, p. 3
The dough is then left: ibid., p. 4
The boiled dough: ibid., p. 6
Just like the *obwarzanki*: Kirshenblatt, p. 44
By 1900 it had risen: Balinska, p. 50
Yehuda Elzet, who was born: Elzet, p. 99
In mark darf men loyfn: Ginsburg-Marek, No. 78, p. 69
Soaking it in light brine: Marks, p. 370
Regelson's suggestion: Regelson, *passim*
Others, like Gil Marks: ibid., p. 36
Sam Lender mixed the bagel: Daniel Thompson, http://www
    .bagelproducts.com/bagel_formers/history.htm Retrieved
    Jan. 12, 2013
With the advent: ibid., my italics
Isaac Mayer Dik: quoted Elzet, *Melokhes*, pp. 17–8
You've got to spend all: Wex, pp. 40–41
Leo Rosten: Rosten, p. 42.
In an unpublished essay: Joselit 1994, p. 202
On Sunday, one had: quoted Cooper, p. 158
In *Eat and Be Satisfied*, John Cooper: ibid., p. 158
Yehuda Elzet says that Jews: Elzet, p. 30
An inexpensive communal snack: Abramovitch,
    col. 421–2
Peter Paul Jonitis: Jonitis, pp. 60–1

EPILOGUE
A Bessarabian dish: Rabinovitch 1912, p. 54
David Sax: Sax, p. 196
Figures from 1902: Diner, p. 202
One hundred restaurants: Heinze, p. 118

Bibliography

Abramovitch, Hirsh. *"Akhiles bay yidn in lite."* In *Lite* 1, M. Sudarsky, A. Katzenellenbogen, Y. Kissin, editors. New York: Jewish-Lithuanian Cultural Society "Lite," 1951, cols 417–428.

Abramowitz, S.Y. (Mendele Moykher Sforim), *Geklibene Verk.* 1. New York: YKUF, 1946.

———*Ale Verk fun Mendele Moykher Sforim.* Warsaw: Farlag Mendele, n.d.

Adamson, Melitta Weiss, editor. *Food in the Middle Ages.* New York and London: Garland, 1995.

Agus, Irving A. *The Heroic Age of Franco-German Jewry.* New York: Yeshiva University Press, 1969.

Alon, Gedalyahu. *Jews, Judaism and the Classical World.* Translated by Israel Abrahams. Jerusalem: The Magnes Press, 1977.

Alpern, Laura Manischewitz. *Manischewitz: The Matzo Family. The Making of an American Jewish Icon.* New York: KTAV Publishing House, 2008.

Appadurai, Arjun. "How to Make a National Cuisine: Cookbooks in Contemporary India." *Comparative Studies in Society and History* 30/1 (1988): 3–24.

Appel, John J. "The Trefa Banquet." *Commentary.* February 1966. http://www.commentarymagazine.com/article/the-trefa-banquet/ Retrieved Dec. 1, 2012.

Ashkenazi, David Tevel. *Beys Dovid.* Wilmersdorf, 1734.

Ausubel, Nathan, editor. *A Treasury of Jewish Humor.* Garden City: Doubleday, 1951.

Bahloul, Joëlle. *Le Culte de la Table Dressée.* Paris: Métailié, 1983.

Balinska, Maria. *The Bagel: The Surprising History of a Modest Bread.* New Haven and London: Yale University Press, 2008.

Baron, Salo Wittmayer. *A Social and Religious History of the Jews* 12. New York: Columbia University Press, 1967.

Baskerville, Beatrice C. *The Polish Jew: His Social and Economic Value.* New York: The MacMillan Company, 1906.

Berg, Gertrude and Myra Waldo. *The Molly Goldberg Jewish Cookbook.* New York: Doubleday, 1955.

Berman, Jeremiah J. *Shehitah: A Study in the Cultural and Social Life of the Jewish People.* New York: Bloch Publishing Company, 1941.

Bernstein, Ignatz. *Jüdische Sprichwörter und Redensarten*, ed. Hans Peter Althaus. Hildesheim: Georg Olms Verlag, 1968 (rpt. of 1912).

Blaustein, Ozer. *Kokhbukh far Yudishe Froyen.* Vilna: L.L. Matz, 1896.

Blech, Zushe Yosef. *Kosher Food Production.* Ames, Iowa: Blackwell, 2004.

Brickman. Marshall. "Inimitable Perelman," *Saturday Review* (July 1981): 68–71.

Braun, H. *Dos Familiyen Kokhbukh*. New York: Hebrew Publishing Company, 1914.

Bryan, David. *Cosmos, Chaos and the Kosher Mentality*. Sheffield: Sheffield Academic Press, 1995.

Das Buoch von guoter Spise. http://www.uni-giessen.de/gloning/tx /bvgs.htm Retrieved Dec. 1, 2012.

Carlebach, Elisheva. *Divided Souls: Converts from Judaism in Germany, 1500–1750*. New Haven and London: Yale University Press, 2001.

Chotzinoff, Samuel. *A Lost Paradise: Early Reminiscences*. New York: Alfred A. Knopf, 1955.

Coe, Andrew. *Chop Suey: A Cultural History of Chinese Food in the United States*. New York: Oxford University Press, 2009.

Collingham, Lizzie. *Curry: A Tale of Cooks and Conquerors*. Oxford and New York: Oxford University Press, 2007.

Cooper, John. *Eat and Be Satisfied: A Social History of Jewish Food*. Northvale, N.J. and London: Jason Aronson, Inc., 1993.

Dembinska, Maria. *Food and Drink in Medieval Poland: Rediscovering a Cuisine of the Past*. Edited by William Woys Weaver. Translated by Magdalena Thomas. Philadelphia, University of Pennsylvania Press, 1999.

De Pomiane, Edouard. *The Jews of Poland: Recollections and Recipes*. Translated by Josephine Bacon. Garden Grove: Pholiola Press, 1985.

De Silva, Cara, editor. *In Memory's Kitchen: A Legacy from the Women of Terezin*. Northvale, London: Jason Aronson, 1996.

Diner, Hasia R. *Hungering for America: Italian, Irish, and Jewish Foodways in the Age of Migration*. Cambridge and London: Harvard University Press, 2001.

Erlich, Shoskhke. Untitled letter, *Yidishe Shprakh* 17 (1957): 63.

Ewen, Elizabeth. *Immigrant Women in the Land of Dollars: Life and Culture on the Lower East Side, 1890–1925.* New York: Monthly Review Press, 1985.

Fabre-Vassas, Claudine. *The Singular Beast: Jews, Christians, & The Pig.* Translated by Carol Volk. New York: Columbia University Press, 1997.

Ferris, Marcie Cohen. *Matzoh Ball Gumbo: Culinary Tales of the Jewish South.* Chapel Hill: University of North Carolina Press, 2005.

Fishkoff, Sue. *Kosher Nation: Why More and More of America's Food Answers to a Higher Authority.* New York: Schocken Books, 2010.

Flandrin, Jean-Louis and Massimo Montanari, editors. Translated by Albert Sonnenfeld. *Food: A Culinary History from Antiquity to the Present.* New York: Penguin, 2000.

Fox, Margalit. "Irving Cohen, King Cupid of the Catskills, Dies at 95." http://www.nytimes.com/2012/10/04/nyregion/irving -cohen-catskills-maitre-dhotel-matchmaker-dies-at-95.html Retrieved Oct. 4, 2012.

Freehoff, Solomon B. *The Responsa Literature and A Treasury of Responsa.* New York: KTAV Publishing House, 1973.

Friedenreich, David M. *Foreigners and Their Food: Constructing Otherness in Jewish, Christian and Islamic Law.* Berkeley, Los Angeles, London: University of California Press, 2011.

Frisch, Erich, editor. *Von der Franckfurter Juden Vergangenheit (Sitten und Bräuchen), Aus Johann Jacob Schudt's "Jüdische Merck-würdigkeiten", Franckfurt und Leipzig, Anno 1714.* Berlin: Schocken, 1934.

Fromson, Daniel. "Southern Comfort," http://www.tabletmag .com/jewish-life-and-religion/78224/southern-comfort Retrieved Sept. 15, 2011.

Fuhrman, Y. "Terminlogye fun Bekerfakh Banitst in Bukovina un Mizrekh Galitsiye." *Yidishe Shprakh* 33 (1974): 32–37.

Gabaccia, Donna R. *We Are What We Eat: Ethnic Food and the Making of Americans.* Cambridge, Mass. and London: Harvard University Press, 1998.

Gastwirt, Harold P. *Fraud, Corruption, and Holiness: The Controversy Over the Supervision of Jewish Dietary Practice in New York City 1881–1940.* Port Washington, N.Y. and London: Kennikat Press, 1974.

Ginsberg, Stanley and Norman Berg. *Inside the Jewish Bakery: Recipes and Memories from the Golden Age of Jewish Baking.* Philadelphia: Camino Books, 2011.

Ginsburg, S.M. and P.S. Marek. *Evreiskiia Narodniya Piesni v Rossii.* St. Petersburg: 1901.

Glazer, Ruth. "The Jewish Delicatessen: The Evolution of an Institution." *Commentary* (March 1946): 58–63.

Gold, David L. "Towards a Study of the Origins of the Two Synonymous Yiddish Adjectives: *pareve* and *minikh.*" *Jewish Language Review* 5 (1985): 128–39.

Goldberg, Jacob. "Poles and Jews in the Seventeenth and Eighteenth Centuries: Rejection or Acceptance." *Jahrbücher für Geschichte Osteuropas,* n.s., 22 (1974): 248–82.

Goodman, Martin. "Kosher Olive Oil in Aniquity." In *A Tribute to Geza Vermes.* Edited by Philip R. Davies and Richard T. White. (Sheffield: JSOT Press, 1990) 227–45.

————*The Ruling Class of Judaea: The Origins of the Jewish Revolt Against Rome A.D. 66–70*. Cambridge: Cambridge University Press, 1987.

Goodman, Matthew. "The Rise and Fall of the Bagel." *Harvard Review* (June 1, 2005): 91–99.

Gordinier, Jeff. "Mindful Eating as Food for Thought." http:// www.nytimes.com/2012/02/08/dining/mindful-eating-as-food-for -thought.html Retrieved February 8, 2012.

Gould, Jillian. "Blueberry Buns." http://journals.hil.unb.ca/ index.php/MCR/article/view/17941/22013 Retrieved Oct. 20, 2014.

Greenberg, Betty D. and Althea O. Silverman. *The Jewish Home Beautiful*. New York: The National Women's League of the United Synagogue of America, 1941 (9th printing, 1958).

Greenspoon, Leonard, Ronald Simkins and Gerald Shapiro. *Food and Judaism: A Special Issue of Studies in Jewish Civilization, Volume 15*. Omaha: Creighton University Press, 2005.

Hahn, Joseph Yuspa. *Sefer Yosef Omets*. Frankfurt am Main: Hermon, 1928.

Harris, Marvin. *Good to Eat: Riddles of Food and Culture*. New York: Simon and Schuster, 1985.

Heinze, Andrew R. *Adapting to Abundance: Jewish Immigrants, Mass Consumption, and the Search for American Identity*. New York: Columbia University Press, 1990.

Herodotus. *The Histories*. Translated by Aubrey De Sélincourt. Harmondsworth: Penguin, 1972.

Home on the Range Cookbook. Compiled by The Sisterhood of Beth Israel Synagogue. Camden, N.J., 1959–60.

Hundert, Gershon David. *Jews in Poland-Lithuania in the Eighteenth Century: A Genealogy of Modernity.* Berkeley and Los Angeles: University of California Press, 2004.

Jonitis, Peter Paul. *The Acculturation of the Lithuanians of Chester, Pennsylvania.* New York: AMS Press, 1985.

Joselit, Jenna Weissman. *New York's Jewish Jews: The Orthodox Community in the Interwar Years.* Bloomington and Indianapolis: Indiana University Press, 1990.

———*The Wonders of America: Reinventing Jewish Culture, 1880–1950.* New York: Hill and Wang, 1994.

———and Susan I. Braunstein. *Getting Comfortable in New York: The American Jewish Home, 1880–1950.* Bloomington and Indianapolis: Indiana University Press, 1991.

Joseph Jacobs Handbook of Familiar Jewish Words and Expressions 6th ed. New York: Joseph Jacobs Organization, Inc., 1954.

Kalish, Ita. "Life in a Hasidic Court in Russian Poland Towards the End of the 19th and the Early 20th Centuries." *YIVO Annual of Jewish Social Sciences* 13 (1965): 264–78.

Kasdan, Sara. *Love and Knishes: An Irrepressible Guide to Jewish Cooking.* Greenwich, Connecticut: Fawcett Publications, 1956.

Kirshenblatt, Mayer and Barbara Kirshenblatt-Gimblett. *They Called Me Mayer July: Painted Memories of a Jewish Childhood in Poland Before the Holocaust.* Berkeley: University of California Press, 2007.

Kirshenblatt-Gimblett, Barbara. "Kitchen Judaism." In *Getting Comfortable in New York, the American Jewish Home: 1990–1950.* Edited by Susan L. Braunstein and Jenna Weisman Joselit. (New York: Jewish Museum, 1990) 76–105.

————"The Kosher Gourmet in the Nineteenth-Century Kitchen: Three Jewish Cookbooks in Historical Perspective." *Journal of Gastronomy* 2, no. 4 (1986–1987): 51–89.

Kolp, Tsvi Hirsh. *Mi-Dor Le-Dor.* Warsaw: N. Sokolov, 1901.

Kosover, Mordecai. "Yidishe maykholim: A Shtudiye in kulturge-shikhte un shprakhforshung." In *Yuda A. Yaffe Bukh.* Edited by Yudl Mark (New York: YIVO, 1958): 1–145.

Kraemer, David. *Jewish Eating and Identity Through the Ages.* New York and London: Routledge, 2007.

Kramer, Bertha F. *Aunt Babette's Cookbook, Foreign and Domestic Receipts for the Household,* 11th ed. Cincinnati and Chicago: Bloch Publishing and Printing Co., 1889.

Leonard, Leah W. *Jewish Cookery, In accordance with the Jewish Dietary Laws.* New York: Crown, 1949 (24th printing, 1977).

Levenstein, Harvey A. *Revolution at the Table: The Transformation of the American Diet.* New York and Oxford: Oxford University Press, 1988.

Levin, Meyer. *The Old Bunch.* New York: The Viking Press, 1937.

Levy, Esther. *Jewish Cookery Book.* 1871. Reprint. Bedford, MA: Applewood Books, 2007.

Lew, Myer S. *The Jews of Poland: Their Political, Economic, Social and Communal Life as reflected in the works of Rabbi Moses Isserls.* London: Edward Goldston, 1944.

Liberles, Robert. *Jews Welcome Coffee: Tradition and Innovation in Early Modern Germany.* Waltham: Brandeis University Press, 2012.

Löw, Immanuel. *Die Flora der Juden.* Reprint. Hildesheim: Georg Olms Verlag, 1967.

Maciejko, Pawel. *The Mixed Multitude: Jacob Frank and the Frankist Movement, 1755–1816*. Philadelphia: University of Pennsylvania Press, 2011.

Mann, Thomas. *The Magic Mountain*. Translated by John E. Woods. New York: Vintage International, 1996.

Marcus, Ivan G. *Rituals of Childhood: Jewish Acculturation in Medieval Europe*. New Haven and London: Yale University Press, 1996.

Marcus, Jacob R. *The Jew in the Medieval World, A Source Book: 315–1791*. Philadelphia: Jewish Publication Society, 1938 (Reprint New York, Atheneum, 1975).

Mark, Yudl. *"Undzer Litvishe Yidish,"* in *Lite* 1. Edited by M. Sudarsky, A. Katzenellenbogen, Y. Kissin. New York: Jewish-Lithuanian Cultural Society, *Lite,* 1951.

Marks, Gil. *Encyclopedia of Jewish Food*. Hoboken: John Wiley & Sons, 2010.

Massialot, François. *Le Nouveau Cuisinier bourgeois et royal*. Amsterdam: Compagnie des libraries, 1734.

Meisels, David. *Seyfer Oytser ha-Shabbes*. Brooklyn: Yofi Book Publishing Inc., 2000.

Le Ménagier de Paris. Translated by Janet Hinson. http://daviddfriedman.com/Medieval/Cookbooks/Menagier/Menagier.html Retrieved Nov. 3, 2012.

Miller, Hanna. "Identity Takeout: How American Jews Made Chinese Food Their Ethnic Cuisine." *Journal of Popular Culture* 39, no. 3 (June 2006): 430–465.

Molokhovets, Elena. *Classic Russian Cooking: Elena Molokhovets' A Gift to Young Housewives*. Edited and translated by Joyce Toomre. Bloomington: Indiana University Press, 1998.

Neil, Marion Harris. *The Story of Crisco*, 3rd ed. Cincinnati: Procter and Gamble, 1914.

Opatoshu, Yoysef. *In Poylishe Velder*. Vilna: Farlag fun B. Kletzkin, 1928.

Parker-Pope, Tara. "The Kugel Challenge." well.blogs.nytimes .com/2012/11/09/the-kugel-challenge/ Retrieved Nov. 9, 2012.

Pinkwater, Daniel M. *Young Adults*. New York: Tor Books, 1985.

Pollack, Herman. *Jewish Folkways in Germanic Lands (1648–1806)*. Cambridge, Mass, and London: M.I.T. Press, 1971.

Rabinovitch, Sholem (Sholem Aleichem). *Ale Verk*. Warsaw and Vilna: Farlag fun B. Kletzkin, 1925.

———*Blondzhende Shtern*. New York: Jewish Press Publishing Co., 1912.

Regelson, Stanley. "The Bagel: Symbol and Ritual at the Breakfast Table." In *The American Dimension*. Edited by W. Arens and S. Montague. Port Washington: Alfred Publishing Co., 1976.

Roden, Claudia. *The Book of Jewish Food*. New York: Alfred A. Knopf, 1996.

Rosenblum, Jordan D. *Food and Identity in Early Rabbinic Judaism*. New York: Cambridge University Press, 2010.

Rosenfeld, Isaac. "Adam and Eve on Delancey Street." *Commentary* (October 1949). https://www.commentarymagazine.com /article/on-the-horizon-adam-and-eve-on-delancey-street/ Retrieved Sept. 6, 2015.

Julius Preuss' Biblical and Talmudic Medicine. Edited and translated by Fred Rosner. New York and London: Sanhedrin Press, 1978.

Rosten, Leo. *The Joys of Yiddish*, 13th ed. New York: Pocket Books, 1970.

Roth, Philip. *Portnoy's Complaint*. New York: Random House, 1969.

Rubenstein, Jeffrey L. *The Culture of the Babylonian Talmud*. Baltimore and London: Johns Hopkins University Press, 2003.

Salsitz, Norman with Richard Skolnik. *A Jewish Boyhood in Poland: Remembering Kolbuszowa*. Syracuse: Syracuse University Press, 1992.

Selected Letters of Henry Adams. Edited by Ernest Samuels. Cambridge: Belknap Press of Harvard University Press, 1992.

Sarna, Jonathan D. "How Matzah Became Square: Manischewitz and the Development of Machine-Made Matzah in the United States." Sixth Annual Lecture of the Victor J. Selmanowitz Chair of Jewish History. New York: School of Jewish Studies, Touro College, 2005.

Satlow, Michael L. *Tasting the Dish: Rabbinic Rhetorics of Sexuality*. Atlanta: Scholars Press, 1995.

Schisgall, Oscar. *Eyes on Tomorrow: The Evolution of Procter & Gamble*. Chicago: J.G. Ferguson Publishing Company, 1981.

Sax, David. *Save the Deli: In Search of Perfect Pastrami, Crusty Rye, and the Heart of Jewish Delicatessen*. Boston and New York: Houghton Mifflin Harcourt, 2009.

Du fait de cuisine/On Cookery of Master Chiquart (1420). Edited and translated by Terence Scully. Tempe: ACMRS, 2010.

———*The Viandier of Taillevent: An Edition of all Extant Manuscripts*. Ottawa: University of Ottawa Press, 1988.

Seyfer Khsidim. Edited by Jehuda Wistinetzki. Frankfurt am Main: M.A. Wuhrmann Verlag, 1924.

Shachar, Isaiah. *The Judensau: A Medieval Anti-Jewish Motif and its History.* London: The Warburg Institute, 1974.

Shtam, Sholem E. *Zeykher Tsaddik.* Vilna, 1905.

Shteyngart, Gary. *The Russian Debutante's Handbook.* New York: Riverhead Books, 2002.

Sklare, Marshall and Joseph Greenblum. *Jewish Identity on the Suburban Frontier: A Study of Group Survival in the Open Society,* 2nd ed. Chicago and London: University of Chicago Press, 1979.

Sperber, Daniel. *Minhagey Yisrael.* Jerusalem: Mossad ha-Rav Kook, 1991–2007.

Spielman, Ed. *The Mighty Atom: The Life and Times of Joseph L. Greenstein.* New York: The Viking Press, 1979.

Greek and Latin Authors on Jews and Judaism, 3 vols. Edited and translated by Menahem Stern. Jerusalem: Israel Academy of Sciences and Humanities, 1974–1984.

Stomma, Ludwik. *Campagnes Insolites.* Lagrasse: Éditions Verdier, 1986.

Strasser, Susan. *Satisfaction Guaranteed: The Making of the American Mass Market.* New York: Pantheon Books, 1989.

Swasy, Alecia. *Soap Opera: The Inside Story of Procter & Gamble.* New York: Times Books, 1993.

Tacitus. *The Histories.* Translated by Kenneth Wellesley. Harmondsworth: Penguin, 1992.

Taub, Harold Jaediker. *Waldorf in the Catskills: The Grossinger Legend.* New York: Sterling, 1952.

Tempting Kosher Dishes, 4th ed., Jersey City and Cincinnati: The B. Manischewitz Co., 1940.

Thompson, Jim. *The Grifters*. New York: Regency Books, 1963; Berkeley: Black Lizard, 1985.

Trachtenberg, Joshua. *The Devil and the Jews*. New Haven: Yale University Press, 1943.

———*Jewish Magic and Superstition*. 1939. Reprint, New York: Atheneum, 1975.

Trillin, Calvin. *Alice, Let's Eat: Further Adventures of a Happy Eater*. New York: Random House, 1978.

Apicius: Cookery and Dining in Imperial Rome. Edited and translated by Joseph Dommers Vehling. Chicago: Walter M. Hill, 1939; New York: Dover, 1977.

Visser, Margaret. *Much Depends on Dinner: The Extraordinary History and Mythology, Allure and Obsessions, Perils and Taboos of an Ordinary Meal*, 2nd ed., New York: Grove Press, 2008.

Weinreich, Max. *History of the Yiddish Language*, 2 vols. New Haven and London: Yale University Press, 2008.

Wex, Michael. *Born to Kvetch: Yiddish Language and Culture in All of Its Moods*. New York: St. Martin's Press, 2005.

Williams' Cincinnati Business Directory for 1910. Cincinnati: Williams Directory Co., 1910.

Acknowledgments

My agent, Richard Pine, suggested this book to me a few years ago and kept at me about it until I finally realized the wisdom of his idea. Nichole Argyres at St. Martin's Press was willing to take a chance on it, and she and her assistant, Laura Chasen, have been an unfailingly pleasant source of support during the writing and preparation of the book. Donna Bernardo-Ceriz, Melissa Caza, and Dara Solomon were gracious and patient with the often silly requests that I made at the Ontario Jewish Archives. Heiko Lehmann in Berlin and Hans Waalwijk in Amsterdam went scouting for *Kugeltöpfe*, while Mark Orlan and Barbara Kirshenblatt-Gimblett, the *doyenne* of Ashkenazi foodways, contributed valuable information about blueberry buns. Susan Leviton provided a number of vintage cookbooks and Michael Derbecker tracked down a few hard-to-find DVDs of old movies for me.

My wife, Marilla, and daughter Sabina suffered through more research-begotten upset stomachs than any human being should be forced to endure. I am happy to acknowledge their patience and superior cooking skills, along with Marilla's unwavering support in our quest for kosher brains. The greatest debt of all, though, is the one I owe to the hundreds of kosher cooks, from my mother on, who forced most of the dishes discussed in this book down a throat crying out for Marshmallow Fluff.

Index